World Wide Web Starter Kit

World Wide Web Starter Kit

Kevin Coffee

Ross Scott Rubin

Hayden
Books

World Wide Web Starter Kit

Library of Congress Catalog Number: 95-60410
ISBN: 1-56830-176-6

97 96 95   4 3 2 1

Interpretation of the printing code: the rightmost double-digit number is the year of the book's printing; the rightmost single-digit number is the number of the book's printing. For example, a printing code of 95-1 shows that the first printing of the book occurred in 1995.

Trademark Acknowledgments: All products mentioned in this book are either trademarks of the companies referenced in this book, registered trademarks of the companies referenced in this book, or neither. We strongly advise that you investigate a particular product's name thoroughly before you use the name as your own.

Apple, Mac, and Macintosh are registered trademarks of Apple Computer, Inc.

The Hayden Books Team

Dedication

This book is dedicated to the open exchange of ideas and information through the World Wide Web, and to better understanding the real links that connect us all.

Acknowledgments

This book, like the Web itself, is the result of a collaborative process.

First of all, it is the distillation of hundreds, if not thousands, of hours spent using the Web and the Internet to learn, share information, and explore. The millions of people who use the Internet regularly have, in one form or another, provided the network this book describes, the standards that network uses, and the software that links us all together.

This book would not be in your hands if not for the people at Hayden Books, and especially Brian Gill, Brad Miser, Jane Corn, and Oliver von Quadt. The difference between what I originally wrote and what you are now reading is a factor of their intelligent work.

Thanks also goes to the technical reviewers of the manuscript, especially Tonya Engst, who slogged through every paragraph, spotted potential and real problems, and reminded me for whom I was writing.

Finally, I thank Rachel, who provided (alternately) advice, criticism, encouragement, and consolation throughout the months spent tack-tack-tacking away at my Macintosh.

About the Authors

Kevin Coffee is an artist, designer, and writer, with a special interest in multimedia information delivery systems, especially the Web.

From 1988 to 1995 he developed and designed exhibitions about human history and the natural sciences, including multimedia and Web presentations, at the American Museum of Natural History in New York, where he was manager of exhibitions.

Currently, he is a design and communications consultant and teaches design at Columbia College in Chicago.

Ross Scott Rubin has been writing professionally about the Macintosh since 1989. He is the author of *Yakety Mac: The Telecom Tome, Cool Mac After Dark* and the original edition of *Hayden's PowerBook Power Book.* He also contributed to *The Macintosh Bible, Fifth Edition, Guide to System 7.5,* and *The Virtual Playhouse for Macintosh.* He has served as a development or technical editor for *eWorld: The Official Guide for Macintosh Users, The Hitchhiker's Guide to the Electronic Highway, The Hitchhiker's Guide to America Online, The Mac Power Toolkit,* and the first edition of *Cool Mac Sounds.* He contributes regularly to *MacWEEK, Web Week,* and other publications. He welcomes feedback at rossrubin@aol.com.

Contents at a Glance

Table of Contents

5 Using HTML   91

Introduction

The Internet has been around for years, peacefully minding its business, moving email and files between universities and research laboratories with only occasional mention in the mass media, and then only when something rude happened with a computer virus or runaway auto-program.

In 1989, a few computer scientists working at the CERN European Particle Physics Lab started developing a new way to exchange information on the Internet, called the HyperText Transfer Protocol. They coined a term to describe their distributed information system: the World Wide Web.

The development of HTTP and the related HyperText Markup Language document structure that developed along with it continued at a gradual pace through the early 1990s, largely unnoticed even by many daily users of the Internet.

Then, in 1994, something really big happened. Some university students wrote a client application for HTTP that allowed users to combine pictures with hypertext and provided an easy-to-use interface for the Web. They called this application NCSA Mosaic.

Since the advent of NCSA Mosaic, use of the Web and the Internet has exploded. The Mosaic browser has been followed by other graphical browsers, including MacWeb and Netscape Navigator, and almost overnight the World Wide Web has become synonymous with Internet communications.

Web browsers provide a common and easy-to-use interface for the Internet. Arcane and mysterious commands typed on a computer keyboard have given way to point-and-click hypertext documents.

Using the information encoded in hypertext documents, a mouse click can take you to a computer halfway around the world, or call up a photograph of rare Pre-Columbian sculpture, or play a motion picture clip using the software on your own computer.

In the calendar year 1994, the number of Web severs on the Internet grew from a few hundred to over ten thousand. Individual hypertext documents on the Internet number in the millions. And there are millions of people now browsing their way across the Web.

If you have a computer and a modem, there is no reason why you can't be using it, too. The purpose of this book is to help you learn how.

The Text

This book follows a logical progression beginning with an introduction to basic Web concepts, moving through information browsing, explaining how to write hypertext documents, and showing you how to set up your own Web server on a Macintosh computer.

There are several graphical Web browsers for the Mac, but we've chosen to focus primarily on the MacWeb browser, published by TradeWave and included on the disk in the back of this book. We used four different browsers while writing this book, and do not intend to spark a "religious war" over the advantages/disadvantages of any of them. Kevin believes that of the (purposefully unnamed) four, MacWeb has proved to be the most reliable.

Chapter 2 provides you with a user's guide to MacWeb and the Netscape Navigator browser.

Chapter 3 takes you on a world tour that includes a few of the servers that we've found unique and also explains how you can use a Web browser to communicate with other kinds of servers (like Gopher and FTP) on the Internet.

Chapter 4 provides a run-down of where else on the Internet you can find the latest news and technical information about browsers, servers, HyperText Markup Language, and Internet standards for the Web.

The Web is not just about grazing for information. The Web enables users to serve up their own information, and so this book examines the formatting language (HTML) used to write hypertext documents and the transfer protocol (HTTP) required to publish documents on the Web.

Chapter 5 is an introduction to the HyperText Markup Language, which is used to edit documents for the Web. Included in this chapter is a step-by-step tutorial that explains how to write your own documents, including your own home page, a personal entrance-way onto the Web. (You can set up your browser to open this home page every time you start a Web session.)

Chapter 6 includes a short tutorial to guide you through the Web server configuration process and demonstrate how to serve documents and images using HyperText Transfer Protocol.

Web servers rely on other, smaller applications, called Common Gateway Interface programs, to process certain kinds of information sent to the server. Chapter 6 also steps you through writing your own simple CGI, using the AppleScript language, in order to process a fill-out form.

Chapter 7 takes a look into the future, including the next generation of hypertext markup language, multimedia, network security, and some of the other trends that will affect how you use the Web a year or two from now.

Throughout this book, we've cited dozens of Uniform Resource Locators. These are addresses used by Web software to identify servers, files, and other resources on the Internet.

Also throughout this book, we've cited many lines of HyperText Markup Language. This is the formatting language used to markup parts of hypertext documents.

HTML statements are composed of elements, attributes, and text. Wherever we refer to an individual markup element, it is written between less-than and greater-than characters, **<like this>**.

The Disk

With this book you also get the World Wide Web Starter Kit Disk, jammed to the last sector with software and other files that will help you get started on the Web.

First of all, we include the software that allows your computer to dial in and communicate with the Internet: MacPPP and MacTCP. These will connect your computer to the Internet.

Then there's a copy of TradeWave's MacWeb 1.1.1 browser, which will allow you to use the World Wide Web.

To help you write your own hypertext documents, the WWWSK disk includes a copy of BBEdit Lite, a great text editor published by Bare Bones Software.

Believe it or not, this is all the software you need to write documents using the HyperText Markup Language.

But in case you'd like to automate the process, we've also included two sets of formatting extensions for BBEdit, specifically written for editing hypertext markup language: HTML Extensions (written by Carles Bellver), and HTML Tools (written by Lindsay Davies).

Last, but not least are the tutorial files on disk that you can use to learn how to write hypertext, following the examples in Chapter 5, and set up a Web server, using the examples in Chapter 6. These files include sample text documents, images, and an AppleScript program that processes fill-out forms.

The Appendices

Appendices A and C list the standard HTML markup for elements, attributes, and special characters, as well as the nonstandard markup implemented by the Netscape Navigator browser.

Appendix B includes a Glossary of Internet Terms that will help you decipher some of the jargon encountered on the Internet.

The Web is full of pictures and sounds, interesting stories and useful information, but most of all it's people, like yourself, creating digital links that reflect the real links that connect the human experience. We hope this book will help you add to those connections.

Welcome to the Web: A Whole New World

The captains of the computer industry may not be fine artists, but they're fond of painting pictures. They foretell a world where people easily and naturally traverse huge repositories of multimedia and information regardless of its location. Considering the difficulties that many computer users endure today just trying to connect to a local network, such talk seems like a distant pipe dream. The World Wide Web, however, is providing a glimpse of effortless access to rich, globally distributed content, a glimpse that is bright enough to draw millions of users.

The World Wide Web (WWW or "the Web" for short) is a large group of computers that communicate using the global Internet. What distinguishes machines on the Web from the other Internet machines is that they exchange information using a special system of codes. These codes allow them to display documents with a multimedia flair that's much more appealing than the staid text of traditional Internet resources. These documents, or pages, are combined into Web sites, which are merely a group of pages that are maintained by a person or group of people. The page you usually first encounter when you visit a Web site is called the "home page."

The Web's versatility has unleashed a flood of infotainment from the likes of corporate conglomerates and radical revolutionaries who fill their pages with styled text, graphics, forms, buttons, sounds, and video. As you'll discover in chapter 3, you can view film clips, request information, hear interviews and music clips, and even purchase things through the Web.

This media mix may not entice those who have seen arresting CD-ROM titles. However, as any sausage connoisseur will tell you, the difference is in the links. What distinguishes Web pages from those in a desktop publishing program or on a CD-ROM is that clicking certain phrases in text or parts of images can transport you to another page. The new page may reside in the same folder as the original page, or it might be halfway across the Earth. Links have made the Web truly worldwide, allowing people to conveniently access resources thousands of miles away with a click of the mouse.

If you want to be the one doing the clicking, this book will be your guide to accessing the Web, sampling its riches, and, should you so desire, weaving your own Web pages that can be read by other travelers on the information highway. So get comfortable; you've just purchased a ticket for the next flight into cyberspace.

Why the Web?

The idea for the Web began in 1990 when two scientists, Tim Berners-Lee and Robert Cailliau, sought a way to share particle-acceleration research at the CERN laboratory. Berners-Lee and Cailliau outlined a scheme for "forming a web of information nodes" that would allow data to be shared among a large number of users and computer systems.

From such humble beginnings, the Web has quickly evolved to become the information distribution vehicle of choice on the Internet, encompassing and surpassing many older ways of communicating via the Internet. Computer companies post information about their latest products. Record companies post sound clips from their newest CDs, and fans of all sorts of trivia have made the Web one of the most entertaining and erudite ways to communicate information. Want to find out about video games of the 80s? A movie history of Buster Keaton? Get some pictures of your favorite soft drink? If it is interesting to anyone, it's on the World Wide Web.

There are several reasons for the Web's popularity, among them the broad range of content, global reach, multimedia, interactivity, standards adherence, platform independence, and ease of navigation.

The Web is a global resource. Virtually anyone who has a direct or dial-up connection to the Internet can access the Web. Online services like CompuServe and America Online, which have millions of members who use their services for news, electronic mail, and discussion forums are enabling their Macintosh members to access the Web, providing a new level in ease of use for Web exploration.

Once you've learned the fundamentals, the Web is very simple to use. You can hop from site to site or start sophisticated database searches with a mouse click. Most Web access software will track where you've been, and you can save your favorite sites in a menu for easy recall.

More than any other Internet application, the Web embraces multimedia. By themselves, most programs that access the Web can handle graphics and styled text together on a page. In theory, though, the Web can support any kind of media, even those that haven't been invented yet. New technologies for virtual reality fly-throughs of scenes, panoramic views of distant settings, and advanced multimedia presentations can be supported by the Web with a few mouse clicks.

The Web is also cross-platform. Any computer that can run the Internet access software and connect to the Internet can use the Web. Macs, PCs, Unix, Amigas, and NextStep PCs are among the variety. The Web is a great way of getting information to people without worrying what kind of computer they use. Furthermore, the demands placed on a machine accessing the Web are minimal, even though some Web browsers can consume computing resources with advanced features. A fast modem also helps if you're dialing in.

Although it is not as interactive as the Usenet bulletin boards (a global electronic bulletin board with thousands of subjects for posting and replying to messages) or the Internet Relay Chat (in which a group of people connected at the same time can type messages among themselves), the Web is moving from an online publishing tool to an online transaction system. Once certain security provisions have been addressed, you'll be able to shop and buy things through the Web. And software is on the way that will let the Web become even more interactive.

Finally, the Web provides an interface for other Internet services. Traditionally, a person had to use one program for email, another for file transfers, another for database searches, and another for Usenet newsgroups. The Web can provide all of these through a single program. And while the specialized applications may still fill their respective niches best, it's hard to beat the convenience of a single, easy-to-use interface.

We can tell from the sweat on the pages that you're hooked, so let's debrief you for your expedition.

Plug In

Technically, you don't need to have an Internet connection to reap the benefits of Web technology. For example, many companies are deploying Web sites internally to make information more easily available. You don't even need a network connection to read Web pages that reside on your hard disk. But, the Web and the Internet make a powerful pair, and it is through the Internet that one can find the broadest array of Web content.

There are many ways of accessing the Internet, depending on what services you'd like to be able to use. Virtually all universities and many large companies these days have at least email access to the Internet. Some companies do not allow access to the Web because of security concerns. Check with your network administrator. Generally, connecting to the Web requires that your Mac be able to communicate using TCP/IP, which defines how computers talk on the Internet.

Note

> *For those of you who are interested, TCP/IP stands for Transmission Control Protocol/Internet Protocol. Simply put, TCP/IP is the Internet's native language.*

If you're going it alone, the good news is that connecting to the Internet is easier than ever. At press time, America Online and eWorld were preparing to unveil Web browsers that took advantage of their services' automatic configuration. The bad news is that you must use the browser that they supply to connect to the server. Web exploration, especially at first, can consume lots of time, and the clock is always ticking on America Online. CompuServe's Web access for Mac users was more similar to the method that independent service providers use without some of the configuration hassles. However, better deals can be found outside its vast network.

Because many of them charge a flat rate for 60 or more hours per month, independent Internet service providers are an attractive option for those who want to enjoy cyberspace without minding the clock. Most Internet service providers will offer a low price of about $10 per month for a "shell account," which means that you'll have to use a text-only display. They may even advertise that this includes Web or WWW access. Web access is possible through a shell account using a program called Lynx, but you will be missing the richness of the Web that has made it so appealing.

The bottom line is that, while online services can ease many of the configuration issues typically associated with Web access, and may offer interesting features to their members (such as vendor support or regular chats), they are typically more expensive for those who wish to spend a lot of time on the Internet. Furthermore, online services have traditionally been slow to keep up with the latest advances in Web technology. In contrast, since most Web applications are available freely (at least in a trial version), those who use a service provider (as opposed to an online service) and know how to choose their own software are able to use new Internet goodies first.

To fully realize the benefits of the Web through a service provider, you'll need to sign up for SLIP (Serial Line Internet Protocol) or (PPP) Point-to-Point Protocol, the latter of which is becoming more popular these days. Both of these protocols allow TCP/IP to be used over a remote connection. The main difference between SLIP and PPP is that the former supports only TCP/IP, while PPP can support a variety of protocols. Only PPP allows your Mac and a modem to speak to other machines on the Internet in its native tongue, TCP/IP. You'll also need two control panels (MacTCP and Config PPP) and an extension (PPP) on your Mac to allow it to use a PPP connection.

MacTCP was created by Apple to allow Macs to speak TCP/IP on a network. Many corporations and universities use TCP/IP for their internal networks, and MacTCP was originally created for their use.

By the time you read this, Apple will have released a successor to the MacTCP control panel called Open Transport, which is designed to make it easier for Macintosh computers to use "foreign" network languages like TCP/IP.

MacPPP has two parts: an extension and a control panel, both of which were written by the Merit Network, Inc. These allow Macs to speak TCP/IP over a modem connection.

These items will be discussed in further detail in chapter 2 when you sign up for your Internet connection.

Browsing for Browsers

Once you have a way to access the Internet, you'll need a Web browser for viewing Web pages and some auxiliary programs called "helper applications" to display file types that the browser cannot view (these will be explained in a moment). You will also need a connection through the Internet, whether it be a network connection at your workplace, school, a local trendy Internet cafe, or via an independent service provider or online service.

Your literal window into the World Wide Web is called a browser. The browser's job is to translate and display the codes that get sent from the hosts that you visit. There are many different browsers for different platforms. Almost all are distributed via the Web itself, but some incur commercial fees if you use them beyond an evaluation period.

Netscape Communications Corporation's **Netscape** is currently the most popular browser. It is available for the Mac, Windows, and the X Windows graphical interface for Unix. Netscape delivers a well-designed interface, unique display features, and excellent speed (see Figure 1.1). Its popular design is not surprising considering that it was developed by many of the same people who designed NCSA Mosaic, the browser that set the Web on fire.

Unlike many of its competitors, Netscape's browser (with its trademark "N" logo in its window's upper right corner) is integrated into its own Web site. The company has become an enthusiastic evangelist for Web-based technologies and electronic commerce. It has placed an excellent aggregation of Web tools and knowledge at its Web site.

MacWeb is published by EINet. It supports all the critical features you need to access the Web. Its resource requirements are more modest than Netscape's. MacWeb can be identified by the "EINet" logo in its window's upper left corner. This program is included on the disk in the back of the book.

TCP/Connect II by Intercon is the Microsoft Works of Internet access software. It's a commercial offering and provides features for file transfer protocol (ftp), terminal access, and Usenet discussion groups—all with a fairly consistent look and feel. Version 2.1 marked the debut of its Web browser, which is relatively quick and one of the few that supports Macintosh Drag and Drop, letting you quickly move text and Web locations out of the application. Intercon is planning to beef up and break out its Web browser into a new product called WebShark, which should be available by the time you read this.

NCSA Mosaic by the National Center for Supercomputing Applications at the University of Illinois was the free browser that started the Great Data Rush of the 90s. The original Mosaic, with its telltale spinning globe in the center of an "S," was written to run on top of the UNIX operating system and was released in February 1993. In September of that year, versions were ready for Macintosh and Windows platforms. NCSA Mosaic will continue to evolve, although it is starting to trail behind many browsers that have commercial companies backing them. The purpose of NCSA is systems research, and the continued development of Web software fits right into that mission. Mosaic for Macintosh 1.0.3 was released in January 1994. A final version of Mac Mosaic 2.0 for both Macs and Power Macs is due in 1995.

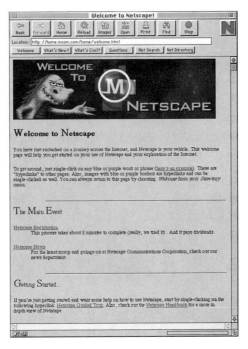

Figure 1.1 *The Netscape home page as seen through Netscape's browser.*

Figure 1.2 *The EINet Galaxy Directory Services home page as seen through MacWeb.*

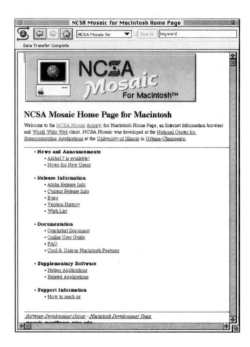

Figure 1.3   *The NCSA Mosaic home page as seen through the Mosaic for Macintosh web browser.*

Enhanced Mosaic by Spyglass is a supported version of its NCSA namesake. While not as flashy as Netscape, it's also commercially supported and is more conservative in generating Web traffic.

InternetWorks is a forthcoming browser that also resembles Netscape. Currently, it is available only for Windows, but a Mac version is due later this year. It was created by what is now the Internet Services division of America Online. While it supports the same access methods of other browsers, it will be the Web interface for millions of America Online's Windows users and, eventually, Mac users. InternetWorks takes advantage of Microsoft's OLE technology to easily exchange Web data with other applications, and can also save both pictures and text from a Web page into a single file.

Internet Assistant for Word by Microsoft is another Windows-only product that will probably make its way to the Mac before year's end. While most Web browsers are individual applications, Internet Assistant turns Microsoft Word 6.0 into a formidable Internet surfboard. Not only can you use Word to view Web pages, but you can use it to compose them as well.

Browsers' Little Helpers

Despite the versatility and volume of Web browsers, they cannot manage the wealth of media found on the World Wide Web alone. While virtually all browsers can accommodate text and certain picture formats, the Web is rapidly expanding to embrace other kinds of media, including sounds, video, electronic documents, and virtual reality walk-throughs. Helper applications are primarily small, focused utilities that specialize in manipulating a certain kind of media. Some of the most popular helper applications are:

JPEGView Before writing the incredible LucasArts game Dark Forces, Aaron Giles wrote this viewer for two of the most popular file formats found on the Web: GIF and JPEG. GIF, or Graphics Interchange Format, was created by the online service CompuServe to allow users of different computing platforms to view pictures on their screen. Although it cannot display more than 256 colors in a file, the format has become very popular in many situations where users need to exchange photographic images (see figure 1.4), and it has become the de facto standard on the Web. Nevertheless, it was recently discovered that a company called Unisys has a patent on an important part of the GIF file format, so CompuServe and other parties are working on a replacement format.

JPEG, which stands for Joint Photographers' Experts Group, is a graphics format for images similar to those used for GIF. The main functional difference between the two formats is that the JPEG format can compress images to a smaller size (than GIF images) because it is designed to compress 24-bit images (thousands of colors); GIFs are based on a maximum 8-bit depth (256 colors). This is important considering many users access the Web over a modem connection, which is relatively slow. Using excessive JPEG compression can reduce an image's quality, but JPEG images typically retain high quality, unless drastic compression is sought.

SoundMachine Since Mosaic first appeared under Unix, and since many users of the Internet use Unix machines, the sound file format for Unix, μlaw has become very popular. SoundMachine is versatile sound player that can play many different sound formats on your Macintosh.

SoundApp This application plays Unix sound files, but can also handle PC sound files, known as .WAV (pronounced "wave") files, and a machine-independent audio file format called AIFF (Audio Interchange File Format). SoundApp also allows you to translate sound files among several formats.

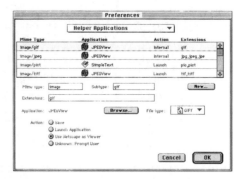

Figure 1.4   *Choosing JPEGView as a helper application.*

StuffIt Expander When the Web spins up a file that you want to transfer to your hard disk, it will often store the file in one of two formats, known as BinHex (in which case it will end in .hqx) or uuencoded (pronounced "you-you-encoded"). These formats are used because there are many machines in the Internet that can only work with textual data. Mac files on these machines must be stored in a special text-based code. StuffIt Expander is a free program that will convert these coded files into standard Macintosh files, and will even decompress them if they've been compressed using standard Macintosh compression programs.

Sparkle While almost all Mac IIs or later machines can play QuickTime movies using the latest version of the free SimpleText program, Sparkle takes advantage of the latest Apple system software to provide great performance for QuickTime movies. Sparkle can also play MPEG movies, which are an industry-standard way to distribute digital video.

As we'll discuss in chapter 7, the Web is poised to encompass even more media—richly laid out Acrobat files, panoramic views or remote locations, 3D walk-throughs of virtual spaces, and intelligent, interactive animations.

Clearly, the Web has come a long way from its text-only origins.

All Wired Up

We've outlined the ingredients for a great time on the World Wide Web; now it's time to start cooking. In the next chapter, we'll explain how to configure your browser and its auxiliary files, connect to the Web and start a near-infinite journey. We'll also point out some great sites for getting a feel of what's on the Web, but once you get online, it's quite possible that you'll start surfing the Web on your own and forget all about us for a while. Once you get the hang of it, come on back to the book and we'll teach you how to create your own web page and server, and we'll talk about what the future will bring. Let's get started.

Chapter

2

Cyberspace Ho!

Learning to surf the Web isn't very different than learning how to drive a car, except your insurance premiums don't go up if you're involved in a crash. There are a few concepts you need to keep in mind, after which it's pretty smooth sailing. And when you're mentioning concepts and computers in the same paragraph, you know there have to be some acronyms waiting in the wings.

In this chapter, we'll start examining the fabrics that link and transmit information across the Web, including how Web sites communicate and present their content. After that, we'll focus on how browsers help you weave your way through the Web, and take off on our maiden Web voyage.

Note

This chapter assumes that you have installed the software that comes on the World Wide Web Starter Kit disk. To install the software, simply insert the disk, double click on the Installer, and you're ready to go. The installer will take care of the rest for you.

If you already have some of the items on the disk, choose "Custom Install" to install the programs that you need.

How Does it Work?

The Web consists of two kinds of machines, clients and servers. Servers contain the content that clients browse. Macs, PCs, and Unix machines can act as a client or a server, or both at the same time, although different software is used for browsing and serving.

Clients and servers typically communicate information on the Web through a language called HyperText Transport Protocol, or HTTP. Unlike many online services, the Web is based on *transactions*; most of the communication that takes place between clients and servers is in the form of short messages. The client sends a request to the server to perform an operation, such as displaying a page. The server responds and complies under normal circumstances. We'll be providing more details on browser and server software for the Mac in this chapter and subsequent chapters.

However, once a Web page is displayed, it appears as if you are maintaining a "live" connection since all the content is in front of you. In reality, the server is paying absolutely no attention to you. This is the great illusion of the World Wide Web.

Most Web pages are constructed using a system of formatting codes known as HTML, or HyperText Markup Language. HTML is intended to describe structured documents. It is a subset of a more comprehensive method of describing the structure of long, often technical documents called SGML, or Standard Generalized Markup Language. SGML remains popular in the federal government and other large institutions, but the creative forces behind the Web are slowly pushing HTML away from its SGML origins. We'll be discussing HTML in depth in later chapters.

Items on the Web like pages, files, graphics and sounds must all have a way of identifying themselves. This is accomplished through a URL (Uniform Resource Locator) URLs are critical to finding information on the Web; its very common for users of the Web to notify each other of interesting Web sites by emailing URLs to each other. Understanding URLs, though, requires a few bits of information about how computers on the Internet are named.

All machines on the Internet have a domain name and an organization name. For example, you may have seen Internet email addresses such as the fictional "ross_rubin@hayden.com". In this case, "hayden.com" is the domain name and ".com" is the domain suffix. Domain suffixes indicate an organization's type (see table 2.1).

Table 2.1
Domain Names and Domain Suffixes

Domain suffix	Organization type
.com	Commercial
.edu	Educational
.org	Non-commercial organization
.gov	Government
.mil	Military

Sometimes, a word will precede the domain name, like "ross_rubin@authors.hayden.com". In this case, "authors" is the machine that hosts my email account. URLs are similar to email addresses except they specify data on computers instead of email accounts.

A URL typically consists of three parts. The initial word indicates the type of protocol being used to access the information. In most cases, this will be HTTP. The protocol is separated from the rest of the URL by a colon (:) and two slashes (//). Next comes the machine name, which is often "www.<name of organization>.<domain name>". So, for example, if one wanted to get to the home page for Macmillan Computer Publishing, the URL would be

```
http://www.mcp.com
```

You'll find this format makes a fine rule of thumb for locating large organizations on the Web, such as:

```
http://www.apple.com (Apple Computer)
http://www.eff.org (Electronic Frontier Foundation)
http://www.cornell.edu (Cornell University)
http://www.whitehouse.gov (Mr. Clinton's digs)
```

These URLs will take you to an organization's "home page," an introductory springboard from which you can often access other pages.

Often, a URL will extend past the domain name to indicate a directory or document on the Web site. While `http://www.apple.com` would bring you to Apple's home page, `http://www.apple.com/dev/qd3d/welcome.html` would display the Web page "welcome.html" in the "qd3d" folder in the "dev" folder on `www.apple.com`.

Special uses of the Web can cause URLs to get very large and unwieldy, such as:

```
http://www.sun.com/cgi-bin/sidMakeMove?1,1,1,-1,
-1,0,0,7,7,X5.035.05.X
```

Take solace in that you'll probably never have to type anything as complex as this.

Now that you have some idea of how the computers on the Web communicate and locate each other, it's time to learn how to get in on the conversation.

Beginning to Browse

Whether it be through an online service or an independent service provider, a browser is your literal window into the World Wide Web. At its heart, a browser has a very simple task—to translate the special codes and file references in an HTML document into meaningful output. Since the Web is so vast and incorporates so many different kinds of media, though, Web browsers generally differentiate themselves on such traits as what HTML commands they can interpret, how fast they access content, and what navigation features they offer, although some, Netscape in particular, are beginning to incorporate other formats and leading multimedia features into its browser.

As we write, online services and certain large Internet service providers like Netcom of San Jose and Pipeline of New York City offer Web access only through their own browsers. Generally, these browsers are not as full-featured as those that can be used with a PPP connection. In any case, a PPP connection offers you much more flexibility in picking a browser that meets your needs and works well with your system software and hardware. While we've furnished a copy of MacWeb on the accompanying disk, we'll also be discussing Netscape Navigator, the developers of which claim is the browser of choice for 75 percent of WWW users.

The most difficult part of using a Web browser is setting up two pieces of software: MacTCP and MacPPP. MacTCP lets your Mac speak TCP/IP, the universal protocol of the Internet, while MacPPP lets TCP/IP travel over a phone wire using a modem. We will discuss configuring both of these as they would relate to an Internet service provider.

The bad news is that it is impossible for you to configure these pieces of software without some information that you need from an Internet Service provider. This is why it is essential that you make sure your service provider is capable of supporting Mac users well. The worse news is that Mac-savvy service providers may be hard to find. Ask if they have instructions on how to configure MacTCP and MacPPP. If they ask you what MacTCP is, apply the gentle art of phone call disconnection.

If you're encountering problems finding an access provider who knows a bit about the Mac, call a local BBS (bulletin board service) or attend a user group meeting. You can be sure local Internet service providers will be a hot topic wherever Mac modem users congregate.

Configuring MacPPP

MacPPP consists of two files, an extension called PPP and a control panel called ConfigPPP. You can install both files by dragging them to the System Folder and restarting. At the time of writing, the latest version of MacPPP was 2.01, which is included on our companion disk.

The control panel ConfigPPP is where you'll enter in the data necessary to set up a PPP connection to your Internet service provider. For purposes of illustration, we'll pretend we're connecting to VaporNet, a local service provider, but any options or numbers given to you by your service provider will supersede the fictional ones we're using here.

To configure PPP, follow these steps:

1. Open the ConfigPPP control panel.

2. Click "New". A field appears in which you should type the name of your service provider.

3. Type the name of your service provider. We'll use VaporNet.

4. Click "Config..." A dialog box appears. Since most Internet Service Providers offer high-speed access at 28,800 KB/second, choose the port speed 57,600 bps, which is the highest speed many Mac serial ports support. This will allow you to take advantage of some of the compression features offered by most modems. Even if you don't have a 28,800 bps modem, you should connect at the highest speed your modem supports. You should consider lowering this value if you have trouble connecting.

5. For flow control, choose CTS Only. This setting assumes you're using a "hardware handshaking" cable that most high-speed modems use. This may be another setting to try changing if you have trouble connecting.

6. If you have Touch-Tone service, click the "Tone Dial" radio button, otherwise click "Pulse Dial".

7. In the Phone Num field, enter the phone number your service provider gave you to access a PPP connection. We'll put in the fictional number (212) 555-1212. You can leave Modem Init field blank unless your modem manufacturer or service provider indicates otherwise.

Configuring the PPP Connect Script

We're not out of this yet. In the service provider dialog, there is a button for Connect Script. This is where you'll enter a short dialog that your Mac will have with the service provider's host machine before it allows you onto the Internet.

As is the case in many human conversations, success hinges on knowing what to say at the right time. Connect scripts watch for certain letters that the host writes and gives an appropriate response. Connect scripts vary by provider, but we'll create an explanatory example for use with VaporNet. Note that you should follow your service provider's instructions for connect scripts.

1. In ConfigPPP's service provider dialog box, click "Connect Script".

2. In the timeout field, enter 60 as the number of seconds before the software decides a connection could not take place.

3. On the first line, we'll type a "greater than" symbol (>). This is where VaporNet asks us the kind of account we're using. Clicking the "Wait" radio button indicates that we are waiting until this symbol is generated by the host software.

4. On the next line, click "Out". This indicates that we will be sending text "out" to the server. We'll enter "ppp" (no quotes) to indicate that we want to start a PPP session. We'll also check the "CR" check box, which has the same effect as pressing "Return" to enter some text.

5. The next four lines continue the dialog we've started. Next, we wait for the word "login:". Click "Wait" and type "login:" (no quotes) on line 3.

6. On the fourth line, click "Out", type the name, in this case "rrubin", and click the "CR" check box.

7. On the fifth line, click "Wait" and type "password:" (no quotes).

8. On the sixth line, click "Out", type your password (your provider may have given you one—otherwise choose your own), in this case "web", and click the "CR" checkbox.

9. Click OK.

You're halfway there. Your computer now knows how to dial into the Internet. Next it needs to know how to talk the Internet language. Luckily, you have a translator. MacTCP.

Configuring MacTCP

MacTCP is a control panel that comes with System 7.5. However, System 7.5 comes with MacTCP version 2.0.4—the version that comes on the World Wide Web Starter Kit disk is version 2.0.6. You should use version 2.0.6 to connect to the Internet. The installer should have placed MacTCP in the correct place for you.

This sample configuration explains how to set up MacTCP so that you appear on the Internet as a customer of VaporNet, a fictional local Internet service provider. Note that this is just an example, and you should use the options and addresses given to you by your service provider.

To configure MacTCP, follow these steps:

1. Open the MacTCP control panel.

2. If it is not already selected, click the "PPP" icon in the MacTCP window.

3. Click "More…" A new window appears with what looks like complicated and jumbled information. Don't worry, you won't have to know what all of this means.

4. In the Obtain Address field (top-left corner of the window), click "Server". This instructs the client to look up your TCP/IP address information from a machine at the host site.

5. A Domain Name Server translates between numeric IP addresses and the domain names used in email addresses and most URLs. In the Domain Name Server Information area, type the name and IP address of your Domain Name Server as given to you by your service provider. For illustration purposes, we'll enter vapor.net as the Server. And we will enter the nonexistent address 300.45.22.1 as the IP address. Often, a service provider will give you multiple name servers. Choose one as the default by clicking the Default radio button.

6. Click OK, or press Return.

7. Close the MacTCP control panel.

You will need to restart your comptuer for your new MacTCP settings to activate.

Let's Get Open

The release of the Power Macintosh 9500 marked the public debut of Open Transport. Open Transport is a breakthrough for Mac network access because it allows the Mac to take advantage of new protocols as they become available. Developers writing to Open Transport will be insulated from whatever happens to be the preferred pipe for data in the future. The extension also increases the number of simultaneous connections a Mac can handle, which is important when it's being used as a Web server.

Open Transport also brings other benefits, such as taking advantage of PowerPC speed, and has other benefits slated for the future. At the time of publication, though, Apple was still ironing out compatibility with older network software and so many Power Mac users are sticking with MacTCP for the time being.

Dialing and Connecting to the Internet

To dial into the Internet, make sure your modem is on and it is connected, then open the ConfigPPP control panel. Since you have everything already configured, all you need to do is click on the "Open" button in the ConfigPPP window.

A series of dialog boxes will show you the connection status. When your connection is live, the status window disappears and you will see smiling faces in the top-left corner of the PPP window. At this point you are connected to the Internet and you are ready to surf.

To disconnect, click on the Hard Close button in the ConfigPPP window. Clicking on this will cut off your Internet connection. If you choose the Soft Close button, you will find that your computer may try to dial to the Internet at seemingly random times. Do not attempt this until you have become more savvy with Internet usage.

If you have trouble connecting, go through the steps again and make sure you have configured everything correctly. Because we do not know which provider you are using, we cannot help you troubleshoot your connection. You need to make a call to your Internet Service Provider, who will help you walk through the connection. It is possible that you received bad information from your provider. If your provider cannot help you with your connection, this might be an indication of the type of service it provides and you may want to consider another provider.

Browsing the Browser

Both MacWeb and Netscape have special features to help you use the World Wide Web. These features enable you to:

- Connect to a "home page" that serves as a launch pad to the rest of the Web.
- Defer the display of graphics for faster access.
- Backtrack sites you've visited in a session a step at a time or from a menu.
- Designate a list of favorite sites maintained between sessions.
- Save URLs for future reference or for use with other applications.

Browser Settings

While Web browsers don't usually need to be configured to work, there are some settings you may want to enter before going online.

Entering MacWeb Settings

You should be aware of a few settings before going online. To adjust these settings:

1. Start the MacWeb application.

2. Choose Preferences from the File menu. A dialog box appears.

   Home URL: This is the address of the page MacWeb displays when you start the application. It could be a file on your local hard disk or a page out on the Web, in which case MacWeb should start the modem dialing after you launch it. For now, let's leave this setting blank.

   EMail Address: Your email address should be your user id@domain. So, if I logged in with the id "rrubin" on vapornet, my email address should be "rrubin@vapornet.com"

3. Choose Format from the popup menu in the dialog box.

   If you'd like graphics to be displayed automatically when you reach a site, select the "Autoload" check box. Not checking this box will speed up the display of Web pages by several orders of magnitude. However, some of the Web's most interesting sites have alluring graphics.

There are other ways to configure Web browsers, especially when it comes to handing off files to other applications, but the settings we've entered would be enough to get us on our maiden voyage.

Let's Surf

Choose "EINet Galaxy" from MacWeb's Navigate menu. You'll see MacPPP's dialing dialog appear. If it does not, you may need to open the PPP connection by opening the MacPPP control panel and clicking the Open button.

After the network connection is established, this preloaded URL takes you to a database that quickly demonstrates the power of the Web (see figure 2.1).

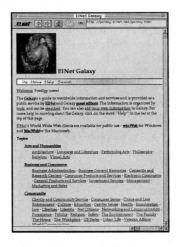

Figure 2.1   *The EINet Galaxy Web page is a directory of hyperlinks to information resources on the Internet. It is the home page for TradeWave, Inc., makers of MacWeb.*

The main EINet Galaxy document displays an index to a wide variety of subjects that you can access through your Web browser. If you scroll to the bottom of the document, you'll see a field in which you can type a keyword and make a search for still other Web pages.

Midway through the page is a category for Science, and a subtopic link for Astronomy. Note that any text that contains a link is blue and underlined. Clicking on "Astronomy" takes you to the URL **http://galaxy.einet.net/galaxy/Science/Astronomy.html**, which is displayed in your browser window. This document contains more links to other documents and servers devoted to the subject of astronomy (see figure 2.2).

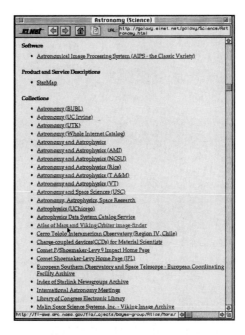

Figure 2.2 *Each of the hyperlinks on the Astronomy index at EINet Galaxy will take you to a server full of information.*

Scroll this new document down to the section titled Collections and the hyperlink for the Atlas of Mars and Viking Orbiter Image-finder. This link sends the URL **http://fi-www.arc.nasa.gov/fia/projects/bayes-group/Atlas/Mars/** to a Web server at NASA's Ames Research Center and returns a list of information and images made by the Voyager spacecraft that visited Mars (see figure 2.3).

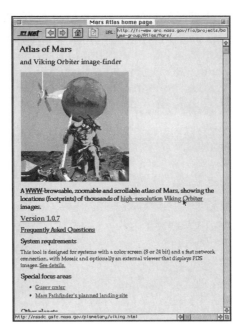

Figure 2.3   *The Mars Atlas collection of documents and images is located at the NASA Ames Research Center, and includes an archive of photographs taken by the Viking Orbiter.*

Toward the top of this new document is a link to "thousands of high resolution Viking Orbiter images." Click on the phrase Viking Orbiter. This sends the URL **http://nssdc.gsfc.nasa.gov/planetary/viking.html** to the NASA Ames server and returns a Web document that describes the Viking Mission to Mars, with a color photograph from Mars across the top of the page (see figure 2.4).

Finally, scroll down this page to a menu list of hyperlinks marked with little color icons and find the link titled Mars Photo Gallery. This sends the URL **http://nssdc.gsfc.nasa.gov/photo_gallery/PhotoGallery-Mars.html** and provides a list of photographs taken by the Viking Orbiter (see figure 2.5).

Figure 2.4 *The Viking Mission to Mars document explains the overall purpose of that space mission and provides hyperlinks to indexes of images sent back by the orbiter.*

The Photo Gallery document displays a series of thumbnail versions of the photographs in the Gallery, together with a short hyperlink description of each one. The first photo is a composite photograph of the planet taken from space. Clicking this link sends the URL **http://nssdc.gsfc.nasa.gov/image/ planetary/mars/marsglobe1.jpg** to the server, requesting that this file be downloaded to your computer. Do it!

Transferring this composite JPEG picture of Mars (see figure 2.6) may take a minute of two. Since MacWeb cannot display JPEG files by itself, it launches JPEGView (if you have it installed on your computer—if not, check Chapter 1 for more information) and open the image. The image is displayed as large as your screen permits.

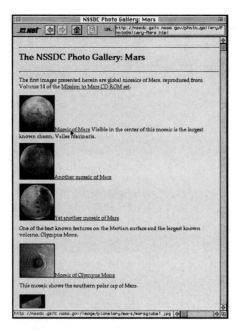

Figure 2.5   *The NSSDC Photo Gallery of Mars provides you with links to a collection of high-resolution 24-bit color photographs of the planet taken at close range from outer space.*

Don't close MacWeb yet. If you're using a dial-up connection to the Internet, you can close that if you'd like, but keep the MacWeb window open. You can use the documents you've just downloaded to check out the rest of the MacWeb interface.

Your test drive just demonstrated how hyperlinks can help you find information on the Internet directly and simply. You also got a taste of the variety of information that is almost immediately available to you if you cruise the Web. You couldn't use any other type of Internet interface to do what you just did; nor could you have retrieved the information more quickly than you just did on the WWW.

MacWeb lets you travel the Web in many ways. A closer look at its interface reveals several ways to take advantage of the links that the Web provides.

Figure 2.6   *This JPEG photograph is a composite made from images captured by the Viking Orbiter.*

MacWeb offers several navigation tools to help you determine where you are and where you're going. Its minimalist toolbar contains left and right arrows. The left arrow returns you to sites you have visited in a given Web session, with the most recently visited sites coming first. The right arrow moves you from the least recently visited to the most recently visited sites. The Home button takes you back to your home page, which can be on your hard disk or out on the Web. You can type in a URL for your home page in MacWeb's general preferences.

MacWeb's Navigate menu contains equivalents for the arrow and home toolbar icons, as well as a History menu item that lets you choose directly the titles of pages you've visited since starting the Web session. The Hotlist menu lets you keep your favorite pages a menu item away.

To the right of the toolbar, MacWeb provides a large field for displaying and typing in URLs. Typing in a URL and pressing Return will take you directly to an item on the Web. By holding the mouse button down on any item that contains a link, a popup menu appears that allows you to retrieve a document to the browser window or to disk, copy its URL to the Clipboard or to the HotList menu. You can also open, save, and print Web pages using the standard Mac commands in the File menu. Keep in mind, though, that saving a Web page saves only the text. The graphics are kept in separate files on the server. Any text formatting will be removed as well.

The Wrap-up

That's about all there is to the basics of how to use MacWeb. You will no doubt hone your MacWeb skills after a few hours of connect time and figure out some power-user shortcuts for the frequent tasks you perform on the Web. The next chapter will help you get into this.

Netscape Navigator

As we mentioned in Chapter 1, Netscape Navigator (commonly just "Netscape") is currently the most popular Web browser (see figure 2.7). While an evaluation copy of Netscape is available freely at the company's Web site `http://www.netscape.com`, you must purchase it if you continue to use it.

Why Netscape?

Among Netscape's advanced features are:

- Disk caching. This technique saves recently retrieved content from the Web on your hard disk, allowing you to reload it quickly.

- Email. Certain links in Web documents, when clicked, allow you to send email to someone. Netscape includes a built-in email sending program. It is also possible to receive and read email through Netscape, although this feature is not included with the product.

- Newsgroups. Netscape allows you to post, read, and reply to messages in any of the 10,000+ Usenet newsgroups.

- Simultaneous image transfers. Netscape can retrieve multiple images at once and supports the gradual display of images. This feature, combined with its caching, helps make Netscape very fast.

■ Apple Events. The Mac version of Netscape supports certain Apple events which allow it to communicate with other Mac applications and to be controlled, to some extent, by scripting languages such as AppleScript.

■ Macintosh Drag and Drop. Netscape's mail window and its history list both support Macintosh Drag and Drop, which lets you drag text between windows and applications.

■ Hierarchical bookmarks. While most Web browsers can maintain a simple list of sites, Netscape allows you to organize your favorite sites into a multilevel, hierarchical menu. Netscape even includes an (admittedly clumsy) editing window for this menu.

■ Popup menus. Netscape uses a different popup menu from MacWeb when you hold the mouse down on an item in a Web page which allows you to, among other things, copy graphics on Web pages directly to the Clipboard. We've heard of drag and drop, but this is grab and cop!

■ Security. Netscape has defined a protocol called Secure Sockets Layer (SSL) to allow confidential information, such as credit card numbers, to travel over the Web without being stolen by hackers. SSL and another standard known as Secure HyperText Transfer Protocol (S-HTTP) will enable commerce over the Web.

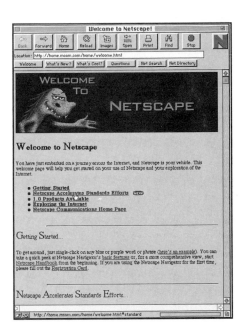

Figure 2.7   *Netscape Navigator Home Page.*

More controversially, Netscape supports many extensions to the HTML language that have not been standardized yet. These features range from the useful, such as tables within Web documents, to the frivolous, such as tiled background pictures. The next major version of MacWeb, version 2.0, is supposed to support many of these enhancements as well. Not surprisingly, Netscape needs more RAM to run than other browsers; a typical RAM allocation is 4 MB.

Netscape's browser is only half of the experience of the product. The company maintains a well-designed Web site with links to many excellent Web resources.

Epilogue

Congratulations. You've taken those first tiny steps into the Web. But as any spider will tell you, once you're in, you're going to get caught up in it quickly. After you've played with your browser's navigation aids, you'll probably go off blazing your own path, but we've decided to highlight some interesting sites in the next chapter.

Chapter 3

Around the World in 80 Clicks

During 1994 alone, the size of the Web grew from 1,000 to more than 12,000 servers. There are more than two million URLs representing documents available on the Web, covering everything from aardvarks to Zimbabwe. With a Web browser and an Internet connection, you can tap into a wealth of information and entertainment recorded on the disks of a vast digital library. One click can summon galaxies millions of light-years away at a NASA laboratory or reveal the strands of DNA in a drop of human blood in a medical research facility.

Furthermore, the Web has extended far past its scientific and research origins. It is a newspaper, a commercial, a stump, a canvas, a teacher, and a playground. It is a source for breaking news and a haven for forgotten trivia.

There are whole books that amount to little more than lists of URLs. This is not one of them. But the first part of this chapter seeks to demonstrate some of the many different ways the Web is being used today.

As we discussed in Chapter 1, one reason for the Web's success has been its embrace of older Internet tools and protocols. The second part of this chapter highlights several Web sites from which you can access pages that were created without the Web in mind, but work smoothly with Netscape.

Windows on the World

In the last chapter, you visited your first Web site; now it's time to take in the riches that the Web has to offer. We will visit sites that demonstrate the cultural, sales, marketing, popular, interpersonal, and entertainment aspects of the Web. In the process, we will explore some special features of the Web and dip into its multimedia mix.

Cultural: ANIMA Arts Network for Integrated Media Applications

```
http://www.wimsey.com/anima/ANIMAhome.html
```

The Arts Network for Integrated Media Applications, located in Vancouver, British Columbia, is run by a group of digital media artists who refer to themselves as the Web Weavers. Derek Dowden is the server administrator and frequent document contributor.

ANIMA is both a resource site and a starting point for art trawling on the Web. In addition to literature and artwork from decidedly nonmainstream Vancouver area artists, ANIMA features several eclectic indexes that match its goal of being a network unto itself. The main page displays a row of buttons across the screen that lead to these major indexes (see figure 3.1). Clicking on any one of these icons takes you to that index.

If you click ArtWorld, you've hit the mother lode. This index is the largest at ANIMA and contains scores of hyperlinks to art sites around the world. These servers cover a broad range of tastes, from more traditional collections-based museum exhibits to electronic outposts of *sturm und drang*.

ANIMA also provides plenty of links to more mainstream art spaces on the Internet, including an array of museums and university art galleries. One collection in particular that I find intriguing is at the University of California, Riverside/California Museum of Photography (UCR/CMP).

UCR/CMP owns the largest collection of stereoscopic photographs in the world. These photographs were made during the late 1800s using twin cameras to produce the first realistic "3-D" images.

Stereoscopic images and viewers were the "virtual reality" device of that time. The Web server at UCR/CMP makes note of this with a GIF file of "Man with Stereoscope", showing an unidentified man's head firmly planted into his stereoscopic viewer (see figure 3.2). The scene bears a striking resemblance to images of people using VR helmets today.

Figure 3.1   *The ANIMA home page.*

Figure 3.2   *A man looking into a Stereoscope.*

Research: NASA Goddard Institute for Space Studies

http://www.giss.nasa.gov/

The National Aeronautics and Space Administration maintains such a broad presence on the Internet and throughout the Web that it is almost impossible to define a single location for information about NASA research activities.

A visit to one of the main NASA Web indexes, like **http://www.sti.nasa.gov/www.html,** is a quick lesson in the complexity of the NASA bureaucracy. Each of NASA's centers is organized into Directorates. Each of these Directorates in turn is responsible for several areas of research. Under the jurisdiction of Goddard Space Flight Center, physically located in Greenbelt, Maryland, is Directorate 940, the Goddard Institute for Space Studies.

The Goddard Institute for Space Studies (GISS) is actually located on the campus of Columbia University, above Tom's Diner, on the upper west side of Manhattan. The diner happens to be one of the locations used for filming the Seinfeld television show (see figure 3.3).

Figure 3.3   Tom's Diner on 112th Street.

NASA provides a tremendous amount of information on the Web, and maintains its own very large network of servers and links to the rest of the Internet. Once you reach one of NASA's servers, you will find connections that lead all over the place. An interesting example at the GISS server is a clickable map of Manhattan that connects to several dozen Web servers on the island.

From the main Goddard Institute page, you can follow links to other earth sciences research facilities, links to World Wide Web facilities, or go deeper into the NASA labyrinth. If you scroll down the page, you'll reach a hyperlink to NASA Hot Topics. One mouse click later, you're on a page full of links to the latest and greatest space research projects (see figure 3.4).

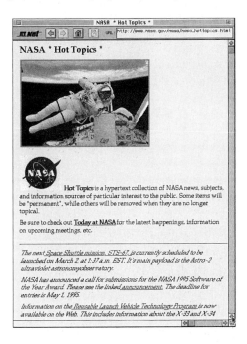

Figure 3.4   *Hot Topics is a directory of the latest activities at NASA*
http://www.nasa.gov/nasa/nasa_hottopics.html.

NASA is a treasure trove of interesting, cool, and exciting visual data. Let's face it, how many times have you been into outer space? Scroll down the Hot Topics page and you'll see a hyperlinked listing for Public Use of Remote Sensing Data. These are your tax dollars at work, so let's use some of the data (see figure 3.5).

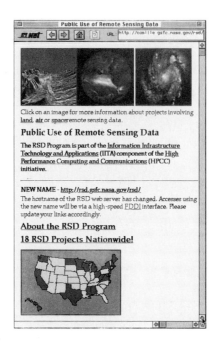

Figure 3.5   *NASA's Web servers are seemingly endless layers of information and images (note the clickable US map).*

Yet another page full of links comes back, with connections to information about remote sensing data. But if you want to see the pictures, scroll down toward the bottom of the page and click on the buttons for Image Catalogue or Movie Catalogue.

You'll be amazed at the energy devoted to making information available through the scores, if not hundreds, of NASA Web servers. If you're looking for ideas on how to use the Web, you'll find them cruising these servers.

If you'd like to start at the top and work your way down, set aside a few days. The administrative NASA Home Page is at: **http://hypatia.gsfc.nasa.gov/ NASA_homepage.html**. A general directory of NASA Web servers is at **http:// www.sti.nasa.gov/www.html** and links to 59 Web servers at various NASA laboratories and space centers.

Sales: The Internet Shopping Network

http://www.internet.net

The creators of the Internet Shopping Network (ISN) have a simple goal: to create the world's largest shopping mall. That dream became much closer to reality when it was purchased by an organization that has sought the same goal through another medium: the Home Shopping Network cable channel.

Unlike its parent cable channel, you must first become a member of ISN before you can purchase anything. Becoming a member requires that you fill out an onscreen form, which acts identically to any you may have used in any database product. Web forms support text fields, popup menus, lists, checkboxes, and radio buttons. However, you're still free to browse even if you don't become a member.

There has been much discussion over how or if commerce on the Web will evolve, or if its even desirable. One key factor in its success is reliable security so that credit card numbers traveling over the wire cannot be picked up by malicious souls looking for such things in Internet transmissions. To that end, Netscape and other companies are working on secure Web servers and browsers that can encrypt any messages traveling along the wire. Encryption makes it virtually impossible for would-be cybercrooks to access confidential information. When Netscape is accessing a secure Web document, a blue line appears above the page and the key icon at the bottom of the window takes on a blue background.

ISN is far from the only company seeking to ensnare hard-earned dollars in its Web site. We'll discuss how to find other sales sites in the next chapter.

Marketing: Batman Forever

http://www.batmanforever.com

By the time this book reaches your hands, time will have judged whether Batman Forever, the third movie featuring DC Comics' Dark Knight, has become a box office smash or headed straight down the BatChute. One thing is certain, though, its Web site is a big hit.

Batman Forever initially presents the Batman logo with some animation below it. While it's not at all intuitive, clicking the logo takes you to Gotham City, complete with its metropolitan skyline. The picture is known as an image map.

Clicking different parts of it will take you to different pages. The Post Office page makes very innovative use of Netscape's tiled backgrounds, crowning them with a graphic to create a convincing illusion of a skyscraper.

Batman Forever is filled with images, profiles of stars, and even a few conundrums from the wily Riddler. While most Web sites are advertised on the Internet, the URL for Batman Forever was plastered all over posters in metropolitan areas. It's one more sign of the Web becoming part of our culture.

Job-Hunting: CareerMosaic

`http://www.careermosaic.com`

While the purple-tented graduates on its home page reveal that this site is geared toward those about to enter the world of employment (and the employers tend to be mostly high-tech at this point), CareerMosaic gives a glimpse of how job-hunting on the Web is evolving. Keep the dime for the shoe shine.

With more than 70 members at this point, some of which participate in online job fairs, CareerMosaic makes it easy for prospective employees to browse a company's vital statistics. The J.O.B.S. (Jobs Offered By Search) link has a database that you can search for current openings and also has a way for you to search across various Usenet newsgroups to see online classifieds. With more newspapers hitting the Web every day, links to your local paper may lie in the future.

CareerMosaic, which is run by recruitment advertising specialists Bernard Hodes Advertising, also hopes to put more career-building resource information on its site.

Entertainment: Virtual Vegas

`http://www.virtualvegas.com`

If you've decided you want to marry your online love in a hurry, Virtual Vegas would be the place. It's an attempt to recreate the City of Sin in cyberspace. Virtual Vegas features a beauty pageant, convention center and, of course, a casino. The site has enough eye-tiring glitz to be mistaken for its namesake as well.

Clicking the Casino button allows you to play roulette and blackjack, among other games. The blackjack game is based on a gaming engine developed by Universal Access, Inc. It's an example of an external program that can be used on the Web through an interface called CGI, or Common Gateway Interface. CGI scripts can be written in a number of different programming languages. On the Mac, for example, they can be written in AppleScript. Another popular language for CGI programs is Perl, which is available on the Mac and popular on Unix machines.

The blackjack rules here are pretty standard, and the bets are funny money for now. There are other blackjack and card game sites on the Web, but we chose this one for its detail, nicely rendered cards, and the virtual winnings we were able to take home after bribing the dealer.

If at First...

As you explore the Web, remember that it's a very fluid network. Some individually maintained servers that existed only a few weeks ago may no longer be operating or may have just moved to a different location on the Internet.

Even in cyberspace, things go wrong. If you try to retrieve a document, but instead get a message that the server is not responding, it does not necessarily mean anything is wrong at your end. The Web's popularity is exploding, and not every server is equipped to handle the volume of requests it is getting. Web servers can only handle so many requests at once. When you address a server that is already handling its limit of simultaneous requests, you may not get any response at all.

While popular sites tend to adopt more powerful computers, components within these machines can fail. Furthermore, remember that news (and rumors) travel very fast around the Internet. When news hits about a popular new Web site or file available through the Web, remember that you may be competing against hundreds of users worldwide to access information or a service. For these reasons, it's always a good idea to try the URL again later.

We hope this section has given you a taste of the different kinds of content you're likely to find on the Web. In the next section, we'll discuss how the Web can be used to access Internet resources other than "Web sites," including gopher document databases and ftp file libraries.

Services with a Smile

Thanks to the ingenuity of Web software designers and the structure of Uniform Resource Locator addresses, Web browsers can interface with many different kinds of Internet servers, even those that were not written with the Web in mind. In this respect, they are the Swiss Army knives of the Internet.

While some limitations on other services exist, you can access the vast majority of Internet information using only a Web browser and an email package, like Qualcomm's Eudora. And it may not be long before Web browsers are able to receive email as well as send it.

This section will discuss using Web browsers to access different kinds of Web services, such as email, gopher, ftp, news and telnet.

Email: Hayden Books

```
http://www.mcp.com/hayden
```

Yes, our beloved publisher is on the Web. Hayden's Web site is part of the Macmillan Computer Publishing Information SuperLibrary, as it's called. At Hayden's site, you can get information on new titles and take advantage of forms to enter contests for win books.

Before the Web, email accounted for the lion's share of Internet traffic. The ability to communicate textual information contrasts sharply to the nature of the Web, which is to publish multimedia information to large groups of people, but the two technologies gel nicely.

On Hayden's Web page, two links at the bottom of the page allow you to send mail. One of these sends mail to the webmaster, which is a de facto title for the person responsible for administering a web site. These links are called "mailto" URLs because clicking them allows you to send mail providing the browser has the ability to accommodate the feature. Clicking a mailto link in Netscape opens an email window preaddressed with your email address and the recipient's. Netscape also has a Mail Document command in the File menu which includes the URL of the document and can include its text as well.

Other browsers may handle email differently. The Web browser for the Mac version of America Online, for instance, uses the regular America Online mail form. Clicking a mailto URL returns you to the America Online program and opens a mail form there. One advantage of this approach is that America Online members don't have to learn another email system to send mail via the Web.

Gopher: Yale Peabody Museum of Natural History Gopher

```
gopher://gopher.peabody.yale.edu:70/1
```

As any summer intern will tell you, a "gopher" is someone who is always asked to "go fer coffee" or "go fer supplies." Internet gophers "go fer" documents.

Gopher is a distributed document search and retrieval service that enables users to search multiple sites by addressing inquiries to any gopher server that has a record of those sites. Gopher has become quite popular among universities, museums, libraries, and other organizations that have large libraries of text-based information. Gopher allows these documents to be publicly searched and retrieved without any changes to the documents themselves.

With its origins at the University of Minnesota, gopher was a popular tool before the Web, but works well with Web browsers. Note that gopher servers, like Web servers, can be accessed through URLs, but "gopher," rather than "http," is used at the beginning of the URL. You can also still use special programs to access gopher servers like the popular TurboGopher program.

When you retrieve a gopher directory, you see a list of files in that directory as well as list items that represent other directories on that server or any other gopher server registered with it (see figure 3.6). To the gopher client, a server directory appears like any other hierarchical file directory, with other Gopher servers represented as subordinate levels to the main directory.

You are probably already familiar with this because your Macintosh also uses a hierarchical filing system. When you open a file folder, you see files stored at that level of the hierarchy as well as folders that are subordinate to that level in the hierarchy.

Using a Web client, gopher directories appear as file or folder icons labeled with hyperlinked text. You can navigate among directories using hyperlinks and the Web browser's navigational buttons.

Like a Web server, a Gopher server only responds to direct requests from clients, and only maintains a connection with a client when receiving a request or sending a response. Unlike Web servers, some Gopher servers can also handle search requests (see figure 3.7). A Web server would have to pass a search request on to an external search program at the server location.

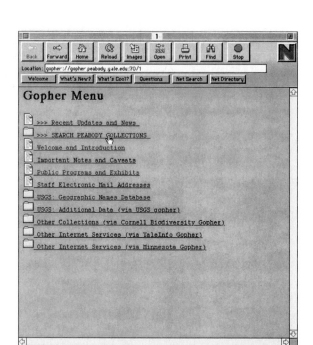

Figure 3.6 *Gopher directories appear as hyperlinked files and folders.*

Each research department at Yale Peabody has its own menu under the main gopher menu. The departmental file areas include an overview of the particular collection area, notes on the gopher data, and items allowing searches of the holdings. There are approximately 375,000 items cataloged on the Gopher server. There are no pictures here, just written systematic descriptions.

Yale Peabody participates with a loose association of other biology-oriented organizations in North America in providing information about their collection over the Internet through a Biodiversity Gopher network. Many of the individual specimen records of the Peabody's collection are readily available by pointing your Gopher or Web client at the Yale Gopher server, or any of the other Gopher servers in this network.

To conduct a search on the Yale Gopher, you click on one of the hyperlinked Search icons represented by binoculars. The browser displays a form with a single field for entering your keywords. You can search using multiple keywords as well as Boolean operators, such as "and," "or," and "not." The search instructions are in the same directory as the hyperlinks to the search functions.

Gopher may not be as versatile as hypertext or as flashy as HTML, but it still represents an important way to access information.

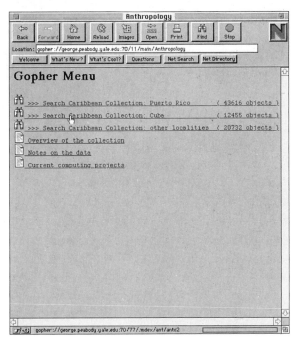

Figure 3.7   *The Museum's Gopher server is capable of performing a search of its own files.*

ftp: The TidBITS File Server

```
ftp://ftp.tidbits.com/pub/tidbits/
```

If you've ever used personal file sharing in System 7.0 or later, you have a good idea of how ftp works. FTP is a networking protocol originally developed for use by UNIX workstations to share files over TCP/IP networks, just like Macs can share files over AppleTalk. Since the Internet is a predominantly TCP/IP network, ftp is the preferred file transfer method for moving large chunks of data around the Internet, too.

There are several good free and shareware ftp programs, such as Dartmouth College's Fetch and Peter Lewis' Anarchie. Just as with gopher, though, Web browsers integrate well with ftp servers, provided they support anonymous log on. As the name implies, an anonymous log on does not require that you have a user account on the server or that you enter a unique password to access certain file directories. Typically, you connect to an anonymous ftp server by using the word "anonymous" as your user ID and your email address as your password.

When using a Web browser, though, the log on procedure is done for you. Most ftp servers ask for your email address as a "password" for anonymous logons. This is yet another reason why Netscape and other Web browsers ask you to enter it.

Web browsers display remote file directories in manner similar to the way they display gopher directories—as lists of file or folder icons labeled with short text descriptions. The description and the icon are shown as a hyperlinked object and clicking on one of these links retrieves that file.

Browsers are not yet fully enabled ftp clients, however. For example, you cannot retrieve multiple files at once nor can you send files to the server. If you need these features, you should try one of the dedicated programs like Fetch.

Hey, even the Swiss Army Knife has its limitations.

But if you are cruising the Web and come across a file that looks interesting, there's no reason to switch to a separate application just to download it. Your browser will do the trick just fine.

Often, anonymous servers are the places where you'll find updates to popular Internet programs, information about software and hardware, information about the Internet, and lots of other interesting files.

Some well-known servers are incredibly busy, and trying to log on to these servers is an exercise in futility. There are several Macintosh software archive servers in the URL directory mainly to provide you with alternative file sources.

One very good source for Macintosh files is `ftp://ftp.tidbits.com`, administered by Adam Engst.

Note

For several years now, Adam Engst and Tonya Engst and a small group of other electronic journalists have published TidBITS, a weekly newsletter about Macintosh computers and telecommunications. Adam Engst is also the author of Internet Starter Kit for Macintosh, *a book that is held in singularly high regard by Macintosh users heading nervously down the nearest on-ramp and out onto that great digital highway.*

You should save this URL to one of your Hotlists. Almost every piece of important Macintosh Internet shareware and freeware is archived at `ftp://ftp.tidbits.com/pub/tidbits/` (see figure 3.8).

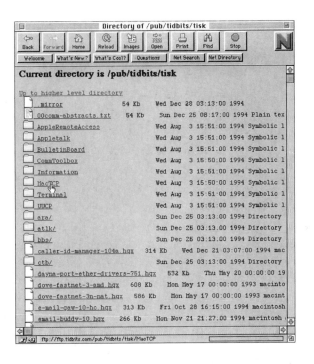

Figure 3.8   *An FTP directory as it appears in the Netscape browser window.*

FTP servers are handled very similarly to gopher servers. Hyperlinks and the navigation buttons are used to traverse the hierarchies. FTP URLs have "ftp" as their prefix instead of "http" or "gopher."

Clicking on the hyperlink anchor for a file begins the downloading process. Clients display downloading progress is the same manner that they display downloading progress for Web documents or graphics.

The TidBITS server is a great resource for Web-related files and information. A variety of HyperText Markup Language text editors are available there, as well as a selection of programs that can be used with the MacHTTP Web server described in Chapter 6. You'll also find several browser Helper applications available at the TidBITS server.

The TidBITS server has been carefully organized to provide all kinds of useful tools to the Macintosh Internet user. You will probably have many reasons to revisit.

News

Usenet is the soul of the Internet. While the Web may make a good place for personal expression, it's far less interactive today than the more than 13,000 Usenet bulletin boards that provide discussions on everything from atheism to Zima. Like the Web itself, Usenet does not exist on any one computer. It is distributed around the world.

Netscape may be the only Web browser through which you can read and post Usenet news. Provided your news server is entered correctly in Netscape's preferences, choosing "Go to Newsgroups" from Netscape's Directory menu or clicking the "Newsgroups" button from Netscape's Directory Buttons toolbar presents a page with several preselected newsgroups for Usenet neophytes.

If you know the name of the newsgroup you want to follow regularly, you can add it to this list by typing its name in the subscribe field and clicking the Subscribe button. You can also view all available newsgroups; it will probably be a very long list. Finally, you can enter the name of newsgroups directly as a URL. Type "news:" (no double slashes) plus the name of the newsgroup. For example, to read alt.drinks.snapple (one of the more ponderous newsgroups), you would type `news:alt.drinks.snapple` in the Location field.

Clicking a newsgroup's name brings you to the newsgroup. Netscape displays a list of posted articles in outline form. A toolbar within the Netscape display window allows you to:

- Post a new message
- Post Mark all articles read
- Post Show the articles that have already been read
- Post Subscribe to the group (add it to Netscape's initial list)
- Post Return to the list of subscribed newsgroups

Messages are listed along with the number of lines they use in parentheses. Clicking a message title displays the full message along with several nice touches. In most newsgroup readers, email addresses and URLs are plain old text, but they become hyperlinks when read in Netscape. The author's name, for example, automatically becomes a mailto URL, and any URLs listed in the message become links. So, for example, if someone puts their home page URL at the end of a message, clicking it would have the same effect as manually entering that URL. The Netscape window accesses the home page to which the URL in the message points.

The Netscape toolbar for Usenet available from a message's page allows you to move among messages and replies in the same discussion topic, or thread, or among threads in a newsgroup. You can also post replies to messages or post and email the author of the post simultaneously.

Be careful of what you say in Usenet. Your message will be transmitted around the world and people will not hesitate to criticize or "flame" you. It's highly recommended that you read a particular newsgroup for a while before posting. FAQs, or Frequently Asked Questions, are files that can be very helpful. They may be posted within the newsgroup or located in a newsgroup called *.answers (* represents the first few letters of the newsgroup, such as alt, comp, sci, rec, talk or soc. So, for example, comp.answers would have the FAQ for comp.sys.mac.hardware).

Incidentally, browsers aren't the only place where Usenet and the Web meet. Popular dedicated news reading programs such as John Norstad's NewsWatcher allow you to select a URL in a Usenet posting and open it in Netscape or another Web browser by using an "Open URL" command.

You can also link newsgroup lists created by Newswatcher with Netscape so that both programs use the same record of groups, read and unread messages, and so on.

To do this, make an alias of your Newswatcher subscription group file and rename the alias "newsrc". Replace this "newsrc" alias file inside the Netscape preferences folder (which is located inside the Preferences folder inside your System Folder).

Netscape will now access the same newsgroup information as the Newswatcher newsreader program.

Spinning New Threads

As versatile as Web browsers are, they can't do it alone. The final section of our Web-wide Tour demonstrates how Web browsers can be used with helper applications. While there is a wide variety of helper applications available, and more coming in the future, this section concentrates on sound and video, and how you can configure Netscape for other kinds of helper applications.

Sound: The Woodstock '94 site

`http://www.woodstock.com/interview/index.html`

If you couldn't get to the original Woodstock, there was Woodstock '94. If you couldn't get to Woodstock '94, there was the Web site. Much like Saugarties, New York, this place seems a bit deserted, but interviews still remain. Clicking on any sound clip title launches the helper application Sound Machine.

Note that SoundMachine isn't the only helper application that can handle sound, which comes in many different formats. Other sound helper applications include the free program SoundApp that handles Windows .WAV sound files and the RealAudio player that plays sound as its being transferred!

Acrobat: Adobe

`http://www.adobe.com/Acrobat/Acrobat0.html`

As stunning as Web pages can be, they can be arduous to create (as you'll discover in Chapter 5), and their graphics don't print well on high-resolution printers. That's where Acrobat comes in. Acrobat is a technology by Adobe (the people who brought us the PostScript language in laser printers) for preserving the layout of complex documents. The file format it uses is called PDF, or Portable Document Format. Simply put, there's a lot you can do in PDF that is not possible in HTML today. Acrobat pages are also easier to create. Virtually any Mac or Windows program that can print can create Acrobat files with the purchase of Acrobat Exchange.

This is why some sites have Acrobat files at their Web site. Netscape is working toward integrating PDF files into its browser, but, at press time, these files had to be viewed with the free Acrobat Reader software, also available from Adobe's Web site at **http://www.adobe.com**.

Once the reader is obtained, you need to configure Netscape to use Acrobat Reader as a helper application. The easiest way to do this is as follows:

1. Click the name of a sample Acrobat file. Netscape displays a dialog box stating it can't find an application to handle

2. Click the Pick Application button. A standard Open dialog box appears.

3. Locate the application Acrobat Reader in the Open dialog and choose it. Acrobat Reader launches and the file is displayed.

If you wish, you can choose Preferences from Netscape's Options dialog box and then choose Helper Applications from the window's popup menu to see how the helper application was assigned.

Cybersmorgasboard

The World Wide Web is truly wide. There is an almost infinite variety of content on thousands of servers in hundreds of formats. That Web browsers can encompass all their riches through clever design and delegation is among their greatest strengths.

Perhaps the Web was originally so dubbed because of its interconnected links, but lately the name has become even more appropriate because it's so easy to get lost in it. The next chapter discusses the express lane on the information highway; it includes excellent resources to help you quickly track down Web sites as methodically as a spider spins a web.

Surf and Ye Shall Find

Information on the Web can be a moving target, and a fast-moving one at that. Matthew Gray has tracked the growth of the Web since the middle of 1993, and has published some interesting statistics based on his program, the Web Wanderer, at:

```
http://www.netgen.com/info/growth.html
```

Using the Web Wanderer, Gray found that the number of servers on the Web grew 10,000 percent in the 18-month period between June 1993 and December 1994. The growth rate during 1994 alone exceeded 50 new Web servers every day.

The estimates of individual documents on the Web range from two million to five million; URLs are constantly being created, removed, and changed. As a result, it's difficult to judge how accurate any estimate of Web files might be.

Trying to pinpoint information browsing such a cyberscape could be like trying to find the proverbial needle in a haystack, if the haystack resembled Mt. Everest. Fortunately, there are a slew of special Internet resources that can act as a supercharged metal detector.

Some of these tools are as simple to use as the Help menu in your browser. Others are programs on servers that help you search broadly through the Internet, or they are documents that keep track of what's new.

Not all of these resources are Web sites, either. Usenet hosts discussion groups where Web users and authors spanning all experience levels share technical information and advice about what they can do with the Web. You can also subscribe to **mailing lists**, in which people email questions and comments about a specific subject to a group address, and these messages are sent to all the subscribers of the mailing list. Mailing lists are a great way to stay abreast of what's happening in a given field, but they can generate a lot of email. Worse, it can sometimes be difficult to get off a mailing list once you're on it.

In this chapter, we'll start with some important ways to find out what's on the Web, and close with a summary of how to stay abreast.

Search Engines

Discovering new resources by chance is a fun way to explore the Web at your leisure. But if you are looking for a specific piece of information, and would like to find it sometime before the universe implodes, you probably don't want to spend hours randomly following hyperlinks around the Web. If you want to make as thorough a search of the Web as possible, you should use more than one of the available search engines:

- Lycos is a research program focused on providing information retrieval and discovery in the WWW. Lycos currently answers browser search requests with relatively complete abstracts of Web documents, including a hyperlink to each document. The name Lycos derives from Lycosidae, a family of large ground spiders, which catches its prey by pursuit, rather than in a web. Lycosidae are noted for their running speed and are especially active at night. To again stress how fast the Web is growing, Lycos grew from two million to nearly four million URLs in the time we wrote this book. It is located at:

```
http://lycos.cs.cmu.edu/
```

- TradeWare Galaxy is a Wide Area Information Service search engine maintained by TradeWare, publishers of MacWeb and winWeb client applications. The TradeWare Galaxy directory provides a list of major topics that link to indexes of documents organized in categories (see figure 4.1). Its interface is similar in form to the Yahoo index. It is located at:

```
http://galaxy.einet.net/galaxy.html
```

- The WebCrawler was developed by Brian Pinkerton at University of Washington in 1994. In June 1995, the WebCrawler was acquired by America Online and is maintained by AOL as a public service to the

Internet. The WebCrawler database contains more than 150,000 visited documents and another 1,500,000 URLs for documents yet to be catalogued. It is located at:

```
http://webcrawler.com
```

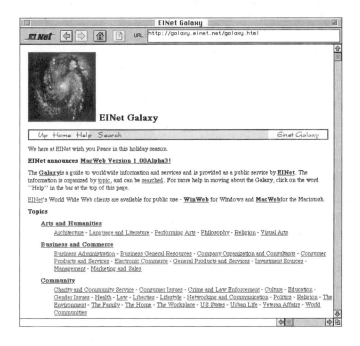

Figure 4.1   *Tradeware Galaxy, formerly the EINet Galaxy, is an index and hyperlinked directory of documents that can be used for either browsing or searching.*

■ The WWW Home Pages Broker was built using the Harvest search software system. The Broker searches by keyword and returns a numbered listing of documents and URLs that match the search criteria. The WWW Pages Broker is located at:

```
http://www.town.hall.org/brokers/www-home-pages/query.html
```

Resource Guides

There are also several general resource guides that provide hyperlinks to index documents and search engines on the Web. You can always use one of these resource guides to look for places to start a search:

■ The Internet Resources Meta-Index is a listing of Web, Gopher, and other indexes, listings, searchable indexes, server indexes, and catalogs of WWW-provided information. It has been compiled by the National Center for Supercomputing Applications (NCSA)/Software Development Group, which writes and distributes the Mosaic browser. It's located at:

```
http://www.ncsa.uiuc.edu/SDG/Software/Mosaic/MetaIndex.html
```

■ The Internet Search page at Netscape Communications (see figure 4.2) is a comprehensive directory of Web search engines, and includes hyperlinks to Lycos, the WebCrawler, WWW Pages Broker, and other large Web document indexes. `Internet Search` is located at:

```
http://home.netscape.com/home/internet-search.html
```

Figure 4.2   *The Internet Search page maintained by Netscape Communications, Inc.*

■ The World Wide Web Consortium publishes a General Overview of the Web that provides links to the Virtual Library and Virtual Tourist lists of registered HTTP servers. These servers are organized by country and continent, according to access protocol (HTTP, Gopher, FTP, and so on) and are currently accessed through:

```
http://www.w3.org/hypertext/DataSources/Top.html
```

- The W3 Search Engines page points to all of the most useful search engines available on the WWW. The page contains links to 46 different engines and 46 submit forms for searching any (or all) of the engines (see figure 4.3). The W3 Search Engine administrator encourages users to install a copy of this document on their local machine. The original list is located at:

```
http://cuiwww.unige.ch/meta-index.html
```

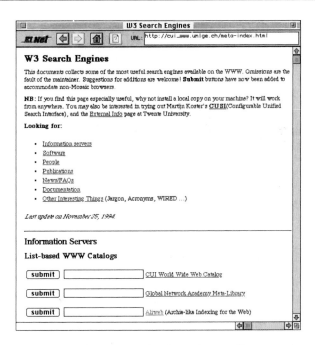

Figure 4.3   *The W3 Search Engine is a form for sending queries to any or all of the major document indexes on the Web.*

The variety of documents you can find on the Web covers a broad spectrum—lists of graphics and sound files, indexes of software files, catalogs of museum objects, and abstracts or full texts of technical publications.

As you move from one hyperlinked phrase or word to another, an inquiry starting with a single Web page can easily lead all over the world. If you try to keep track of individual documents that you've visited, you may create a thoroughly unmanageable Hotlist menu.

Let's examine some of these engines in depth.

Lycos

`http://lycos.cs.cmu.edu/`

The Lycos catalog is maintained at Carnegie-Mellon University, one of the primary computing centers on the Internet in North America. Lycos is actually several computers that can run searches concurrently on the same database. The Lycos database is fed by an automated program (the Lycos Web Explorer) that runs daily searches of the World Wide Web, looking for new URLs. Based on these searches, the index in the Lycos catalog is revised weekly and new URLS are added.

Lycos takes advantage of forms to let you narrow your searching criteria.

The home page for Lycos provides you with a directory of hyperlinks (see figure 4.4). The first two hyperlinks are used for starting a document search on any of the several servers available. Although you can conduct the search from any of the servers, each server can handle only so many requests at one time. Having a variety of servers available provides access to as many concurrent users as possible. If your first server choice is busy, you can simply try another one.

Figure 4.4   *The Lycos home page.*

You can use the Lycos home page to get information about Lycos and you can add your own URL to the Lycos directory. The Lycos Web Explorer (a separate program) validates these user-submitted URLs before they are entered into the database.

Traffic into Lycos can be heavy. Browser requests generally hit a peak about 2 p.m. Eastern (U.S.) time but, even at its low point (around 6 a.m. EST), Lycos is serving about 8,000 accesses each hour. In the late afternoon, the number of requests hovers around 18,000 an hour. When you have trouble getting your search request to run, note the time and try again later.

Lycos has a catalog of approximately 4.2 million documents, so running a search can sometimes take a few minutes. Lycos, however, is one of the most comprehensive search engines on the Net, consistently finding more references than other fine searching tools on the Web.

To use Lycos, first click on the link in the first line of servers. This returns a page that displays a single field and reads "This is a searchable index" (see figure 4.5).

Figure 4.5 *Single keyword searches are easily run on Lycos.*

Let's say you've been browsing hither and thither for information on zithers to no avail. Enter the word "zither" in the search field and press Return. This sends the keyword as part of a URL to the Lycos server and starts a search of the database for all entries that contain the word "zither."

Lycos returns detailed information. When you run a search, you don't just get a list of hyperlinks, you get brief descriptions of the various index entries that tell you something about the specific citation. You also get a hyperlink leading to the cited document (see figure 4.6). Based on the description, you can decide if the cited document is what you're looking for or if it's way off track, and thus save yourself the trouble of checking each document. You'll save download time, too.

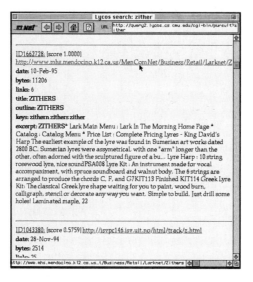

Figure 4.6   *Lycos returns comprehensive index information about documents.*

Now let's look at the index entries Lycos sent to you. The list returned from the "zither" request isn't very long. One entry in the list is for a musical instrument dealer in California. The second line of that entry is a hyperlink that can be used to go to that dealer's home page.

The Lark in the Morning main menu indicates that this dealer probably doesn't do a lot of business with the heavy metal crowd. Nonetheless, zithers are here and in three different models. The two concert models are shown through inline GIF images (see figure 4.7).

Our music dealer does not represent the last word in zithers. At the bottom of the page is a hyperlink to more citations for zither. Clicking on this link will display additional pages of entries from the Lycos database, including one that lets you hear the sound of the instrument.

Returning to the first page at the Lycos site, you'll notice a second set of hyperlinks leading to the Lycos servers. This set of links includes a form, which provides a few more options for conducting your search, including specifying the number of citations that will be displayed.

Searching again reveals additional records for "zither," including one that lets you hear the instrument. Virtual Planet Three does include a rather large .wav (a type of sound file) recording of some Vietnamese musicians jamming with a zither (see figure 4.8) and a guitar.

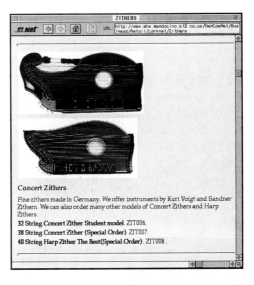

Figure 4.7   *My first search returns some pictures of concert zithers.*

Figure 4.8   *Searching again leads straight to an audio file of a zither performance.*

Clicking the name of the sound file launches SoundApp, a helper application for handling Windows sound files. SoundApp was mentioned in Chapter 1 as a helper application. You can download it from many places on the Internet, such as one of the many Info-Mac archives.

Lycos may be the best overall search engine, but it's far from alone. Other search engines are the World Wide Web Worm at the University of Colorado, the Web Crawler at the University of Washington, and ALIWEB at Nexor, Ltd. in the UK. You can find indexes of these and many other search engines at several locations on the Web (see figure 4.9), including on a document at:

```
http://www.ncsa.uiuc.edu/SDG/Software/Mosaic/Demo/metaindex.html
```

Figure 4.9   *The Internet Resources Meta-Index at NCSA lists most, if not all, of the directories, indexes, and search engines on the World Wide Web.*

Nevertheless, using several other popular Web search engines to search for "zither" yielded these results:

Table 4.1
Searching for Zither

Search engine	Number of hits
Lycos	33
Yahoo	0
ALIWEB	0
WebCrawler	3
TradeWare Galaxy	1
JumpStation	0

You can find an index of hyperlinks to all of the larger document and URL indexes at many locations on the Web, including:

```
http://cuiwww.unige.ch/meta-index.html
```

Yahoo

```
http://www.yahoo.com/
```

If you couldn't tell from its name, Yahoo is worth getting excited about.

After a few hours of wandering around the Web, it's easy to compile a long Bookmarks menu of Web sites that you're sure you'll want to visit again. But there is hope for the very curious Web surfer, and its name is Yahoo.

Yahoo is a subject-oriented database, written and maintained by David Filo and Jerry Yang at Stanford University. The Yahoo database is presented on the Web as a hierarchical directory of hyperlinks organized by subject category. Filo and Yang aptly describe it as a hierarchical hot list.

The main Yahoo page lists several dozen broad subject categories (see figure 4.10). Clicking on any of these categories takes you ever deeper into the database records for that group.

Eventually, you reach indexes of hyperlinked Web documents. None of the documents indexed in the Yahoo database are actually at the Yahoo server—it only contains the URLs that lead to them.

The URL references are compiled through a form at Yahoo that Web authors can use to submit a document URL to the database. URLs are also compiled from automated searches of other directories on the Web.

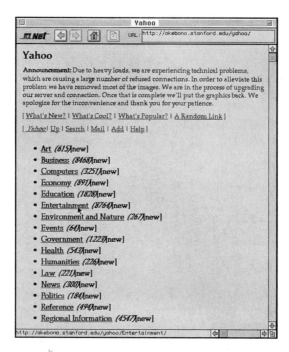

Figure 4.10   *Yahoo is a Web-wide hotlist maintained by David Filo and Jerry Yang.*

During a recent visit, the database was reportedly growing at a rate of about 540 documents a day. There are already tens of thousands of URLs indexed at Yahoo.

The subject categories on the Yahoo list attempt to be broad. The main directory lists categories in Art, Business, Computers, Economy, Education, Entertainment, and other general topics.

You can quickly search the Yahoo database through a form linked to the main page. Searches for art or entertainment are bound to find something worthwhile. While "zithers" have escaped Yahoo's notice, online comics have not. The Entertainment link on the main page leads to long list of possibly entertaining subjects, including Amusement Parks, Cooking, Home and Garden, and Comics. Each link shows the number of entries to which it refers. Comics listed 160 entries.

The Comics page itself is a list of URL entries and other links that lead even deeper into the Yahooian labyrinth. For example, a link to Comic Books advertised another 49 links available at the click of a mouse. This discussion will stick with Online Comics, which returned a page full of descriptions and links to graphics from a Web server at: `http://www.eden.com/` (see figure 4.11).

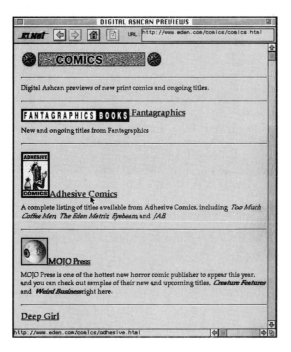

Figure 4.11   *Yahoo leads to this page describing Online Comics.*

The Online Comics index features brief descriptions and eye-catching graphics, as one might expect to find at the cutting edge of popular illustrated text on the Internet. If you are interested in Adhesive Comics, you're in for a treat.

The listing advertised a new comic that was "a dizzying Foray into The Never-so-Placid World of Substance Abuse for the Common Man.... Sell your kids, if you have to, to procure a copy of this final word in print..." How can you resist? (see figure 4.12).

Yahoo is an excellent resource for what's new and hip, but may not fare as well on the obscure subjects as Lycos does.

Figure 4.12   *Adhesive Comics promotes its latest creation.*

Subject-Oriented Internet Resource Guides

http://www.lib.umich.edu/chhome.html

Imagine if you could go to the local library and, instead of shuffling through the card catalog, click through listings of all of the books on the shelves. Now imagine if you had immediate access to this service, not only in that library, but in several thousand others as well.

Today, many public libraries contain computerized databases of books and periodicals. In big cities, like Chicago or New York, these databases already display the collections at all the various branches. You just walk up to any terminal and stare at the screen, trying to figure out how to find the book you seek. These interfaces are so obscure that you're likely to go to the card catalog and look it up the old-fashioned way.

It's bound to work better someday, and those improvements may arrive by way of hyperlinked indexes using the Web. The University of Michigan's University Library, New York Public Library, and the School of Information and Library Studies (SILS) are attempting to build a library reference service for electronic information (see figure 4.13).

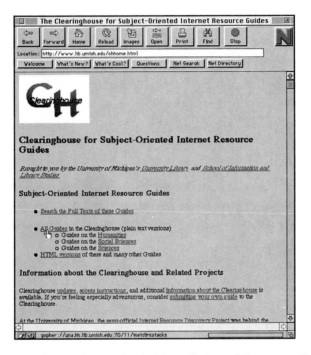

Figure 4.13   *The Clearinghouse for Subject-Oriented Resource Guides is like a card catalog for the Internet.*

The goal of the Clearinghouse for Subject-Oriented Internet Resource Guides is to collect information about everything on the Internet and provide a summary index that lists subjects, authors, locations, and other pertinent information. While most of this information takes the form of plain text, many of the resource guides are beginning to appear as hypertext, or are indexed using hypertext (see figures 4.14 through 4.16).

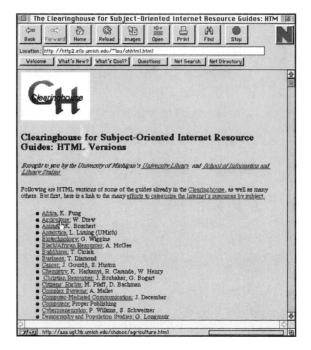

Figure 4.14 *The Clearinghouse includes hypertext versions of subject guides.*

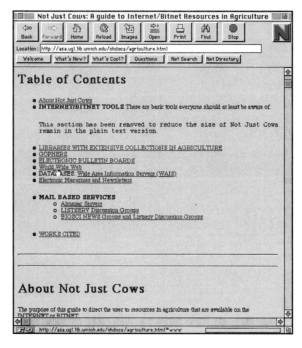

Figure 4.15 *Documents related to agriculture are indexed on the hypertext directory titled Not Just Cows.*

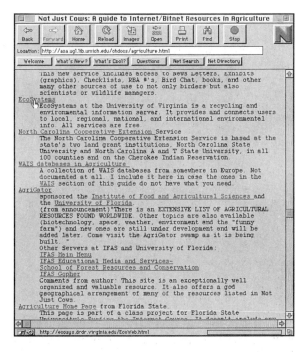

Figure 4.16   *Not Just Cows provides hyperlinks to other resources in many separate locations on the Internet.*

Each subject category is its own resource gathering project. The categories have been produced by members of the Internet community and by SILS students who participate in the Internet Resource Discovery project at the University of Michigan.

These resource guides are primarily written as plain text documents and served using gopher. Users making a gopher request to server Zebra see directories for many other servers. Users can browse or make keyword searches of the information indexed or stored at any of the gopher sites registered with server Zebra, using a gopher client application.

Given the tremendous amount of text involved in these guides, new contributors are urged to edit their entries using HyperText Markup Language and take advantage of the Web as an easy to use and powerful interface.

There is clearly demand for the Clearinghouse, judging from the number of users who access it. By mid-1995, it was being accessed more than 174,000 times a month—a tenfold growth rate for the year.

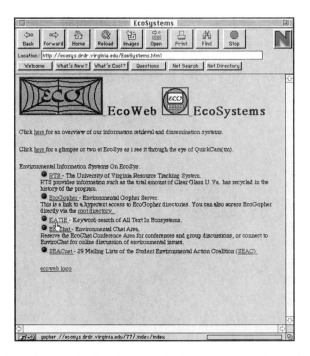

Figure 4.17 *Jumping to the EcoSystems index turns up a hyperlink to a gopher search engine called KATIE.*

The Clearinghouse is the type of electronic resource that would be a great addition for any classroom, school, or public library, to say nothing of providing a valuable tool for mining the Internet for virtually every bit of data out there.

The World Wide Web Consortium

http://www.w3.org/

On October 1, 1994, the center of the World Wide Web jumped a few thousand miles west. On that date, the original center of the Web was reorganized and relocated from Geneva, Switzerland to Cambridge, Massachusetts.

The Web server at CERN, http://info.cern.ch/, had become the central point for software, information, and extensive directories of Web servers around the world.

The announcement of the World Wide Web Consortium (W3C) indicated that a refocusing period was in the works. The other shoe dropped in February 1995, when CERN announced that it was transferring its core Web development activities to the French National Institute for Research in Computing and Automation, INRIA.

CERN still maintains its own Web servers and provides information about the Web, hypertext, and Web software, at http://www.cern.ch/ExpSupport/. But the major effort of coordinating the architecture of the Web has moved to the World Wide Web Consortium.

The W3 Consortium is located in the Laboratory for Computer Science on the Massachusetts Institute of Technology campus, and is being administered by MIT. Tim Berners-Lee and several other prominent architects of HTTP and HTML have moved to Cambridge, and Berners-Lee is now Director of the Consortium.

For now, all of the fundamental information about the Web, including its structure, HTML, HTTP, URLs, software, and related discussions, are documented or linked at MIT. In fact, the pages at MIT are indistiguishable from the pages that had been served up in Geneva, including the green Ws designed by Robert Cailliau (see figure 4.18).

And, like the old CERN site, the W3C server provides information and links to Web servers around the world. If you are interested in finding servers in distant places, the W3C is now the place to start.

The opening page at W3C is a general directory of hyperlinks to major categories of Web developer information. You can follow these links resources to help you develop and run your own Web server, and you should check them out. But I'd rather show you the Web server directories that are linked to this page under the heading How to find things on the Web.

These directories take very different routes to provide you with similar results. One is a list organized by continent and country. The second is a list organized by subject matter. A searchable catalog of servers helps round out the presentation.

The List of Servers link moves you to a long list organized by continent and country. You could scroll though this list to find the geographic area that interests you, or you could try the clickable world map hyperlink toward the top of the page. This link leads to another server at the State University of New York at Buffalo, and a rather unique interface (see figures 4.19 and 4.20). Bear in mind that the list of test hyperlinks will be faster, because there are no inline graphics to download.

Chapter 4
Surf and Ye
Shall Find

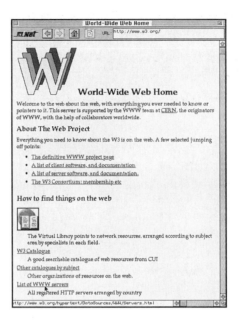

Figure 4.18   *The World Wide Web Consortium home page maintains the look and feel of the old CERN site.*

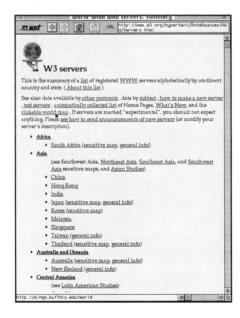

Figure 4.19   *The W3 servers page lists servers by geographic regions and provides a link to a clickable world map.*

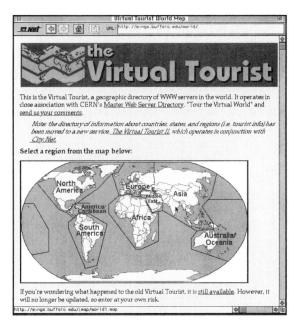

Figure 4.20 *The world map of servers provides a graphic interface to different regions of the world.*

The Virtual Tourist is certainly a more colorful method for locating servers on the Web than paging down a list of names. It also helps users maintain a sense of where in the world they are going. This is a good example of an interface that is tailored for use in public settings and with less experienced users, like a classroom or library.

A second and very useful directory to Web servers is also linked to the main page at W3C. Choosing the link to Other catalogues by subject on the main W3C page takes you to the first level of the Virtual Library directory at W3C (see figure 4.21).

The Virtual Library is a more complex directory method, since individual servers might each be listed within several categories. As a matter of fact, if not necessity, the Virtual Library is a distributed cataloging system. There are many Virtual Library servers, and each provides listings for specific subject categories.

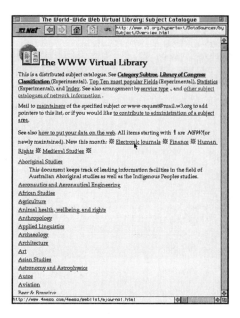

Figure 4.21   *The Virtual Library catalogues Web servers by subject matter and is accessed through a central page at the W3C.*

The first level listing provides general categories of subject matter. Each of these links leads to a separate server elsewhere on the Web, where that section of the library is maintained. Toward the top of the page is a series of recently added links leading to new additions to the Virtual Library network.

One recent library addition is a catalogue of Electronic Journals. Clicking on this link will take you to the home of this area of the library, a server at:

```
http://www.4mesa.com/
```

The World Wide Web Consortium is poised to lead the Web through the second five years of its life. The tremendous growth in the Web, both in numbers of new servers and in numbers of new clients, has certainly stimulated several corporations to join.

Up until now, the Web has been developed through a laissez-faire blend of individual initiative and organizational support. This gradual evolution was only recently punctuated by the widespread acceptance of graphical browser software. It remains to be seen how well the W3C plays its role as facilitator of standards and software, and whether the Web developer community fractures into Insiders and Outsiders.

Spider Anatomy

Search engines rely on programs known as worms, spiders, and robots to compile databases of Web resources according to unique routines. In general, however, they all work according to a few common principles.

First, they must determine what's out there. This can be done in a number of ways, but a typical method is gradually polling the Internet for URLs that begin with "http://" or that end with ".html". Using these search criteria, the spider will avoid other files, like GIF images or QuickTime movies, because the files would end with a .gif or .mov filename extension.

Using this list of document URLs, you can make a second exploration of the Web. This time your program will scan through the text content of these documents in an attempt to determine the subject matter within the documents.

As you'll discover in Chapter 5, there are a variety of HTML conventions for specifying everything from major subject headings in the document to the email address of the document's author. A properly written program could be sent to look through each document and retrieve information that has been tagged as an HTML element. For example, to find the titles of documents, the spider only needs to retrieve text that is marked up as <TITLE>.

Furthermore, the entire displayed content of the document resides between a pair of <BODY> tags. A spider might scan everything between these tags. In order to determine the subject matter more accurately, it could ignore certain very common words, or words that appear either too often or too infrequently.

Using moderately powerful UNIX computers and relatively simple computations, some of the existing spiders, worms, and robots can find hundreds of documents per minute. Scanning each document individually is a lengthier process.

What's New?

Search engines may help reduce overall Internet traffic and save you time when you already know what you want. But even the best search engine can't keep up with the growing number of documents on the Web.

At a rate of 50 or more new servers a day, keeping up with the new and noteworthy could become a full-time job, as it most likely is for someone at the NCSA Mosaic What's New index server (see figure 4.22).

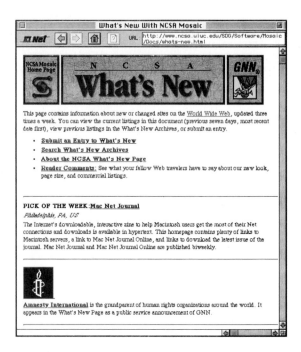

Figure 4.22   *NCSA's What's New page is updated three times each week with announcements of Web servers and documents.*

The NCSA What's New list is one of the main ways that new servers are announced to the rest of the Web. For inclusion in the list, anyone can submit a description of his server or new documents, along with the URLs, to the What's New editors. Currently, What's New is updated three times each week.

The URL for NCSA Mosaic What's New is:

```
http://www.ncsa.uiuc.edu/SDG/Software/Mosaic/Docs/whats-new.html.
```

Mosaic browser users can also access the NCSA What's New page through the Mosaic Navigate menu.

The typical What's New page is a 40K document of hyperlinks and brief descriptions of the new server or documents. Although a document of this size is not too large to browse, if you'd like to search the document for specific words, go to Edit in your browser menu bar and use the Find command.

The most recent weeks' pages are also available through the Recent Updates link on the main What's New page.

Full monthly indexes are available from the main What's New page through a hyperlink to the What's New archives. These archives are listed by month, beginning with the most recent and going back to June 1993, when the What's New page began. The archive index page contains a hyperlink to each monthly list.

Some of these documents may be 700K or 800K in size. Downloading a document of this size over a modem connection will take several minutes. Searching it with the Find command will also take some time.

Fortunately, all the monthly archived lists have been cataloged, and you don't have to download the archives and scroll through them. Instead, you can use a search engine to make a much quicker scan of all the archives at once. This search engine is available through the CUI W3 Catalog hyperlink on the archive index page.

The CUI W3 Catalog is maintained at the same server as the World Wide Web Search Engines page, and you can reach it directly at:

```
http://cuiwww.unige.ch/w3catalog
```

The kind of information you can find using this type of search differs from the information found by searching an index compiled by a spider program.

Unlike index entries compiled by a spider program, the What's New entries are composed from blurbs written by the person(s) who submitted the new listing, and do not necessarily reflect the full or current document content at those sites.

There are various other What's New types of lists on the Web, none of them come close to the breadth and frequency of the NCSA What's New pages. The closest runner-up is the What's New on Yahoo document at:

```
http://www.yahoo.com/new
```

There are over 50,000 entries in the Yahoo database, and 300 to 500 new entries are added daily. Because Yahoo tends to attract entries from the arts, entertainment, and business end of the spectrum, you should look there first for new sites related to art, culture, and commerce.

A hyperlink on the main Yahoo page leads directly to the What's New on Yahoo index, which maintains hyperlinks to new URL entries for each of the past five days (see figure 4.23).

**Chapter 4
Surf and Ye
Shall Find**

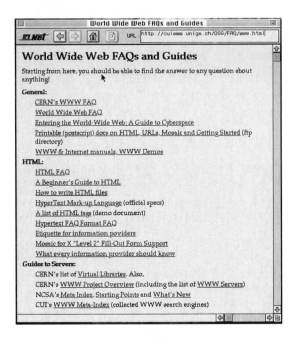

Figure 4.23   *What's New on Yahoo lists the most recent additions to that database.*

The individual daily indexes are organized along the same hierarchy as the main Yahoo index, and include hyperlinks up to the major subject listings as well as hyperlinks down to the newly added documents.

Newsgroups

On the Internet, newsgroups are a global town hall meeting. While the newsgroup structure actually predates the Internet, it now represents a good chunk of the information that is passed back and forth there daily.

There are more than 14,000 individual newsgroups. Each is organized around a specific topic and newsgroup subscribers use the newsgroup as a place to both post and read messages about that topic (see figure 4.24).

Several newgroups are important forums used for discussing the growth, the content, and the technology of the World Wide Web among the larger Internet community.

Figure 4.24   *Newsgroups are open forums for discussion on the Internet.*

Each new message posted to a newsgroup includes a subject heading, along with other headings that show who wrote the message and when it was written. Replies to the original message assume the same subject heading as the first message, and are grouped with it in a "thread." Subject threads are supposed to enable readers to easily locate comments on a specific message or subject matter.

There are 21 active newsgroups that focus solely on discussions about the World Wide Web. Internet newsgroups are referred to by their name in the newsgroup hierarchy. For example, **comp.infosystems.www.misc**, tells you that the newsgroup is found under the general category of **comp** (for computers) and subcategory **infosystems** (for information systems, like WAIS, gopher, or the Web). Periods are used to separate the hierarchical levels shown in a newsgroup address.

Newsgroups can also be located on the Internet using a URL address. The Uniform Resource Locators for some of the Web-related newsgroups are:

```
news:comp.infosystems.www.announce
```

```
news:comp.infosystems.www.misc
```

```
news:comp.infosystems.www.providers
```

```
news:comp.infosystems.www.users
```

```
news:comp.infosystems.www.authoring.cgi
```

```
news:comp.infosystems.www.authoring.html
```

```
news:comp.infosystems.www.authoring.images
```

```
news:comp.infosystems.www.authoring.misc
```

```
news:comp.infosystems.www.browsers.mac
```

```
news:comp.infosystems.www.servers.mac
```

I'll explain more about how to connect with newsgroups a little later in this section. First, let me explain what these newsgroups are.

comp.infosystems.www.announce is a relatively low-volume newsgroup. It is used to place announcements about new Web servers and home pages. It is not moderated, meaning there is no person or group of people who monitor the newsgroup for improper postings.

Sometimes, overcome with excitement about their own success, new Web server operators post their announcements to newsgroups other than **comp.infosystems.www.announce**. This practice is considered bad form and can result in small conflagrations of ill temper from those who tire of wading through inappropriate news articles.

More frequently, new server operators also submit their announcement to the What's New page at NCSA or What's New on Yahoo.

comp.infosystems.www.misc serves a large volume of messages that cover a range of discussion topics. It was set up to handle messages that do not apply to any of the other Web related newsgroups. It is unmoderated.

Included in miscellaneous news are announcements about meetings, discussions, or Web-related events, discussions about HTML or HTTP, discussions about software developers or network resources, or general discussions about the Web and its future. Keep in mind that subscribers may be located anywhere in the world and that participants are not mainly Macintosh users.

comp.infosystems.www.providers carries the largest volume of messages of any of the Web related newsgroups and focuses on the server side of things. It is unmoderated.

Messages and threads in `comp.infosystems.www.providers` focus on questions related to network connections, server software, Common Gateway Interface programs, operating systems, and other matters related to setting up and operating a Web server. It is also a place to discuss writing Hypertext Markup Language documents as well as topics related to server security.

Many major software developers, such as Netscape, Spyglass, Spry, and TradeWare, visit this newsgroup regularly, so it is a good place to follow or participate in discussion about topics related to server software.

`comp.infosystems.www.providers` is gradually being replaced by the new `comp.infosystems.www.servers` in newsgroups, and may no longer be active by the end of 1995.

`comp.infosystems.www.users` is a high-volume group that focuses on Web browser software and issues related to using a Web browser. It is unmoderated.

Discussions in this group focus on specific browser software but often overflow into general discussions about Web sites, modems, service providers, and other tangential topics.

Appropriate topics for this newsgroup include browser setup questions, bug reports, comparisons of browser programs, or other topics that specifically relate to using the Web.

If you have a question about your browser, this is a very good place to start looking for answers. You should also read the Frequently Asked Question (FAQ) document, written by Thomas Boutell, and posted to this group (and the other Web groups) every four days.

`comp.infosystems.www.users` is gradually being replaced by the new `comp.infosystems.www.browsers` newsgroups, and may no longer be active by the end of 1995.

`comp.infosystems.www.authoring.cgi` is a moderate-volume group used to discuss Common Gateway Interface programming for the Web. CGIs are small programs written to extend the functions of Web servers. Programs that process information submitted by a fill-out form or image map are examples of CGIs.

Keep in mind that subscribers may be located anywhere in the world and that participants are not only Macintosh users. The newsgroup is not moderated.

`comp.infosystems.www.authoring.html` is a high-volume group used to discuss the HyperText Markup Language, which is used to build the hypertext documents served over the Web.

Discussions in this newsgroup range over basic questions about existing HTML practice, the proprietary elements used by Netscape or other browsers, HTML editing software, and the various new elements being proposed for the next generation of hypertext, HTML 3.0.

Because HTML is not platform-specific, neither is this newsgroup, and the discussion can provide insight into how different browser software interprets the "common" hypertext language.

`comp.infosystems.www.authoring.images` is a low-volume group intended to discuss the creation and editing of graphic images used for Web publishing.

The judicious use of graphics in page design, the difference between compression schemes, and the use of imagemaps are all acceptable topics for discussion in this group, which is not platform specific or moderated.

`comp.infosystems.www.authoring.misc` is a high-volume group intended for topics that don't fit into the other `www.authoring` newsgroups. The high number of postings betrays the fact that it also plays the role of catch-all authoring group.

The authoring.misc discussion is intended for topics like using audio, video, and "virtual reality modeling language" over the Web.

It is not platform-specific, and because the A/V capabilities of browsers, desktop computers, and workstations vary greatly, so does the discussion in the group. It is not moderated.

`comp.infosystems.www.browsers.mac` is a low-volume group created for discussing Web browsers specific to the Macintosh computer.

Acceptable topics for discussion include browser configuration questions and problems, helper applications, bug reports, and on-going comparative analysis of MacWeb, Netscape, and Mosaic. The newsgroup is not moderated.

`comp.infosystems.servers.mac` is a low-volume group dedicated to discussing Web server software designed for the Macintosh.

Currently there are only a couple of Mac server applications, and the dominant Mac server is MacHTTP/WebStar. The newsgroup is not moderated.

Whatever newsgroup you read and post messages to, you should observe the basic rules of polite behavior for the Internet. A central principle of newsgroup decorum is that messages posted to the group must be on the topic. Off-topic postings waste readers' time as well as disk space on the news servers.

Existingpostings also indicate the appropriateness of a subject to the newsgroup. You should familiarize yourself with the kind of discussions being conducted through the newsgroup before posting a message of your own. You should also read the Frequently Asked Questions document posted in the newsgroup for the answers to basic questions about the subject matter. It's possible that your question has already been answered, perhaps repeatedly, and is already contained in the FAQ.

Mailing Lists

Electronic mail predates the Web by many years. But it still is the most common form of communication on the Internet and the most convenient way to disseminate information to specific individuals.

One way that email is used to organize group discussions on a topic is through a mailing list. Unlike a newsgroup that stores messages on a server for you to browse when you have the time, messages posted to a mailing list are rebroadcast back to the mailboxes of list subscribers. If you subscribe to one of these lists, the news will come to you via email.

Like newsgroups, subscriber-participant lists may be moderated or unmoderated, and like the newsgroup, netiquette dictates that postings stay on topic.

Unlike the newsgroup, where you can pick and choose which messages to read, every message to a participant mailing list is resent to every subscriber. Floods of off-topic messages are seldom appreciated, even by the most encyclopedic of list readers. Nobody likes downloading and wading through junk mail.

Chapter 4
Surf and Ye
Shall Find

Subscribing to Lists

The World Wide Web Consortium maintains several mailing lists for discussing the technical aspects of the Web. The W3C provides a description of its own lists at:

```
http://www.w3.org/hypertext/WWW/Mail/Lists.html
```

W3C also maintains a listing of other web-related mailing lists (not W3C-run) at:

```
http://www.w3.org/hypertext/WWW/Mail/Outside_mailing.html
```

These pages are not complete catalogues of all the Web-related lists on the Internet, but they are a good place to start, and both pages include hyperlinks to mailing list archives for many of the lists they describe.

To subscribe to a mailing list, you address a message to the server address, not the address for the mailing list. The body of the message is reserved for the function command(s) you want the server to execute. For example, the word **subscribe** is the common prefix for a subscription request command, followed by the name of the list you wish to subscribe to and your name or email address.

FAQs and other documents

A Frequently Asked Questions document (FAQ) may be written to explain the fundamentals about a topic, to provide a list of informational resources, to describe the ground rules for a mailing list or newsgroup, or all of the above.

FAQs are typically the effort of one or a few knowledgeable individuals who have taken it upon themselves to coordinate the collection and dissemination of introductory information on behalf of a larger group of Internet users.

For example the World Wide Web FAQ describes what the World Wide Web is, what kinds of browsers are available and who publishes them, and where to find browser software on the Internet. It also describes how to use helper applications, what kinds of Web servers are available and where to find them, on the Internet, and a dozen pages of other basic information about the Web.

If the mailing list or newsgroup that you subscribe to (or intend to subscribe to) has a FAQ, you should seek out and read it. The FAQ will probably answer some of your initial questions, and save you the trouble of posting questions that have already been answered (see figure 4.25). Reading the FAQ may also save you the possible embarrassment of being taken to task by others subscribers for asking a beginner's question, but then there's no accounting for personality disorders on the Internet.

The World Wide Web Frequently Asked Questions document is written by Thomas Boutell and is frequently posted to several newsgroups, including **comp.infosystems.www.users** and **comp.infosystems.www.misc**. This FAQ answers all the basic "where do I find it?" questions about Web browsers, helper applications, and servers, as well as simple configuration instructions (see figure 4.26).

It is written for all Web users, so it covers Macintosh, Windows, and UNIX software and hardware. The document is available as hypertext at:

```
http://sunsite.unc.edu/boutell/faq/www_faq.html
```

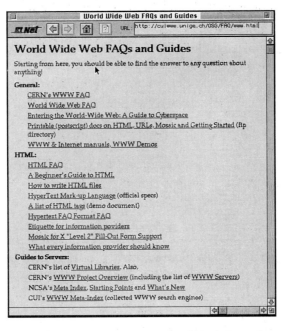

Figure 4.25 *A hypertext listing of Frequently Asked Question documents is kept at* `http://cuiwww.unige.ch/OSG/FAQ/www.html.`

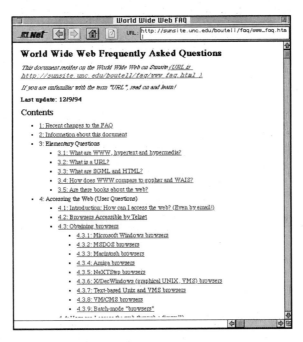

Figure 4.26 *The World Wide Web FAQ is kept at* `http://sunsite.unc.edu/boutell/faq/www_faq.html.`

NCSA's *Mosaic Demo Document* contains links to documents that demonstrate the capabilities of the Web, including how to use graphics, sound, and compressed video. These documents also provide answers to basic questions about clients, servers, HTML and other topics. The Beginner's Guide to HTML is a very good starting point for writing documents using HTML 2.0.

The Mosaic Demo Document is available as hypertext at:

```
http://www.ncsa.uiuc.edu/SDG/Experimental/demoweb/demo.html
```

The *Netscape Communications How to Create Web Services* page contains links to information sources for HTML specifications and editors, including beginner's guides to writing hypertext documents. This document is itself hypertext at:

```
http://home.mcom.com/home/how-to-create-web-services.html
```

The *World Wide Web Primer* by Nathan Torkington is written as a "gentle primer" for users who have heard of the Web and wish to learn more. It explains the basic concepts of the Web, and explains how to get started wandering the Web. The document is available as hypertext at:

```
http://www.vuw.ac.nz/who/Nathan.Torkington/ideas/www-primer.html
```

It is also available as a text document that can be downloaded using anonymous FTP at:

```
ftp://rtfm.mit.edu/pub/usenet/news.answers/
```

An *Information Provider's Guide to Web Servers*, by Nathan Torkington, is an introduction to the server applications that provide information on the Web. It focuses on HyperText Transfer protocol applications and their use. This FAQ is available as text and can be downloaded using anonymous FTP at:

```
ftp://rtfm.mit.edu/pub/usenet/news.answers/
```

An *Information Provider's Guide To HTML*, by Nathan Torkington, is an introduction to the HyperText Markup Language used to format all of the documents presented on the Web. The third document in Torkington's trilogy, this FAQ is also available as text and can be downloaded using anonymous FTP at:

```
ftp://rtfm.mit.edu/pub/usenet/news.answers/
```

World Wide Web Security is published by Rutgers University Network Services and provides information about security for WWW, HTTP, HTML, and related software, including proxy servers, and other internal network security methods.

It is available as hypertext at:

```
http://www-ns.rutgers.edu/www-security/index.html#list
```

The FAQ Resource is a hypertext document that contains links to several dozen information and FAQ documents about the Web, and is at:

```
http://www.charm.net/~web/Vlib/Misc/FAQ.html
```

Entering the World Wide Web: A Guide to Cyberspace by Kevin Hughes, was published by Honolulu Community College in October 1993. It is still a good introduction to the World Wide Web and is available as a hypertext document at:

```
http://www.hcc.hawaii.edu/guide/www.guide.html
```

The NCSA *Mosaic 2.0 Quick FAQ* is basic information about NCSA Mosaic version 2.0, currently available for X-Windows on UNIX-based workstations. The FAQ explains new features of Mosaic 2.0, which hopefully will be available in finished form for Macintosh computer soon. The document is available as hypertext at:

```
http://www.ncsa.uiuc.edu/SDG/Software/Mosaic/Docs/faq-quick2.html
```

The NCSA *Mosaic FAQ: Something Doesn't Work Right* document covers most of the basic new user configuration problems facing NCSA Mosaic users. The document is available as hypertext at:

```
http://www.ncsa.uiuc.edu/SDG/Software/Mosaic/Docs/faq-broken.html#5
```

The *Guide to Network Resource Tools* page has been compiled and produced by the EARN Association and includes information and links to documents about the Internet and the Web, information databases, network resources, methods for locating people and computers, getting files, network software file sites, and just about anything else you might be looking for (see figure 4.27). The Guide is at:

```
http://www.earn.net/gnrt/notice.html
```

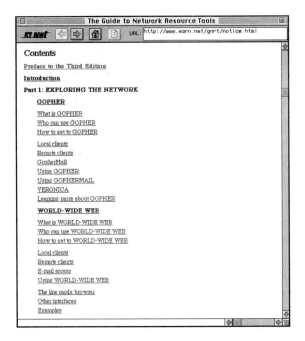

Figure 4.27   *The EARN Association has compiled and produced the Guide to Network Resource Tools at* `http://www.earn.net/gnrt/notice.html`.

The *World Wide Web FAQs and Guides* hyperlink page contains links to many FAQs covering a wide range of topics, including CERN, HTML, Servers, Communication, HTTP, Client/Server architecture, and Tools. The author claims, "Starting from here, you should be able to find the answer to any question about anything!" So you might just want to start at:

`http://cuiwww.unige.ch/OSG/FAQ/www.html`

Dozens of other documents provide beginning and intermediate information about client applications, server software, HTML specifications, the HyperText Transfer protocol, and other topics of relevance to Web users and authors.

The best way to find these or other supplemental documents is to check the Resource Guides at the University of Illinois/National Center for Supercomputing Applications, the CERN laboratory, and the World Wide Web Consortium.

Staking Your Ground

Feeling like the great Web parade is passing you by? The key to getting your name in lights in these great catalogs is creating your own Web pages using HTML. The next chapter explains how to make Web magic using this language of links.

Hyperlinks to many of the resource guides, search engines, and FAQ documents described in this chapter are located on the *World Wide Web Starter Kit* pages at:

http://www.panix.com/~kcoffee

Using HTML

In the previous chapters you've seen some of the many ways that information is conveyed by the Web using text, graphics, and sound. You've also seen how different sources of these media can be interconnected using hyperlinks. And you've seen how hyperlinks can be used to connect a text phrase or picture on one document with almost any other bit of Web information on other documents and servers, no matter where these bits are in the world.

The Web owes its flexible information structure to the HyperText Markup Language (HTML), which is used to construct Web documents. The easiest way to learn HTML is by using it, so this chapter illustrates how to write a Web document and use it as your home page.

This home page will contain links to other Web information sources for authoring documents and preparing a Web server. You will also write an interactive form for your home page that allows you to search the Web for information.

HTML documents are written in a modular fashion—each document is a collection of elements that you can easily modify in order to add or change the information presented.

You can immediately see your results using any browser that complies with the HTML standards, but beware of browsers that bend the rules. Just because your document "looks good" on your screen doesn't necessarily mean it translates the same way on someone else's browser. Learning to check your work before you put it on the Web is an important authoring step.

Netscape is a good tool to use for proofreading your documents because it closely adheres to the current HTML standard, HTML 2.0. The HTML Tools extensions set for BBEdit Lite also provides a method for comparing your document to the standard descriptions for HTML 2.0.

Before you begin writing your own HTML documents, let's take a look at the structure of a typical document. This one happens to be located on a Web server Kevin prepared at the American Museum of Natural History in New York.

Basic Elements of an HTML Document

All HyperText Markup Language documents share some common elements and use a common style for formatting these elements. One way to learn how HTML is used is to look at how other authors have written their documents.

Note

You can download the source HTML for any document on the Web by choosing "Save As..." from the File menu and choosing "Source" from the popup menu in the Save dialog box.

The example shown here is a short hyperlink directory of QuickTime files made to showcase video productions made for exhibitions at the museum (see figure 5.1).

While you won't need to download the file to follow the explanation, a current version of this page is at:

```
http://exhibition.amnh.org/video/videofilm.html
```

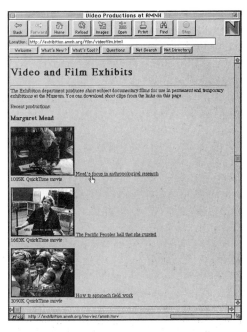

Figure 5.1   *A simple HTML document that provides hyperlinks to QuickTime files.*

This document provides a brief description of how video is used in exhibitions, and provides some still images from recent productions.

Clicking one of the highlighted descriptions or still images downloads a QuickTime movie file to your computer. From there, you can play the video clip in a small window and listen to the soundtrack using a movie player. (If you use a modem connection to the Internet, beware, the files are all larger than 1 MB.)

What Your Browser Doesn't Tell You

If you were to save the document in figure 5.1 to your hard disk as an HTML file, or choose Source from the View menu in Netscape to open a copy of the source HTML on your screen, you would see a text document similar to that shown in the bottom half of figure 5.2. To view the source in MacWeb, choose View Source from the Options menu, then choose Retrieved from the popup menu.

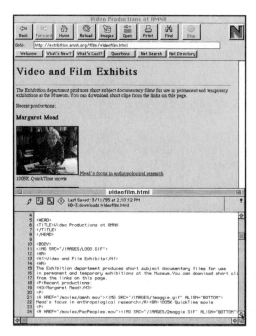

Figure 5.2   *Using the View Source command in Netscape 1.1 to view an*
             HTML document.

Since it's nearly impossible to read the text in that diagram and actually learn
from it, here is the complete document's HTML source code. While this is
confusing right now, each of the items is explained in the next few pages.

```
<HTML>

<HEAD>
<TITLE>Video Productions at AMNH
</TITLE>
</HEAD>

<BODY>
<IMG SRC="/IMAGES/LOGO.GIF">
<HR>
<H1>Video and Film Exhibits</H1>
<HR>
<P>The Exhibition department produces short subject
documentary films for use
in permanent and temporary exhibitions at the Museum. You can
```

```
download short clips
from the links on this page.
<P>Recent productions:
<H2>Margaret Mead</H2>
<P><A HREF="/movies/amnh.mov"><IMG SRC="/IMAGES/1maggie.gif"
ALIGN="BOTTOM">
Mead's focus in anthropological research</A><BR>1005K
QuickTime movie
<P><A HREF="/movies/PacPeoples.mov"><IMG SRC="/IMAGES/
2maggie.GIF" ALIGN="BOTTOM">
The Pacific Peoples hall that she curated</A><BR>1683K
QuickTime movie
<P><A HREF="/movies/anthro.mov"><IMG
SRC="/IMAGES/4maggie.GIF" ALIGN="BOTTOM">
How to approach field work</A><BR>3090K QuickTime movie
<P><A HREF="/movies/media.mov"><IMG SRC="/IMAGES/5maggie.GIF"
ALIGN="BOTTOM">
Mead as a role model for the Woodstock
Generation</A><BR>2983K QuickTime movie
<HR>
<ADDRESS>Geralyn Abinader, Film and Video Developer,
gabin@amnh.org</ADDRESS>
<HR>
</BODY>
</HTML>
```

Interpreting the Tags

Sure, it makes for fascinating reading, but what does all that <XYZ> stuff mean?

Let's start at the top. The portion of this document that states **<HTML>** is known as an "element" or a "tag." This particular tag tells the Web browser to interpret the text that follows as HyperText Markup Language. Tags are not shown in the browser window, which is why you do not see them on any home pages. Tags are surrounded by the characters **<** and **>**; tags tells the browser what to do.

You may notice, in this document and throughout all HTML documents, that tags are usually written in pairs, such as **<HEAD>** and **</HEAD>**. This tells the browser when a tag opens and when a tag closes. Closing tags almost always include a slash mark.

Inside the **<HEAD>** element of this document is the **<TITLE>** of the document. The information contained by this markup is displayed in the title bar of the browser window. If you save the URL of a document to your Hotlist or Bookmark list, the **<TITLE>** of the document is saved also. The head element is closed using **</HEAD>**.

The **<BODY>** tag marks the content of the document. Everything in between **<BODY>** and **</BODY>** is displayed in the browser window. All other document content markup is subordinate to **<BODY>**.

Just below the body tag is an **<IMG>** element that describes an inline graphic. As the browser downloads and reads this document, it requests this inline graphic URL when it reads this line. If you have turned off the command to AutoLoad Images in your browser, all inline requests like this one are ignored.

Below the inline image is an **<HR>** tag that tells the browser to draw a horizontal rule line at the location of the tag. The horizontal rule written here is used as a visual aid to separate the inline image from the rest of the document.

The main heading for this document is **<H1>Video and Film Exhibits</H1>**. There are six levels of text headings specified in HTML, with **<H1>** being the primary (and largest) level heading. In this document we use an **<H1>** heading to describe the subject of the entire document.

After another horizontal rule, we provide a short, descriptive paragraph about film and video production at the museum. Every paragraph in an HTML document ends with a **<P>** tag.

<P> is one of a few elements that does not require a closing tag. According to the Document Type Definition for HTML, this tag is intended to define a section of text as a separate paragraph. **<P>** is not intended to define a space between paragraphs, although some authors may use it as one.

This document is a directory to samples of several video productions, so we've placed a second level heading **<H2>Margaret Mead</H2>** to describe the four links written next as one subgroup. As you add other video clips, you order them under other subheads using **<H2>** headings.

Each of these QuickTime files is referred to by a hyperlink anchor. Anchors are written using the **<A>** and **</A>** tags and display on your screen as highlighted text or graphics. Take a close look at the HTML structure of these anchor statements.

Each of the four anchors are defined as separate paragraphs because we are using each as a separate description. The main part of the anchor statement follows the **<P>** tag. The first one reads:

```
<A HREF="/movies/amnh.mov"><IMG SRC="/IMAGES/1maggie.gif" ALIGN="BOTTOM">
```

This very long tag indicates that this anchor **<A** is a hyperlink to the file described by the **HREF="/movies/amnh.mov"** statement. The **HREF=** statement is an *attribute* of the anchor and specifies the Uniform Resource Locator of the file that this anchor points to.

In this example the **HREF=** statement uses a *partial URL* that points to another folder on the same server, **/movies/**, and to the **amnh.mov** file inside that directory. If you click on the highlighted text in this paragraph, your browser requests **amnh.mov** from the server.

This hyperlink is a bit more complicated. Immediately after the opening anchor tag is a second tag **<IMG SRC="/IMAGES/1maggie.gif" ALIGN="BOTTOM">**. This tag identifies the URL for an inline image that should be downloaded and displayed at this location in the document, inside the hyperlink anchor.

This inline image is described by the partial URL **/IMAGES/1maggie.gif**, and is a GIF file stored on the same server. The attribute **ALIGN="BOTTOM"** tells the browser that the adjacent text in the paragraph should be displayed aligned with the bottom of this inline image.

Notice that **<IMG>** elements do not use a closing tag. All of the information required to download and display an inline image is contained within the **<IMG>** tag itself.

Because this inline image is located inside an anchor tag, it is displayed as part of the hyperlink. Clicking on the image or the text tells the browser to request the URL in this anchor.

Following the inline image tag is a text description **Mead's focus in anthropological research**. This text is displayed as a highlighted hyperlink in the document because it is written between the opening anchor element and the closing anchor element </A>. If you look back at figure 5.1, you see that this text is underlined.

The **
** tag after the closing anchor tag tells the browser to cause a line break in the display. The file size description that follows begins a new line of type beginning at the left side of the browser window.

The rest of the paragraphs in the document follow the same format as this first hyperlink.

Toward the bottom of the file is an **<ADDRESS>** tag that is used to indicate the author of a document. Addresses are usually displayed in italic typeface and use the closing tag **</ADDRESS>**.

Right after the address is a closing tag for the body of the document </**BODY**>, followed by a closing tag for the entire document </**HTML**>.

In one document we have incorporated text, graphic images, and hyperlinks to compressed video files. The most time-consuming aspect of preparing this document was editing segments of video tape into QuickTime movies.

Writing the text and HyperText Markup Language instructions for this Web page probably didn't take as long as it took for you to read the description.

Of course, there is much more to HyperText Markup Language than what you've just seen. We'll cover additional elements throughout this chapter. This example, though, describes the basics of how to assemble an HTML document. Any plain text document can be converted to HTML by adding a few basic tags. And HTML documents plus a Web server (described in Chapter 6) enable anyone with a computer and an Internet connection to become an electronic publisher.

As you work through the tutorial documents, you will learn more frequently used parts of HyperText Markup Language. When you've finished this chapter, you should understand how some lines of text typed like this:

```
<HR><CENTER><H1>Welcome to the Exhibition department!</H1></
CENTER>
<P><IMG SRC="/images/hhbe.gif" ALT="picture of Human Biology and
Evolution exhibit"><BR> <B>Mezhirich diorama in the Hall of Human
Biology and Evolution</B>
<P>If you'd like to drop us a line, please do. If you are using
Netscape, <A HREF="mailto:kcoffee@amnh.org">you can post from
here</A>. Or you can get help <A HREF="help/netpref.html">setting
your Netscape preferences</A> here, so that you can mail from
Netscape. Otherwise, use your mail client to send mail to
<B>kcoffee@amnh.org</B>
<HR><H2>Expedition: Treasures from 125 Years of Discovery</H2> <A
HREF="http://www.amnh.org/html/treasures/treasures.html"> Photo-
graphic images</A> of some of the highlights of the Museum's work
and collections.<HR>
```

end up in your browser window looking like figure 5.3:

Figure 5.3 *HTML enables you to become a World Wide Web author.*

HTML Basic Terms and Concepts

Markup and formatting languages are ubiquitous in computer software. Word processors, for example, are written for the primary purpose of formatting text documents for display and printing.

When you decide to use boldface type for a document heading, the word processor inserts instructions into your document through a menu, command, or dialog box that mark up the words you want in bold. The marked-up parts are displayed in bold on your screen, and are printed in bold type. But the instructions written into the document that specify bold type are hidden from you by the word processing program. This kind of markup describes the document format.

HTML takes a different approach. Instead of markup that describes the display or print characteristics of a document, HTML is meant to describe document structure. There is a compelling reason for this.

The Web is intended as a cross-platform, content-based information retrieval system. The same text/HTML document that you read on your Mac can be read on someone else's IBM-compatible, or Sun workstation, or VAX terminal.

HTML markup indicates the structure of the document content: title, headings, paragraphs, links to other information, graphics, lists, author names, etc. These markup notations are written using plain text that can be read by any computer system.

As a Web document author, you are writing for an audience of millions of other computer users on the Internet. You can't know what kind of computer each member of your audience uses, much less what kind of monitor each has, or which fonts their operating system can display. Therefore, document display is not directly tied to HTML.

Instead, display formatting is primarily controlled by the individual browser that matches display format to document parts.

By writing your documents to conform with the current HyperText Markup Language specification, you ensure that your documents are readable to most people using the Web.

Markup Tags

HTML uses a series of tags to mark up text documents. These tags are *containers* for sections of the document and tell your browser how to interpret those sections.

On the Web, the terms "tag" and "element" are used interchangeably. As a general rule, tag is applied more frequently to describe actual markup notations in HTML documents whereas element is more frequently used to describe the complete function of specific markup.

A typical HTML container begins with an opening tag written inside angle brackets and ends with a closing slash+tag written inside brackets, as in the heading `<H1>Video and Film Exhibits</H1>`.

Some elements do not require a closing tag and are referred to as empty containers. The markup for paragraph `<P>` is one example of an empty container.

HTML tags mark all of the parts of every HTML document. As a document is downloaded, your browser reads through these elements and uses the markup information to determine how it displays the document to you.

Markup is also used to instruct your browser to perform additional tasks, like requesting an inline image identified with an `<IMG>` element.

Major Document Parts

HTML elements are written in a loose hierarchical order. When a browser downloads a Web page, it interprets markup tags according to this hierarchical structure.

For example, when your browser encounters the tag **<HTML>** it interprets everything after that tag as HyperText Markup Language until it encounters the tag **</HTML>** signaling the end of the document.

Within the **<HTML>** element, other tags are interpreted according to the same type of structure. The opening tag signals the beginning of an element and indirectly indicates what other markup may be included within this element. The closing tag indicates the end of that sub-part of the document.

This syntax is part of the common language of the Web and should be used in your documents if you want other browsers (and people) to understand you.

The **<HTML>** element includes two subordinate elements, **<HEAD>** and **<BODY>**.

<HEAD> </HEAD> contains markup and information that describes the entire document and the document's relationship to other documents on the Web.

<BODY> contains markup and information being conveyed to the reader of the document. Every other HTML element that is to be displayed by the browser or used for interaction with the reader is written between the **<BODY></BODY>** tags.

Head Elements

Only a few elements are allowed within the **<HEAD>** part of a document. A typical document **<HEAD>** might look like this:

```
<HTML>
<HEAD>
<TITLE>Kevin Coffee's Help Page</TITLE>
<BASE HREF="http://exhibition.amnh.org/kevin/kevinpage.html">
</HEAD>
```

These elements describe the title of the document, and the location of the document on the Web as described by a Uniform Resource Locator.

Every document you write should include a title element that provides a description of the document's content. Title information is often used to catalog documents and is saved along with the document URL to Hotlists and Bookmark files, so write descriptive titles.

The **\<BASE\>** element shown here records the Uniform Resource Locator for the document. Base elements provide a reference for partial URLs if the document is moved from its original location.

A partial URL is a hyperlink that records only the filename or directory/ filename of a linked document. The partial URL "**/images/1maggie.gif**" used in the Film and Video document shown at the beginning of this chapter is an example. The full URL for that graphic file is:

`http://exhibition.amnh.org/images/1maggie.gif`

As long as documents are stored in the same location, hyperlinks between those documents can be written using partial URLs. If a document containing partial URLs is moved (say someone saves it to his own disk), those partial URLs no longer function properly. This happens unless the document also includes a **\<BASE\>** element showing its original location (and thus providing the correct path for the partial URLs).

The other **\<HEAD\>** elements, **\<ISINDEX\>**, **\<NEXTID\>**, **\<LINK\>**, and **\<META\>**, are used less frequently, and have special relevance for Web servers and search programs.

Body Elements

The markup used within **\<BODY\>** consists of elements that define structure or an interactive function.

All text within the body of a document is marked up according to its place in the organizational structure of the document. Commonly used text markup includes tags for paragraphs, headings, lists, and type styles.

Some **\<BODY\>** elements are interactive hyperlinks to other documents or resources on the Internet, including indexes, databases, graphics, or sound files.

Anything that is to be displayed onscreen, or that requires a user's interaction, is written within the **\<BODY\>** element.

Attributes

Elements in HTML are sometimes modified with additional statements called attributes.

The exact meaning of any attribute depends upon the element that it is being used to modify.

For example, the **<INPUT>** element can be modified with the attribute **NAME=**. The function of this **NAME=** attribute is to identify data entered into an **<INPUT>** field in a fill-out form.

The anchor **<A>** element also uses an attribute called **NAME=**, but the function of the anchor attribute **NAME=** is to create a text anchor in a document.

Attributes usually take the form of a pair of terms separated by an equal sign. The value in an attribute statement is almost always placed inside a pair of straight quotation marks.

There is one exception to this rule. The **METHOD=** attribute used in a **<FORM>** element can be written either with or without quote marks; this is explained later in the chapter.

Don't confuse the value part of an attribute statement with the **VALUE=** attribute. **VALUE=** attributes are used to assign a default value to an element.

Hyperlinks

What would hypertext be without hyperlinks?

Hyperlinks are elements that refer to other documents, images, files, or programs on the Internet. These elements always include an attribute that specifies a Uniform Resource Locator.

There are two main types of hyperlink elements.

Anchors use the tags **<A>** and **</A>** to mark up text or graphics as clickable links to other elements, images, documents, or servers.

Anchor markup looks like this:

```
<A HREF="http://www.w3.org/hypertext/WWW/Clients"> World Wide Web
browsers </A>
```

The phrase **World Wide Web browsers** in this markup appears in the browser window as highlighted and underlined text. If you click on the phrase **World Wide Web browsers**, your browser sends the URL request **http://www.w3.org/hypertext/WWW/Clients**.

In this example, the statement that begins with **HREF=** is an attribute that identifies the hyperlink reference URL for this anchor.

A pair of anchors can be used to create links between parts of documents. In this usage, one anchor points to a second target anchor. Target anchors use the attribute **NAME=** to identify themselves. The anchor pointing to the target uses an **HREF=** statement that is formed with that name preceded with a **#** character.

For instance, the link **`<A HREF="#zither">more info about zithers</A>`** could be written to point to other text in the same document that was marked up as **`<A NAME="zither">musical instruments in our collection</A>`**. Clicking on the first anchor would move you to the second anchor.

You would point to a named anchor in a different document by adding the anchor name to the end of the URL for that document. For example, **`<A HREF=http://www.dog.org/hypertext/catalogue#zither">`**.

The hyperlink tag **`<IMG>`** is used to specify a graphic file that should be auto-matically downloaded and displayed within a document.

Markup for an inline image looks like this: **`<IMG SRC="/IMAGES/1maggie.gif" ALIGN="BOTTOM">`**.

When a browser downloads this markup, it automatically sends the URL specified by the attribute statement **`SRC=`**, unless the browser cannot display inline graphics or is set to ignore inline graphic markup.

You can (and usually should) write your inline image markup to include an alternate text description, like this: **`<IMG SRC="/IMAGES/1maggie.gif" ALT="photo of Margaret Mead 24K" ALIGN="BOTTOM">`**. If a browser reading this markup does not display inline graphics, it displays the text specified by the attribute **`ALT=`**.

The third image attribute, **`ALIGN=`**, indicates the display position of adjacent text relative to the inline image. In this example, text written immediately after the **`<IMG>`** tag is displayed starting at the bottom-right corner of the picture.

Inline images are usually small Graphic Interchange Format (GIF) or Joint Photographic Experts Group (JPEG) files.

This whirlwind tour of basic HTML terminology is only a beginning explana-tion, but it's enough to get started with writing one of your own, so let's do that next.

Home Page Tutorial

You've heard about them, seen them, even download onto your computer screen. Now live the excitement of writing your very own Home Page!

Just what is a home page supposed to be?

In its most basic sense, a home page is a hyper-notebook about servers and documents that you've found and that you refer to frequently while your browsing the Web.

The home page you're about to write in this exercise is one that loads every time you launch your Web browser and that you can use to teach yourself more about the World Wide Web.

To write this home page, we recommend that you use the text editor BBEdit Lite.

Make sure you have also decompressed and copied the folder containing MacWeb to your hard drive.

On the WWWSK disk is a folder named Chapter 5. Copy the **home.gif** file in this folder to the Documents folder inside your MacWeb application folder.

Launch BBEdit Lite and create a new (empty) document. Choose "Save As" from the File menu command to name it **homepage.html** and save it also to the Documents folder in your Web browser's application folder (see figure 5.4).

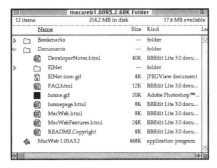

Figure 5.4 *Your Web browser's Documents folder should contain the* home.gif *and the* homepage.html *files.*

BBEdit is a plain text editor published by Bare Bones Software. Despite the name, BBEdit does include some useful features for editing text, including HTML. We leave you to discover most of these features on your own, but for the purpose at hand you should make a few adjustments to how BBEdit displays text on your screen.

Choose "Preferences" from the Edit menu. Choose "Editor" from the popup menu at the top of the window and select the Wrap While Typing check box, and deselect the Smart Quotes check box.

The first setting enables BBEdit to automatically wrap the text you enter according to the width of your document window. Size your document window accordingly. The second setting keeps BBEdit from inserting "curly" quote marks into your HTML document. Curly quotes are not legal characters in the HTML character set and you cannot use them! You need to use straight quote marks in HTML attribute statements.

Now, choose "Window" from the Preferences popup menu. In this dialog box, select the Status Bar and Philip Bar check boxes. The status bar displays across the top of the BBEdit window. The Philip Bar is a thin vertical line that indicates the width of smaller display screens.

Finally, choose "Wrapping" from the Preferences popup menu. In this dialog box, select the radio button for Philip Bar in the Default Wrap Settings. This causes text you type into a document to wrap at the location of the Philip Bar.

In your new, empty BBEdit document type in the elements for the beginning of your home page (feel free to make up your own title):

```
<HTML>
<HEAD>
<TITLE>My WWWSK Home Page</TITLE>
</HEAD>
```

Every document begins with an opening **<HTML>** tag to indicate to the browser that what follows is HyperText Markup Language. This tag is followed by the **<HEAD>** part of the document, where you describe the document generally. In this case, you've written a **<TITLE>** element that describes the document.

Close the **<HEAD>** portion of the document with the tag **</HEAD>**.

Now let's start the body of the document. You can add any information that you'd like, but let's start by creating a collection of hyperlinks to information about the Web, about HyperText Markup Language, and about HyperText Transfer Protocols.

Type the following:

```
<BODY>
<HR>
<H1>World Wide Web Starter Kit Guide</H1>
<P>Notes and hyperlinks to information about HTML, HTTP, and
Web wanderings generally.
<HR>
```

The substance of every HTML document is written inside the **<BODY>** element, so you need to write the opening tag for **<BODY>**. We've entered a horizontal rule **<HR>** tag before the heading just to break up the page. This is followed by a heading that describes the content of the document. This heading is the primary heading for the document, so mark it with a first level heading tag, **<H1>**, and close it with the tag **</H1>**.

Generally, document headings are followed by text, so start a new paragraph with a **<P>** tag and enter a short description of your home page. We've entered a second **<HR>** tag after the description, again just to provide a visual break in the page.

Save the changes you've made to your document. Launch MacWeb and use Open command in the File menu to open your **homepage.html** document in the browser window. Your document should look something like figure 5.5.

Figure 5.5   *The beginnings of a great Home Page.*

Note

*A common mistake in writing elements is to forget a special character here or there. If your highlighted text is not displaying correctly, check to make sure you wrote your anchor tags enclosed in brackets **<>**. If more text is highlighted than should be, check that you wrote the closing anchor tag **</A>** in the right place. If the link doesn't work, check that the **HREF=** URL is written between quote marks.*

OK, it's a bit stark. But we can fix that with a few hyperlinks to information about HyperText Markup Language. Write a second level heading for this new section:

```
<H2>HyperText Markup Language</H2>
<P>Documents that contain useful information about
hypertext on the Web.
```

Now we start getting tricky. The next couple of paragraphs are going to include entries written as hyperlinked text. Follow along closely.

```
<P><A HREF="http://www.ncsa.uiuc.edu/demoweb/html-primer.html">A
Beginner's Guide to HTML.</A> A
primer for producing documents in the markup language used by the
World Wide Web, from the National Center for Supercomputing Ap-
plications at the University of Illinois.
```

Maybe that wasn't so hard after all. But let's review. It's a separate paragraph so you entered a **<P>** tag. This is followed by an opening anchor tag **<A** that contains an **HREF=** attribute.

Attributes are used to qualify specific elements, in this case, the **HREF=** attribute is part of the anchor element and indicates the document being pointed to by the anchor.

All attribute statements contain two parts. The first part is the attribute class, the second part is the attribute value. These pairs are separated by an equal sign (**=**), with the value written inside straight quotation marks. There are no additional spaces in an attribute statement. After the attribute statement, the tag is completed with a greater-than (**>**) sign.

Hyperlinks are interactive text or graphics. You activate the hyperlink by clicking on it. The active part of the link is highlighted in the browser window.

In order to mark up text as a hyperlink, the linked text is placed between an opening and closing anchor tag. In this example, you marked up the phrase **A Beginner's Guide to HTML** as the hyperlinked text, and followed it with a closing **</A>** tag.

This phrase by itself is not much to go on, and this page is supposed to be helpful, so it's followed by a short description of where the link leads.

Save your changes to **homepage.html** and close the document window. Open the document using MacWeb. Your home page should now look something like the one shown in figure 5.6.

Figure 5.6   Your first hyperlink!

OK, let's add a few more hyperlinks. Enter the next heading and link:

```
<H2>HyperText Transfer Protocol</H2>
<P>Documents that explain how browsers and servers
communicate with each other.
<P><A HREF="http://info.cern.ch/hypertext/WWW/Protocols/Relevant-
Protocols.html"> The HyperText Transfer protocol</A> A
description of HTTP from the original authors of the standard
at the CERN physics lab in Geneva.
```

This is marked up just like the first one; however, this one leads to a document at the CERN lab that explains what the HyperText Transfer Protocol is and does. (Hint: HTTP is how browsers and servers communicate.)

Let's keep going.

```
<P><A HREF="http://www.biap.com/machttp/machttp_docs.html"> In-
formation about MacHTTP server</A> with hyperlinks to archives of
the MacHTTP mailing list, FAQs, and tutorials, maintained by BIAP
Systems, Inc.
```

This link leads to a directory of resources related to the MacHTTP server application. It provides you with lots of useful information about setting up and operating the MacHTTP Web server described in chapter 6.

Now add another heading for the next section, about Uniform Resource Locators.

```
<H2>Uniform Resource Locators</H2>
<P>Documents that explain how documents and servers are
identified on the Web.
<P><A HREF="http://www.ncsa.uiuc.edu/demoweb/url-
primer.html">Beginner's guide to URLs</A> A primer
for understanding Uniform Resource Locators, written by the
Mosaic software developers at the National Center
for Supercomputing Applications.
```

Finally, for now anyway, let's add a section for links that enable you to go looking for more information.

```
<H2>Search Engines</H2>
<P>Databases of documents available on the World Wide Web.
<P><A HREF="http://akebono.stanford.edu/yahoo/search.html">The
Yahoo Web Directory</A> The search form for finding information
in the Yahoo index of Web documents at Stanford University.
```

Save your changes. Choose "Open" from the File menu or "Reload" from the View menu to view your home page. Your document should look like the one in figure 5.7.

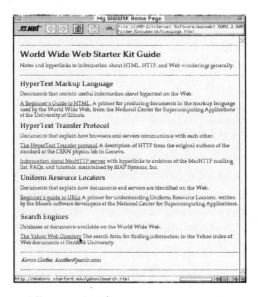

Figure 5.7   *Your rapidly growing home page.*

Your new document is functional, and it looks pretty good, but a little bit of color could really help. Let's add an inline graphic.

At the start of this lesson, you were asked to copy the file **home.gif** to the Documents folder inside your MacWeb folder. Link that file to your home page.

Go back to the top of your HTML document. Just after (below) the first **<HR>** horizontal rule and just before (above) the **<H1>** heading of your document, add another piece of markup: <IMG SRC="home.gif" ALT="20K picture of the rings of Saturn">.

This is an image element that tells your browser to place the file **"home.gif"** at this location in your document. The **<IMG>** element is always used with a **SRC=** attribute to specify the URL of the image file. Like all attribute values, the URL specified in **SRC=** is placed inside straight quote marks.

The second attribute in this element, **ALT=**, specifies a text string that is displayed by text-only browsers, and some graphical browsers, in place of the image. We've written the **ALT=** text string to tell users the image size and description. The **home.gif** file is a picture of Saturn's rings taken by the Hubble Space Telescope.

You probably want to stop now and reload your document in Netscape.

Like any master artist, you must now save your work. Even though nobody but you may ever see your new document, you should get into the habit of providing an address for all your HTML documents. A couple more horizontal rules won't hurt, either.

Type in the following text and markup:

```
<HR>
<ADDRESS>your name and address</ADDRESS>
<HR>
</BODY>
</HTML>
```

Remember, it's important to close both the **<BODY>** element and the **<HTML>** elements. It won't make a big difference to a document like this one because it's loaded from your own disk drive, but it can make a difference for documents that you serve on the Web.

You may have noticed that Netscape displayed your document contents just fine without either closing **</BODY>** or **</HTML>** tag. Not all browsers may be as forgiving.

The closing **</HTML>** tag also signifies the end of a file to a browser and that the connection to the server can be closed. Of course your new home page document is not being served over the Web, so there is no active connection to open or close, but again, we're talking about the proper way to write all your HTML documents, not just this one.

When you've finished typing these last pieces of text and markup, save your changes and reload your home page in MacWeb. It should look like figure 5.8.

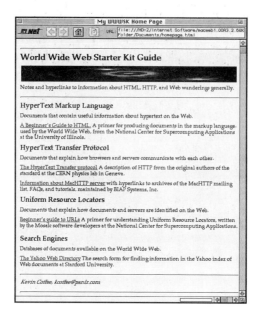

Figure 5.8   *Your first HTML document.*

Text Markup

There are several groups of HTML elements specifically designed to format text information. You use these elements frequently in your documents, so let's examine them next.

Headings

As we've already described, text headings are marked up according to their position within a document. There are six levels of heading markup.

Primary headings are written between **<H1>** and **</H1>** tags, secondary headings are tagged with **<H2></H2>**, and so on through the lowest heading level: **<H6></H6>**.

Browsers usually display headings in decreasing type sizes and in bold type styles (see figure 5.9), but more browsers now allow you to set your own display characteristics for headings and all other elements. In Netscape you customize how type is displayed by choosing Preferences from the Options menu and choosing "Fonts and Colors" from the popup menu.

Some programs look for prioritized heading tags and use them to extract an outline from a document, or to list the major topics within a document.

You should not use heading markup as a typographical device; in other words, don't use **<H1>** just because you want to see big type.

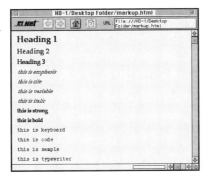

Figure 5.9   *Headings and styled text formats displayed in MacWeb.*

Paragraphs and Line Breaks

Individual sections of text in an HTML document are marked up using the paragraph tag **<P>**. A closing **</P>** tag is optional, but rarely used. Browsers usually separate individual paragraphs with a line space.

Some browsers may interpret **<P>** markup as a line space. Browsers that conform to HTML 2.0 ignore **<P>** markup that is not followed by text.

Normally, the line length of paragraphs and other text in an HTML document is governed by the size of the browser window. If your window is five inches wide, text wraps at five inches. If your window is ten inches wide, text wraps at ten inches.

Line breaks can be marked up using the **
** tag. This tag forces a line break in a line of text at the location of the tag. The **
** tag does not cause a line space.

Text Styles

Words and phrases can be marked up using a series of logical and physical style elements. Physical styles are meant solely to indicate typographic style, such as bold or italic. There are only a few physical style tags in HTML 2.0, but more are planned for HTML 3.0.

Logical style elements are meant to mark up text according to its meaning in the document. There are several logical markup tags. More will be added in HTML 3.0.

You may reset different browsers to display logical styles in whatever way you'd like.

For example, the default display style of **<EM>** is black italicized type. You could reset MacWeb so that it displays **<EM>** markup in red-colored, bold type.

<EM> is for adding emphasis to a word or phrase, the logical style **<CITE>** marks up text as a citation (from a published work), the logical style **<VAR>** marks text as a variable in a computer language phrase. These all default to italic type. The physical style markup for italics is **<I>**.

<STRONG> is used to add emphasis to a word or phrase. It defaults to bold type. The physical style markup for bold is **<B>**.

<KBD> is used for indicating text as it might be entered using a keyboard, **<CODE>** marks up text that represents computer language, **<SAMP>** marks up text that indicates a sequence of literal characters. These logical styles all default to monospaced type. The physical style for monospaced type is **<TT>**.

Which to use for what? If you are marking text that has a specific meaning in your document corresponding to a specified logical style, use that style element. Otherwise use one of the physical style elements.

Blocks of text in an HTML document can also be formatted according to their function in the document and these are also linked to how the text block is displayed.

You used **<ADDRESS> </ADDRESS>** to mark up your home page. The function of this tag is to signify an actual address and is often used to mark up the author's address in an HTML document. The address tag should not be used as a generic marker for italic type, but addresses should be marked up with the **<ADDRESS>** tag so that programs capable of extracting address information from a document can find it.

The **<BLOCKQUOTE>** tag is used to identify text as a quotation. Text marked up with **<BLOCKQUOTE></BLOCKQUOTE>** is indented from the left side of the browser window as a block separating it from the rest of the document.

Preformatted text in monospaced typeface displays exactly as you have typed it into your text/HTML document. Text that is marked up between **<PRE>** and **</PRE>** maintains all of the character spacing and line breaks of the original entry. Tab spaces are converted as character spaces, however, because the tab character is not allowed in HTML.

```
<PRE>
you could use     pre-formatted  text markup
to specify        how text       lines up
in a document     and simulate   columns of type,
or numbers,       or whatever    you want to format.
</PRE>
```

This markup would display exactly as it is typed here (see figure 5.10).

Until very recently, using **<PRE>** was the only way to enter text or numbers as a table in an HTML document. However, a new **<TABLE>** element is proposed for HTML 3.0, and is already implemented in NCSA Mosaic 2.0 and in Netscape 1.1. It will soon be implemented into MacWeb.

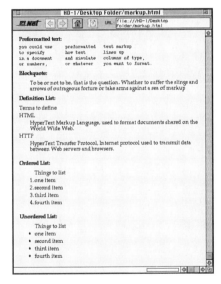

Figure 5.10   *Block text and list styles as displayed by MacWeb.*

List Elements

HTML includes several different kinds of markup for formatting lists. Each list type uses one set of tags to define the entire list and another tag or set of tags to mark up the individual items in the list.

The entire list is contained between opening and closing tags. List items do not use closing tags. All lists are indented to the right.

Definition lists are used to present information in glossary-like form, listing a specific word or phrase and then providing one or more sentences to define the word. The tags **<DL></DL>** enclose the entire list. Terms are marked up with **<DT>** and definitions are tagged with **<DD>**. Here's an example:

```
<DL>Glossary of Terms
<DT>HTML
<DD>HyperText Markup Language, used to format documents shared on
the World Wide Web.
<DT>HTTP
<DD>HyperText Transfer Protocol, Internet protocol used to trans-
mit data between Web servers and browsers.
</DL>
```

Directory lists are used to present information in the form of a directory or listing with no special marking or bullets. The entire list is enclosed between **<DIR>** and **</DIR>**. Each list item is tagged with a preceding **<LI>** and appears on a separate line.

Menu lists are used to present items in the form of a menu, and resemble directory lists, except that each item is preceded by a bullet. The entire list is enclosed between **<MENU>** and **</MENU>**. Each list item is tagged by **<LI>** and appears on a separate line.

Ordered lists are used to present items in numerical order. HTML automatically numbers these items beginning with the number 1. The entire list is enclosed between **<OL>** and **</OL>**. List items are tagged with **<LI>**.

```
<OL>An Ordered List
<LI>one item
<LI>second item
<LI>third item
<LI>fourth item
</OL>
```

The ordered list will be greatly extended in HTML 3.0 to include Roman numerals, uppercase and lowercase letters, and to allow the list sequence to begin at a specific letter or number (instead of 1 or A).

Unordered lists are marked up the same as ordered lists, but are used to present items in no special order. Items display in the order you enter them in the HTML document. The entire list is marked up between **<UL>** and **</UL>**, and each **<LI>** is marked with a bullet and appears on a separate line.

If you've noticed some redundancy in list markup, you are not alone. **<MENU>** and **<DIR>** are being phased out beginning with HTML 3.0.

Special Characters

The text contained within HTML documents must conform to a character specification known as Latin 1. HTML uses a subset that includes 127 common characters used in most European alphabets.

The basic HTML character set includes upper- and lowercase letters A through Z, and the Arabic numerals 0 through 9.

This subset does not include all the ASCII characters represented on your keyboard. It also doesn't include the various special characters that are available to Macintosh character sets through ⌘ + Shift and Option + Shift combinations.

As if that wasn't confusing enough, some of the regular Latin 1 characters are ignored by HTML. The space, line feed, and tab characters are examples of ignored characters. Some other characters, such as **<**, **>**, and **&**, are reserved for use only as HTML markup.

In order to write "unsafe" characters that are reserved for markup, or to write special diacritical character markers, you need to use encoded character markup. There is encoded character markup for 63 special characters, and this is listed in Appendix A.

Examples of encoded markup are **&** for the ampersand sign, **<** for the less-than sign, and **"** to display "curly" or "smart" double quote marks. Note the format for this markup. Every code begins with an **&** character and ends with a semi-colon.

Special characters not included in the Appendix A listing cannot be represented by text in HTML documents.

Note

It does not matter whether you use upper- or lowercase type for most markup. HTML is not case-sensitive to text strings inside angle brackets. The one exception, as of this writing, is the value statement for the <FORM> argument METHOD=, which in HTML 2.0, is either GET or POST (this is explained in the next few pages).

Forms and CGI

A useful way to interact on the Web is to use forms that enable users to enter text or data and submit that data to a server. You can use this to conduct a document search, create a new document or document entry, or trigger some other process at the server.

This form interactivity is possible because of the introduction of the **<FORM>** element in HTML 2.0.

The **<FORM>** element is really a suite of elements and attributes that includes the subordinate elements **<INPUT>**, **<OPTION>**, **<SELECT>**, and **<TEXTAREA>**.

These elements are each modified with some or all of the attributes **ALIGN=**, **CHECKED=**, **MAXLENGTH=**, **NAME=**, **SIZE=**, **SRC=**, **TYPE=**, and **VALUE=**.

Information entered into a **<FORM>** is sent by the browser to a remote program for processing. Usually, this program is a Common Gateway Interface program, or CGI. Forms can also be used by the browser to send electronic mail to a remote mail server.

The **<FORM>** element doesn't do anything except accept data entered into the form fields by a user. The browser takes the data input into the form and sends it to a server at the location specified by an **ACTION=** attribute. The **<FORM>** element is a method for organizing information, it does not process any data itself.

Here you will experiment with writing a **<FORM>** and its related markup in an HTML document. Be sure to follow this tutorial all the way to the end.

Use BBEdit Lite to create a new document and name it **form.html**. Save this document to the Documents folder in your MacWeb folder (where your home page is not located).

Since this is a new HTML document, you need to enter the basic markup required for all documents.

```
<HTML>
<HEAD>
<TITLE>A Lesson in Form</TITLE>
</HEAD>
<BODY>
```

Now that you've gotten that out of the way, let's write a document that solicits user feedback about a hypothetical Web server. First, type in a descriptive heading and opening paragraph.

```
<H1>Welcome to My Web Server</H1>
<P>Thanks for stopping by. Please take a minute to let me know
what you think.
```

Every form begins with an opening tag. The **<FORM>** tag is written to include at least two attributes, or statements, that qualify what the form does. The first attribute is the **ACTION=** statement.

ACTION= identifies the location of the Web server and the CGI program that receives the information submitted through this form. This location is written as a Uniform Resource Locator. Like all attribute statements, the value we give to **ACTION=** is written inside straight quote marks.

```
<FORM ACTION="http://exhibition.amnh.org/scripts/foosurvey.cgi"
```

The second attribute needed in this **<FORM>** element is a **METHOD=** statement. **METHOD=** describes the HyperText Transfer Protocol method that is used to describe the information entered in the form to the CGI program (which is on the Web server).

The browser takes the data entered in the form **<INPUT>** fields and adds it to the end of the URL entered in the **ACTION=** statement. This complete string is sent to the Web server for handling.

There are two main types of **METHOD=** values: **GET** and **POST**.

The **GET** method sends the data as one or a few keywords that can be used for a database search. Information sent using **GET** is separated from the main URL string by a **?** (question mark).

The **POST** method is used to send data added to an existing document or data-base, or processed in some other way by the CGI program. Information sent using **POST** is separated from the main URL string by a **$** (dollar sign). For this exercise, you'll use the **POST** method because our form is collecting information to be added to a document on the server.

The **METHOD=** values, **GET** and **POST** are not placed inside quote marks.

Finish writing the **<FORM>** element with a **METHOD=POST** like this:

```
<FORM ACTION="http://exhibition.amnh.org/scripts/foosurvey.cgi"
METHOD=POST>
```

Now you need to create the input fields used to enter information into the form. Let's start with a field for collecting a user's name.

```
<P>Name:<INPUT NAME="name" SIZE="24">
```

The **<P>** tag marks the line as a separate paragraph of the document. The field is displayed in the browser screen next to the text label **Name**.

Input fields are formed by the element **<INPUT>**, which is modified with one or more attributes. The **NAME=** attribute is used to mark the data collected in this field. According to the example here, the data entered in this field is identified using this value, **NAME**, followed by an equal sign and whatever text was entered in the field.

The second attribute in this **<INPUT>** element is **SIZE=**. The default size of an input field depends on the browser. For MacWeb, this default size is 20 characters wide. The 20-character width does not limit the amount of text that can be entered, only the size of the field as it is displayed by the browser. The **SIZE=** attribute can be used to display the field wider or narrower than 20 characters.

The default type of input field is a text entry field. Other types of fields can be specified in an **<INPUT>** element by adding a **TYPE=** attribute. For example, the **TYPE="HIDDEN"** attribute is used to make the field invisible in the browser window. **TYPE="CHECKBOX"** is used to make the field an either/or selection entered by using a checkbox.

Let's try a few combinations:

```
<P>Address:<INPUT NAME="address" SIZE="30">
<P>City-State-Zip:<INPUT NAME="csz">
<P>Email address: <INPUT NAME="email">
<INPUT NAME="ID" VALUE="sample form" TYPE="HIDDEN">
<P>I use MacWeb: <INPUT NAME="macweb" TYPE="CHECKBOX">
```

Save your changes to the document and open **form.html** using MacWeb. Your document should look like figure 5.11.

Figure 5.11   *The fields in your* **<FORM>** *should look like this.*

You'll notice that the input fields are different sizes. The Name and Address fields are the width specified by the **SIZE=** attribute used with that **<INPUT>** element. The width of the Email and City-State-Zip fields are the default size of 20 characters.

You should also notice that the **<INPUT NAME="ID" >** field does not display in the browser window because it contains the attribute **TYPE="HIDDEN"**.

Now let's add a few more entry fields.

You can create a popup or scrolling list of choices in a **<FORM>** by using the **<SELECT>** element. Each of the choices is marked up using the **<OPTION>** element, like this:

```
<P>Please rate this server:
<SELECT NAME="rating">
<OPTION>Very good
<OPTION>Average
<OPTION>Not that great
<OPTION>Poor
</SELECT>
```

As it's written here, this **<SELECT>** element displays a popup list of options. If you add a **SIZE=** attribute that is greater than "1" to the **<SELECT>** element, the list of options displays as a scrolling list. The number specified in the **SIZE=** attribute specifies the height in characters of the window.

Save your changes and reload **form.html** in your browser window. You'll see the first **<OPTION>** item as the default selection. The other **<OPTION>** items are available through a popup menu.

If you want to provide a space for users to write more lengthy comments, you can add a **<TEXTAREA>** element to your **<FORM>**, like this:

```
<P>Your comments:
<P><TEXTAREA NAME="comments" COLS="72" ROWS="12">Please feel free
to speak your mind here</TEXTAREA>
```

Like other entry fields, text area fields are written with a **NAME=** attribute to identify the data collected in the text area.

Unlike other entry fields, the size of a text area is specified for height and width of the field, using the **COLS=** and **ROWS=** attributes. **COLS=** indicates the width of the field according to character width. **ROWS=** indicates the height of the field according to character height.

Any text that you would like to have automatically appear in the **<TEXTAREA>** field can be written between the opening **<TEXTAREA>** and closing **</TEXTAREA>** tags.

In order to send the data collected in the form, you need to provide a way for users to tell the browser to submit their information. This is done through a special **<INPUT>** field of the **TYPE="SUBMIT"**. The submit field appears in the browser window as a button. Clicking on the button tells the browser to submit the form according to the **ACTION=** statement in the **<FORM>** element.

A submit button is written like this:

```
<P><INPUT TYPE="submit" VALUE="Send">
```

The **VALUE=** attribute specifies label text to be written on top of the submit button.

Finish up the **<FORM>** by writing a closing **</FORM>** tag below this last input field and save your changes. Reload **form.html** in the MacWeb window. Your form document should look like figure 5.12.

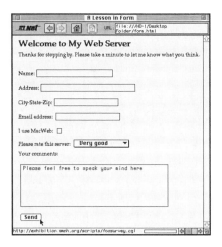

Figure 5.12   *Your sample **<FORM>** should now look like this.*

A Working Form

This exercise demonstrates how to write HTML markup for **<FORM>**, but the **form.html** document isn't functional because it doesn't address a working CGI (Common Gateway Interface) script anywhere on the Web (there is no **foosurvey.cgi** at **exhibition.amnh.org**, sorry).

That doesn't mean you can't create a working form right now. This next exercise creates a form on your home page that you can use to search the Lycos document directory at Carnegie-Mellon University.

Use BBEdit Lite to open the **homepage.html** document you wrote earlier in this chapter. Add the following markup beginning on a new line, after the hyperlink to the Yahoo index but before your address.

```
<H2>The Lycos Search Engine</H2>
<FORM ACTION="http://agent3.lycos.cs.cmu.edu/cgi-bin/pursuit"
METHOD=GET>
```

This form allows you to submit one or more keywords to the Lycos database. The **ACTION=** of this form is to send these keywords to the CGI program **pursuit** on the Lycos 3 search engine computer.

The **METHOD=GET** appends a question mark **?** to the end of this URL followed by your keywords. (Again, **GET** is the usual method used for submitting a search request through a form.)

This next line creates a field for entering the keywords for your search. The **NAME=** of this field must be written as **"query"**. There's room for entering more than one word.

```
<P><B>Query:</B> <INPUT TYPE="text" NAME="query" SIZE="48">
```

The Lycos search program allows you to specify several additional parameters for your document search. The next input fields collect that parameter information. The Lycos program is case-sensitive so do not change the case of the **NAME=** values for these parameters. Note that each of these fields includes a specified **VALUE=** that appears as a default value in the field.

```
<B>Max-hits:</B><INPUT TYPE="text" NAME="maxhits" VALUE="10"
SIZE="5">
<B>Min-terms:</B><INPUT TYPE="text" NAME="minterms" VALUE="1"
SIZE="5">
<B>Min-score:</B><INPUT TYPE="text" NAME="minscore" VALUE="0.2"
SIZE="5">
```

You can also tell Lycos to send you simple listings of documents by sending a "terse" command using this checkbox field:

```
<B>Terse output:</B><INPUT TYPE="checkbox" NAME="terse">
```

You need to add an input field for the submit button. You can also create another button field that allows you to reset all of the fields in the form to their default values. This is done by writing an **<INPUT>** element with the **TYPE="RESET"** value. After you've written these elements, enter the closing tag, **</FORM>**:

```
<P><INPUT type="submit" VALUE="Start search">
<INPUT TYPE="reset" VALUE="Reset">
</FORM>
```

You may recall from Chapter 3 that there are multiple Lycos programs running simultaneously to handle the high volume of requests for information from the database. The computer specified in this form, **agent3**, may be busy some of the times you try to run a search, so adding a link to the Lycos main page is a good backup plan. On the next line of your home page, enter the markup for that hyperlink:

```
<P><A HREF="http://lycos.cs.cmu.edu/">The Lycos main page</A>
```

Now you're done. Reload your home page in the MacWeb window and take it for a test spin (see figure 5.13). Try finding some information about zithers.

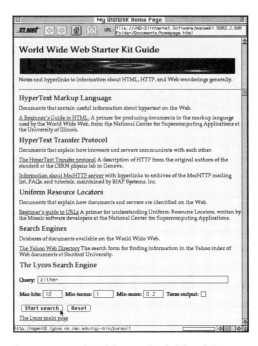

Figure 5.13   *Your home page should now look like this.*

Using Graphics and Sound

Another of the gee-whiz features of the World Wide Web is the capability of Web browsers to receive multimedia information. All of the browsers written for the Macintosh since NCSA Mosaic are capable of displaying inline images as well as using external applications to display color graphics, play sound files, or run compressed video and animation.

Linking text with graphic or sound files and integrating graphics into text documents are things that the Web does better than most other Internet systems, and less expensively than any of them. Using these features is only a bit more complicated than writing a URL that points to the proper file.

Inline Graphic Formats

HTML lets you place graphics directly into a document by simply writing an `<IMG SRC="">` element into your document. The browser automatically handles the rest, and the target graphic file is displayed in the browser window at the correct location.

The most common use of an inline graphic is to display a banner graphic across a page, like a logo or letterhead (see figure 5.14). Inline graphics are also used to display iconic buttons, or thumbnail pictures, colored divider bars, or other decorations. You can write an inline image into a hyperlink anchor and turn a thumbnail photo into a clickable link.

Another use for an inline image is as a graphical interface that serves as a menu of hyperlinks. This kind of inline graphic is called an image map, because Uniform Resource Locators are "mapped" or encoded to pixel coordinates in the graphic (see figure 5.15).

Image maps are controlled by server-side CGI programs. But the presence of the interface must also be marked up in the document by writing an **ISMAP** attribute inside the **<IMG>** element that calls the graphic. Here's an example of the HTML markup used for an image map:

```
<IMG SRC="http://exhibition.amnh.org/hhbe/skulls/map.gif" ISMAP>
```

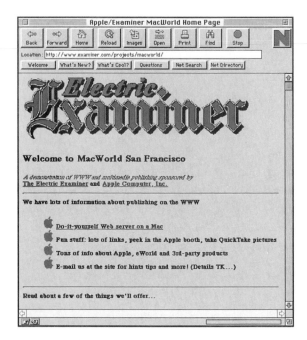

Figure 5.14   *The logo and apple bullets on this page are inline graphics.*

Figure 5.15   *The button graphic across the top of this page is actually an inline image map that has several clickable "hot spots."*

The Web has evolved around the Graphic Interchange Format, or GIF, as the primary format for inline image files. The GIF format can be interpreted by almost all operating systems. The format itself is built on a 256-color palette that corresponds to basic 8-bit color display systems widely used in desktop computers.

The image quality trade-off with the Graphic Interchange Format is that photographic images are reduced to 256 fixed colors. On the other end, there is no way to determine whether the color palette of the receiving computer matches the color palette of the originating system.

For simple graphics, the GIF color-map barrier is not a big deal. Icons and logos displayed on a computer screen aren't usually expected to match a custom color chip book, and the number of colors used is almost always less than 256.

Some newer browsers, including Netscape, are also capable of interpreting and displaying JPEG compressed graphic files as inline images. Other client applications probably will include this capability in future versions.

JPEG is the acronym for the Joint Photographic Experts Group and is also used to refer to graphic files that have been compressed according to the algorithms developed by the JPE Group.

Unlike GIF, the JPEG scheme is designed for compressing photographs and other images that contain 24-bit-per-pixel, or photographic-quality, color data. The JPEG scheme does not require mapping color data to a typical 256-color palette. All of the original image data is compressed.

As a comparison of how the two schemes compress images, a typical 80K RGB color photographic image compresses to 39K using GIF, and compresses to 32K using the highest image quality JPEG compression.

Computers that cannot display a 24-bit color image reduce the amount of image data displayed. The amount of color data contained in the compressed file, however, is greater than the amount of data contained in a GIF file.

A new GIF format is being developed to record 24-bit color images using a rewritten GIF-like compression scheme. If and when this format is finished, it would enable another method for compressing photo-realistic graphics, and perhaps using them as inline graphics on the Web.

For most Web document applications, it really doesn't make sense to use JPEG graphics as inline images. Logos and icons rarely use a color palette of 16 million values. And most of the (IBM-compatible) desktop computers in the world are probably only capable of displaying 8-bit color at best.

The place where it does make sense to use JPEG is for serving larger color graphics as separate files. A discussion of this follows.

A full comparative analysis of JPEG and GIF, or other image compression schemes, is well beyond the scope of this book, but you can find many sources of information about image compression and graphics transmission using your browser.

For a start, try some of these sites:

```
news:comp.graphics
```

```
news:alt.graphics.pixutils
```

```
news:comp.infosystems.www.providers
```

```
http://www.dh.umu.se/
```

```
http://www.wimsey.com/anima/ANIMAwelcome.html
```

```
http://corinthian.mac.cc.cmu.edu/
```

```
http://siva.cshl.org/gd/gd.html
```

```
http://www.ncsa.uiuc.edu/EVL/docs/html/EVL.LAB.html
```

Inline Image Sizes

Although there are no specific rules governing the size or use of inline graphics, a little common sense is appropriate when writing HTML documents.

First, consider that the graphic capability of your clients' browsers and system software is unknown to you. The client may or may not be a graphical browser. If it is not a graphical browser, downloading an inline image is not an option. For these clients, you should always include an **ALT=** statement describing the image.

Second, consider that the remote client system hardware is also unknown to you. For instance, you don't know whether the remote client is using a 9" monochrome monitor or a 21" color screen that displays 24-bit color.

Third, consider that the remote client network connection is unknown to you. The client could be a node on a super-fast Asynchronous Transfer Mode tele-communications network tied by fiber-optic cable directly into the NSF Net backbone; or the client could be using a (considerably slower) dial-up SLIP/PPP account through a 9600 bps modem connected with alligator clips to a phone jack dangling off the wall in a corner of the garage.

Inline images are "automatic" hyperlinks. As soon as the browser gets to the **<IMG>** element, it sends a request formed from the **SRC= URL**.

If the browser has image loading turned off, or if the browser is a text-only applications, the inline element is ignored. If you haven't included an **ALT=** statement, text-only browsers won't even know that the image exists, while most graphical browsers show little PICT icons where the inline graphics are supposed to be (see figure 5.16). The most recent versions of some graphical browsers now display ALT text along with these icons when automatic image loading is turned off.

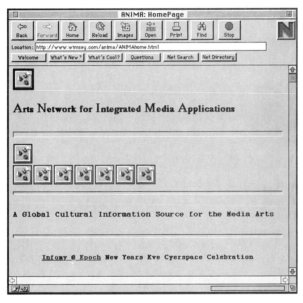

Figure 5.16 *Relying on too many inline images can result in a confusing document.*

If your image size is large, some of the graphic may not fit in the client window. If the file size is very big, transmission time is unreasonably long, and clients may prefer not to download the image at all.

Accordingly, in addition to including alternate text for an inline graphic that makes a note of the image size, it is also good form to try and keep inline graphic files smaller than about 35K. Also be sure not to produce 14" wide banners for a document, especially when a 6" wide graphic conveys essentially the same information.

Most importantly, don't get carried away with using inline images to navigate your server. When a document does not make any sense without the images, it is probably time to rethink the document.

Larger Images

Images that are not decorative or navigational icons (such as illustrations referred to in a document) can also be embedded in the document structure using **<IMG SRC=>**. It may be both convenient and necessary to include line illustrations, graphs, charts, or tables as inline graphics in a text document when you can store these graphics as small GIF files.

For example, simple black and white charts and tables captured as screen shots rarely exceed a few K in size and are much easier to format than **<PRE>** markup.

Images larger than 35K that are supplemental to the content of the document, or that are indexed by the document, should not be retrieved with **<IMG>** elements, but should instead be provided as separate files—just like any other document or file that is linked to your document.

Large graphic images retrieved through anchor statements do not need to be GIF format images. These files can be read by a separate image application acting as a "helper" to the browser. Image files served in this manner can then be stored as JPEG or other higher-resolution data files and referred to with a standard anchor hyperlink.

The practice of writing phrases like "click here" to act as hypertext links in a document is less than helpful. The hyperlinked phrase should state something informative about the target of the anchor, such as "satellite photograph of Grand Canyon, 156K," rather than something less descriptive, like "color picture of pretty rocks" (see figure 5.17).

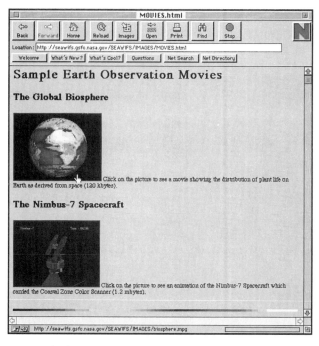

Figure 5.17   *Hyperlinks to graphics and multimedia files should indicate the size of the file so that remote clients understand what they're getting into.*

Audio and Video Files

Digital audio and video files are usually very large. At a sampling rate of 22 kHz (a typical Macintosh sound rate), an uncompressed 8-bit stereo sound file requires about 44K of disk space for every second of sound.

Obviously, musical recordings or other sophisticated sound samples are even larger. A ten-second sample recording of your favorite grunge band might create a 1 MB AIFF file.

Like graphic files, digital audio is stored in compressed form. But even with compression, a few seconds of sound can build a digital file of hundreds of kilobytes. Even if you're using MPEG compression to compact image data, 16-bit video consumes megabytes of disk space per second.

Because of the large file sizes required for digitized audio and video, these types of files are also not used as inline sources of information, but are referenced as hyperlinked files using an anchor element. You should include a note in the text of the hyperlink to indicate the size of the target file so that clients can judge whether to spend the download time.

The current state of multimedia transmission on the Web is that compressed files are downloaded in compressed form by the client application. After the download is completed, the browser automatically launches, or tries to launch, the appropriate external (helper) application to decompress and play the sound or animation file (see figure 5.18).

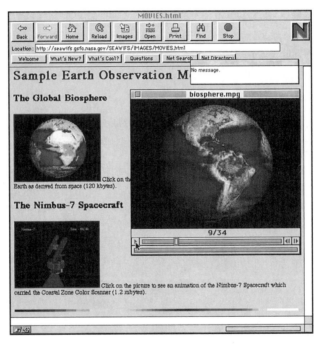

Figure 5.18 *Helper applications are automatically launched by the client application. The remote user controls whether to view the animation or play the sound.*

As a matter of compatibility with the several operating systems used by clients on the Web, the standard file format for audio data is AU mapped to the audio/basic MIME type. The standard file format for animation and video is MPEG mapped to the video/mpeg MIME type.

This does not mean that other file formats cannot be served by HTTP servers or retrieved by browsers. All browsers are capable of re-mapping system extension types; whether the client operating system can handle other types of file formats is another question. In any event, the capability of the remote computer to play downloaded audio or video files depends on the helper applications on that computer, not the browser.

Given the current state of connections to the Internet, real-time video transmission is a rare event. Transmitting real-time video through a dial-up modem connection is virtually impossible. The connection is way too slow. Transmitting even compressed video over anything less than a 1.5 Mbps T-1 connection is bound to result in choppy sound or pictures.

And, unlike television, signals on the Internet have to be addressed to specific computers. Under normal transmission circumstances, communication is point-to-point, involving one sender and one recipient. This impacts real time audio and video intended for any audience greater than one.

Currently, the Internet Engineering Task Force (the body that develops technical standards for the Internet) has set up an experimental audio/video multicasting scheme that can route video over the very-high-speed backbone sections of the Internet. This MBone scheme transmits video quickly enough so that it can be displayed as it is downloaded, as opposed to downloading it completely first and then playing the video file. The data can also be addressed to many recipients simultaneously.

The transmission rates required for multicasting according to this scheme are high—at least 500Kbps, but not beyond the bounds of current technology. Still, a T-1 connection is required, along with a workstation fast enough to process the data as it is received. Currently the software required for routing multicast data runs only on UNIX workstations.

In spite of current limitations, it may not be too long before hyperlinks in a Web document can display a video window transmitting something live and in full motion from the other side of the world.

HTML Editing Tools

The most direct method for writing HTML documents is by using a plain text editor, such as BBEdit Lite. Marking up text through your own keyboard entry can be fast, and it's a good way to familiarize yourself with the syntax of elements and attributes.

If your documents are small, using the keyboard entry method is probably faster than other methods, too.

If you're unsure about how to write specific markup elements, you can also take the easy route of copying the markup from someone else's document. Any document you display in your browser can be saved as HTML text by choosing "Source" from the View menu of MacWeb.

MacWeb, Netscape, and NCSA Mosaic all provide an option in the Save As dialog to save the document as "HTML" or "Source" (depending on the browser). You can open these saved HTML documents with BBEdit, or any other application that can open plain text documents.

Keyboard entry markup is not your only option, however, and there are certainly instances where more automated formatting methods can be faster and more efficient.

Repetitive markup jobs, like preparing existing text documents for publishing on the Web, are logical tasks for an editing tool designed to add basic document tags, headings, paragraph markers, and hyperlink anchors.

There are several specialized HTML editing and conversion programs that have been written for the Macintosh. One of the most popular authoring tools, though, and the one that Apple bundles with its own Web servers, are built on BBEdit and its freeware sibling, BBEdit Lite.

BBEdit Lite

BBEdit Lite is a versatile text editor for the Macintosh that is a scaled-down version of the program BBEdit, written by Bare Bones Software. BBEdit is aimed at programmers. The "Lite" version is distributed as freeware and shares some of the features of the full version.

Computer language is written with special characters and with strict orders of hierarchy and syntax. Coincidentally, HTML also uses special characters and adheres to a simple hierarchical structure. Consequently, the BBEdit Lite program lends itself well to writing hypertext markup.

Using BBEdit, you can search through a document for exact or approximate text matches, you can change text case with a single menu command, and you can use a menu command to select by line (as well as Select All).

BBEdit and BBEdit Lite also support adding functions to the program through the use of formatting extensions. These extensions are coded routines that automate formatting tasks and can be loading into the basic editor by copying them to the application folder.

Two sets of extensions have been written for formatting HTML: BBEdit HTML Extensions written by Carles Bellver and BBEdit HTML Tools written by Lindsay Davies; both are in the following discussions.

BBEdit HTML Extensions

BBEdit HTML Extensions are written by Carles Bellver <bellverc@si.uji.es> and provide automated formatting for hyperlink anchors, headings, forms, and images. The latest version is Release 8 and is included on the WWWSK disk. It is also available at:

```
http://www.uji.es/bbedit-html-extensic .html
```

Two very useful extensions in this set are Specials Translation and Template, because they take care of some the most tedious aspects of formatting an existing text document according to basic HTML markup.

The Release 8 version of HTML Extensions performs tasks that cannot be undone using the Edit menu. Each time you select one of these extensions, BBEdit asks you to confirm your selection. You can turn off these notifications by choosing "Editor" from the popup menu in the Preferences dialog box and selecting the No "Can't Undo" Alert checkbox. The Release 9 version of HTML Extensions are undo-able.

Here's what HTML Extensions do, and why they do it.

Figure 5.19   *The BBEdit Extensions menu, showing HTML Extensions written by Carles Bellver.*

The Anchor extension marks up a selected piece of text as a **NAME=** anchor. **NAME=** anchors are used as targets for hyperlink anchors within the same document, allowing readers to quickly jump to a reference point within the document.

The extension displays a dialog box asking for the **NAME=** value and then generates an element written like this:

```
<A NAME="donkey">donkey</A>
```

This NAME anchor would be referred to by a hyperlink elsewhere in the document that was written like this:

```
<A HREF="#donkey">another use of the word donkey</A>
```

The Comment extension is used to insert markup at the beginning and end of a line of text so that it is not be processed by a browser. This is known as "commenting out" the text.

The expression and function is borrowed from computer programming, where it is often applied to blocks of source code in a program.

In order to comment-out a line of text in an HTML document, you need to begin the line with the characters **<!--** and end the same line with the characters **-->**. The Comment extension applies this markup for you to selected text:

```
<!-- selected text -->
```

Forms are written using four complex elements, **<FORM>**, **<INPUT>**, **<SELECT>**, and **<TEXTAREA>**, as described earlier in this chapter. The Form extensions automate writing each of these elements and can help ensure that you get the syntax right.

Form provides a dialog box for entering the **ACTION=** and **METHOD=** to be used in the form. You type in the ACTION URL and select **GET** or **POST** with radio buttons. The extension writes the markup including a closing tag:

```
<FORM METHOD="POST" ACTION="http://exhibition.amnh.org">
</FORM>
```

Form Input provides a dialog box for entering the values for the **TYPE=**, **NAME=**, **SIZE=** and **MAXLENGTH=** attributes used in an input field.

```
<INPUT TYPE="text" NAME="address" SIZE="24" MAXLENGTH="48">
```

Form Select is supposed to insert markup for a multiple-choice pop-up menu, and it does indeed add markup to a selected list of text items. However, it always seems to run the last two items in a list on the same line (see grape and lemon in the example below), which is not what you normally want to have happen. You have to tweak your markup if you use this extension, but it may still be faster than doing it manually. A fix is planned for Release 9.

An example of the resulting markup is:

```
<SELECT NAME="Your favorite flavor" SIZE = "1">
<OPTION>vanilla
<OPTION>strawberry
<OPTION>chocolate
<OPTION>raspberry
<OPTION>grape
lemon</SELECT>
```

Form Text Area marks up a text area field for a form. A dialog box allows you to enter values for **NAME=**, **ROWS=**, and **COLS=**. If you have selected any text, this text is bracketed by the opening and closing tags appear within the text area entry field.

The extension generates markup like this:

```
<TEXTAREA NAME="flavor comment" ROWS=4 COLS=40>
Your favorite flavor </TEXTAREA>
```

Format is a versatile dialog box that lets you quickly format text as a series of list elements, as a blockquote, an address, or as pre-formatted text. Radio buttons allow you to choose the markup that is applied.

Format works, as advertised, for blocks of selected text that require only an opening and closing tag, like **<PRE></PRE>** or **<ADDRESS> </ADDRESS>**. It has a problem with lists, similar to the problem encountered with the Form Select extension, and runs the last two items together.

```
<OL>
<LI>vanilla
<LI>strawberry
<LI>chocolate
<LI>raspberry
grape</OL>
```

The Heading extension simply inserts an opening and closing tag around the selected text. You choose the level (1 through 6) in a dialog box.

```
<H2>Heading extension inserts heading tags!</H2>
```

Image quickly writes out markup for an inline image, including the URL for the picture, **ALT=** text description, an **ALIGN=** attribute if you want one, and also adds an **ISMAP** attribute for marking up graphics as image maps.

This is an example:

```
<IMG ALIGN=bottom SRC="/images/maggie.gif" ALT="photo of Margaret
Mead">
```

Link creates a hyperlink **<A>** anchor, not a **<LINK>** element, which is OK since you'll probably write zillions more hyperlink anchors than you'll ever write LINK elements.

This extension provides a dialog box to enter the URL for the hyperlink and inserts anchor tags around your selected text. It generates markup that looks like this:

```
<A HREF="/movies/mead1.mov">video of Margaret Mead</A>
```

Paragraph inserts a **<P>** tag at the beginning of the selected block of text. It considers blocks of text to be single paragraphs and does not mark up multiple paragraphs unless they are separated by a blank line.

As explained earlier in this chapter, HTML allows only the use of 127 alphabetic and numeric characters. Diacritical alphabetic characters and characters reserved for HTML markup must be encoded in order to be used in an HTML document.

The Specials Translation extension reads through selected text and perform encoding for you, automatically. This is a great help if you are converting text documents for the Web. Hunting through a long document to encode every "smart quote" mark as **"** is not recreational.

This extension sorts through selected text fairly quickly and converts unsafe characters into encoded markup. It also translates special characters used in some European alphabets, like ñ, ø, and ü.

The Template extension is used to apply a set of predetermined markup to a new or existing document.

The Template extension automatically writes a SGML prologue statement to the first line of the file. This prologue statement tells programs that understand Standard Generalized Markup Language that this document is written in HTML 2.0.

The prologue is followed by the basic document elements, **<HTML>**, **<HEAD>**, and **<BODY>**. Template provides a dialog box for writing **<BASE>** and **<TITLE>** elements into a document **<HEAD>**, and provides options for marking paragraphs and translating special characters in the **<BODY>** of the document. You also can specify text to be placed in a document as your address element.

BBEdit HTML Tools

BBEdit HTML Tools is written by Lindsay Davies at **<LD11@unix.york.ac.uk>**. You can find the latest version at:

```
http://www.york.ac.uk/~ld11/BBEditTools.html
```

BBEdit HTML Tools are more complex than HTML Extensions. For example, there are Preference settings for the Tools, and balloon help that can be activated from within any of the Tool dialog boxes. All of the Tool operations can be undone using the Edit menu.

Each extension can be selected using ⌘+Option+key shortcuts and many selections in the dialog boxes can also be selected using ⌘+key shortcuts. The dialog box shortcuts are shown by pressing the ⌘key while the dialog box is open.

Several settings for HTML Tools are recorded using the Utilities Tool and stored as preferences by BBEdit. A button in the lower left corner of the Utilities dialog box takes you to dialogs for defining your Web server's URL, your browser, and your Hotlist file.

Recording your server URL speeds up writing hyperlinks with the Anchor Tool and defining your browser allows you to preview your HTML documents quickly using the Preview Tool.

Anchor allows you to mark up any type of anchor element, using either full or partial URLs. The dialog provides popup menus for URL schemes (**http://**, **gopher://**, etc.), and a list of the last ten URLs that you have written using the tool.

You can use the extension to scan the current document for existing URLs or anchor **NAME=** values and insert one of these in the current markup. A File button in the dialog box also enables you locate a file on your drive and create a URL pointing to that file.

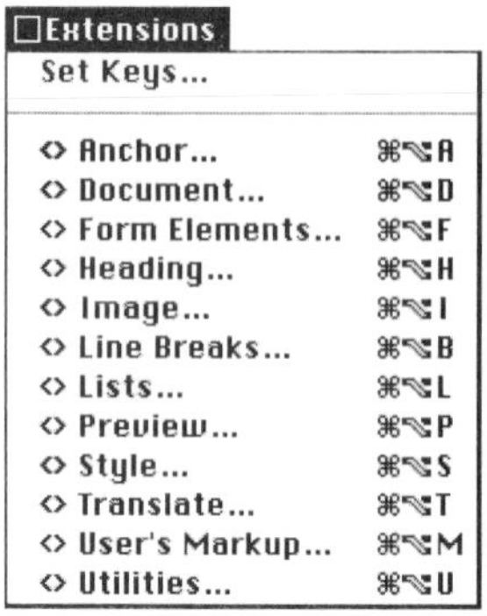

```
☐Extensions
  Set Keys...

  ◇ Anchor...          ⌘⌥A
  ◇ Document...        ⌘⌥D
  ◇ Form Elements...   ⌘⌥F
  ◇ Heading...         ⌘⌥H
  ◇ Image...           ⌘⌥I
  ◇ Line Breaks...     ⌘⌥B
  ◇ Lists...           ⌘⌥L
  ◇ Preview...         ⌘⌥P
  ◇ Style...           ⌘⌥S
  ◇ Translate...       ⌘⌥T
  ◇ User's Markup...   ⌘⌥M
  ◇ Utilities...       ⌘⌥U
```

Figure 5.20   *The BBEdit Extensions menu showing HTML Tools extensions.*

Anchor generates the following markup:

```
<A HREF="http://foo.bah.org/directory/file.html"></A>
<A NAME="example"></A>
<A HREF="#example"></A>
```

The Document extension creates new HTML documents or can be used to add markup to an existing document.

Fields in the dialog box allow you to enter standard **<HTML>, <HEAD>, <TITLE>, <BASE>, <LINK>, <ISINDEX>**, and **<BODY>** markup. The extension can also create an SGML prologue statement.

The Insert Template button allows you import the contents of other text or HTML documents. This is a very useful feature if you write complex **<FORMS>** or other elements as standard document markup and store examples of these for use as templates. You can use the command to import these templates directly into your current document.

The Form Elements tool provides dialog boxes for marking up all of the elements used with a **<FORM>**. If a form element has not already been written, a opening dialog box asks for the **ACTION=** and **METHOD=** for the form.

A second dialog is used to create the markup for **<INPUT>, <SELECT>**, and **<TEXTAREA>** elements in the form. These are created one at a time, using entry fields, checkboxes, and radio buttons in the dialog box. You need to reselect the extension for each element you mark up.

Form Elements automatically add **<HR>** horizontal rule tags above and below the form markup. In earlier versions, this feature was selected in the dialog box. You can't turn it off in version 1.3.

Because **<FORM>** is the most complex bit of HTML 2.0 markup, this tool may help you avoid making syntax mistakes, especially with the attributes used with **<INPUT>** and **<SELECT>**.

Heading quickly marks up selected text with heading tags according to the level number you enter in the dialog box.

Image marks up inline image links using either a URL that you enter or one of the 10 most recently created image URLs that you wrote using this tool. Image provides an entry for **ALT=** text and for marking an image as a **ISMAP** coordinate map.

You can also use Image to write an anchor hyperlink for a regular graphic file.

The dialog box includes a checkbox for automatically adding paragraph **<P>** tags above and below the image markup, like this:

```
<P>
<IMG SRC="sample/image.gif" ALT="Alternate Text">
<P>
```

Line Breaks is used to insert the elements for paragraphs, line breaks, and horizontal rules. This extension makes sense only if you can type ⌘+Option+B *plus* ⌘+P (or R or B) faster than you can type **<P>** or **
** or **<HR>**.

Lists mark up ordered **<OL>**, unordered **<UL>**, directory **<DIR>**, menu **<MENU>**, and definition list **<DL>** elements. It also marks up items simply as list items **<LI>** omitting any major list tags.

Best of all, the List tool works perfectly, and it makes sense because you *can* type ⌘+Option+L followed by ⌘+O faster than you can manually mark up an ordered list.

The Preview tool enables you to open the document you're editing with your Web browser. You select your browser initially through the Tools preferences setting. After that, it's a lot faster to use Preview than it is to switch applications and use the Open command in the File menu in MacWeb, Mosaic, or Netscape.

Style marks up selected text according to any of the logical or physical styles currently supported in HTML.

Interestingly, you can also mark up text for the styles subscript, superscript, and strike-through, which are not part of HTML 2.0, and are supported only by the latest version of NCSA Mosaic. These styles may be included in HTML 3.0.

Translate is used to translate "unsafe" characters such as < > & " in an existing text file into code suitable for an HTML formatted document. The Translate extension can also be used to convert an HTML document into a text-only document, stripping out the HTML markup.

The first sentence of the preceding paragraph translates into ISO Latin 1, used by HTML, like this:

```
Translate is used to translate &quot;unsafe&quot; characters such
as &lt; &gt; &amp; &quot; in an existing text file into code
suitable for an HTML formatted document.
```

Users Markup can be used to record and apply custom markup, and to automate various steps taken in writing HTML documents.

For example, let's say you regularly mark up documents with a list element. You could enter the markup for this list in the entry field in the User Markup dialog box and assign it to one of the ten radio buttons shown (see figure 5.21). To apply this list to documents, you use the keyboard combination for that radio button or open the dialog and click the radio button. The list contents and markup is automatically entered in whatever document you are editing (see figure 5.22).

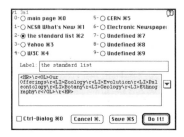

Figure 5.21   *The Users Markup tool allows you to store frequently used markup and paste it into documents.*

Figure 5.22   *The stored markup in figure 5.21 is automatically entered into a document like this.*

You could create entries that format a regularly used set of list markup, or style markup, or a combination of markup elements, according to a set of scripting characters explained in the Tools documentation. This Tool can also be set to automatically apply a selection through a keyboard command, without opening the dialog window.

Lindsay Davies has continued to add features to this Tool so that it now includes a macro editor. The instructions for how to write macros with Users Markup are included in the Documentation for HTML Tools.

The best utility in this extension is Check Markup. This operation checks your document against the Document Type Definition (DTD) for HTML 2.0. The DTD is the "official" description of the elements, attributes, and syntax used for HTML. If Check Markup finds any errors, it opens a new document and show a report of the errors it found with advice on how to correct them. If your markup is OK, it reports that, too.

The Insert Hotlist utility writes the currently selected Hotlist into a document as a list of Anchor elements. Link Summary writes a list of all the anchor URLs in a document as a list at the end of the document.

Open URL attempts to connect to the URL currently selected in the document you are editing using the browser you have identified in the preferences setting for HTML Tools.

Remove Tags removes HTML markup from a selection, or from the entire document if no text is specifically selected. Comment marks up the selected text as commented-out text.

BBEdit HTML Tools also provides for building custom HTML document Templates. Instructions for creating templates and for using the Extensions is included with HTML Tools as a set of HTML files.

In addition to writing your HTML documents with BBEdit, you may want to experiment with one of the customized editing programs written for use on the Macintosh.

Other HTML Editing Tools

Besides writing your HTML documents "from scratch" using a text editor like BBEdit, you may want to experiment with one of the editing programs listed in the following discussion.

A long list of programs that convert text into HTML is available on the World Wide Web Consortium server at:

```
http://www.w3.org/hypertext/WWW/Tools/Overview.html
```

Because word processors add their own formatting instructions, documents created using a word processor need to be converted to plain text in order to be served as HTML/text documents.

Independent software developers, as well as some of the major word processing and desktop publishing program vendors, have released or are readying HTML conversion tools for the latest versions of popular programs. Documents created with WordPerfect 3.5, FrameMaker 5.0, ClarisWorks 4.0, and PageMaker 6.0 can be translated into HTML. Microsoft is allegedly working on a Mac version of Internet Assistant for Microsoft Word 6.0, which turns Word into both an HTML editing tool and a browser.

Astrobyte has created a commercial product called BeyondPress that presents many options for converting QuarkXPress files into HTML. Unlike some of the other products, it also automatically converts graphics in the XPress file to GIF files. Unfortunately, though, it costs nearly as much as QuarkXPress itself. DataViz, the veteran Mac translation vendor, also has updated its MacLinkPlus package to translate HTML bidirectionally.

Information about other conversion tools is also available through the World Wide Web Consortium server.

RTFtoHTML

RTFtoHTML 2.7.5 is a program for converting Rich Text Format (RTF) documents into text/HTML. Any document created by most word processors can be saved as RTF and then processed by this application.

The program does a good job of formatting paragraphs, lists, "unsafe" characters, and other text markup. It works quickly, and can create a separate error.html document to indicate Rich Text formats that were not translated.

The RTFtoHTML package includes style sheets that contain the configuration code used by the program to create HTML markup according to the standard specifications for HTML. These style sheets can be updated or replaced as the specification is changed. Complete documentation is included with the program.

RTFtoHTML is written by Chris Hector. Information about the Macintosh version, and a link to download it, is available at:

```
ftp://ftp.cray.com/src/WWWstuff/RTF/rtftohtml_overview.html
```

HTML Web Weaver

A text editor at its core, HTML Web Weaver uses floating palettes, along with standard menu selections, to apply markup to text that you write in Web Weaver document windows. Dialog boxes help create items like forms and lists. Web Weaver also opens and edits documents created by plain text editors.

A menu bar can also be also used for selecting some of the most frequently applied markup tags. The interface, especially the floating palettes, is easy to understand and includes support for balloon help.

The program can be linked to a web browser on your computer for previewing your documents.

Web Weaver is written by Robert Best as shareware ($25). Information about the program and a link to download it via FTP is available at:

```
http://www.potsdam.edu/Web.Weaver/About.html
```

Arachnid

Arachnid is a freeware HTML editor based on HyperCard. Arachnid uses a floating palette for applying anchor and form markup to text selected in the Arachnid document window. Standard menu commands are used for applying headings and styles.

Working documents resemble HyperCard "stacks" and are created as self-contained files called Projects. Arachnid does not require the HyperCard application. Projects are readable only by Arachnid. Markup must be exported as a plain text/HTML document for use on the Web.

Frequently used URLs (for formatting anchors or other markup that refers to a URL) and document templates can be stored as menu-accessible items. The program is published by the University of Iowa.

Information about the program and a link to download it is is at:

```
http://sec-look.uiowa.edu/
```

HTML Editor for Macintosh

HTML Editor is a "semi-WYSIWYG" (what-you-see-is-what-you-get) text editor that provides a toolbar and popup menus for adding HTML markup to selected text.

Documents created in HTML Editor are text/HTML and can be served "as is," without further conversion.

Among the buttons for anchors, text styles, inline images, and lists, is a button that can be set to launch your browser to preview documents.

Special features in a directory for storing frequently used URLs, and the ability to create and store custom markup. The program requires System 7.

HTML Editor is written by Rick Giles as shareware ($25). Information about the program, with a link to download it, is available at:

```
http://dragon.acadiau.ca:1667/~giles/HTML_Editor/Documentation.html
```

HTML.edit

HTML.edit v1.1.2 is another editor created on HyperCard, but it does not require HyperCard to run. Documents are created in HTML.edit and then saved as plain text/HTML files.

HTML.edit includes a B&W/color palette, and handles multiple documents, master headers, and footers.

HTML.edit is also capable of drag-and-drop editing (with HTML.edit already open), uses hypertext-style help, presents a resizeable editor window, uses command-key equivalents for commonly-used codes, and maintains an HTML code index.

An index within HTML.edit displays all instances of the selected HTML code within your document. It follows the HTML specification for naming conventions and also implements most HTML elements, including lists, images, anchors, and text formats.

HTMLedit is written by Murray M. Altheim as freeware. Information about the program, with a link to download it, is at:

```
http://nctn.oact.hq.nasa.gov/tools/HTMLedit/HTMLedit.html
```

HTML Writer

HTMLWriter 0.9d4 is a specialized text editor written in SuperCard. Documents are written in an editing window. Menu commands are used to mark up selected text in the document window.

The program includes a preview function that displays formatted text, but styles are not displayed. The programs includes online help to explain interface functions.

HTML Writer is written by Jon Wiederspan as freeware. Information about the program, with a link to download it, is at:

```
http://www.uwtc.washington.edu/JonWiederspan/HTMLEditor.html
```

HTML Pro

This custom text/HTML editor displays two windows simultaneously.

One window is used for writing and editing text as HTML. Elements are applied to selected text through menu commands. Many of the most frequently used tags can be applied through keyboard shortcuts. Customized or frequently used formatting can be written to a small macro editor, and saved as a menu command in the Macro menu.

The second window displays the formatted text as it might appear in a browser window. Graphics are displayed as a notation [IMAGE]. Anchors appear as highlighted text. One slight quirk is that the review window does not always ignore irrelevant "white" spaces.

According to the author, HTML Pro works best with System 7.

HTML Pro is written by Niklas Frykholm as shareware ($5). Information about the program, and a link to download it, is at:

```
http://www.ts.umu.se/~r2d2
```

Commercial HTML Tools

As the Web becomes more of a profitable enterprise, third-party vendors are starting to ship commercial authoring tools.

HTML Pro

NaviPress from America Online's Internet Services Division is an HTML authoring program that integrates with the company's NaviServer Web server. The pages it generates, though, can be used with any Web server. NaviPress is also a browser, allowing you to easily incorporate HTML code from other Web sites into your own sites. One nice feature of the product is "mini-Webs" which allow you to plan the links among your HTML pages.

NaviPress can be downloaded by America Online members by using the keyword "navipress" (no quotes). The online service provider is distributing the program freely as it offers users the chance to host their Web pages on the service.

FrontPage

FrontPage from Vermeer Technologies is scheduled to be released for the Mac later in 1995. It has the potential to greatly ease HTML authoring, especially some of the trickier parts of creating engaging Web pages, such as forms and image maps. Like NaviPress, FrontPage works well with Vermeer's Web server, but also generates pages that work with other popular Web servers.

FrontPage uses a number of WebBots and WebWizards to automate and guide users through creating Web pages without programming, according to the company. If it lives up to the hype, it could extend Web publishing to a far greater number of nontechnical content providers.

So now that you can create your own Web page, it's time to learn how to put it on the Internet. In the next chapter, you'll learn how to turn your Mac into a Web server.

Chapter

6

Web Publishing

A Web browser helps you find and download an amazing amount of information from the Internet. You can explore the far reaches of NASA's online photo collections, take a world tour of Web servers through the Virtual Tourist at the University of Buffalo, or listen to clips of baroque chamber music from a Web server in Tokyo.

As wonderful as your browser is, there's at least one thing it can't help you to do on the Internet, and that's serve up your own documents, graphics, QuickTime movies, and sound files.

In order to do that, you need to become an information provider on the Web. One way to do this is to set up your own Web server (see figure 6.1).

Servers are applications that provide data or process information for other computers over a network. If your Macintosh is running System 7, you may already be familiar with built-in File Sharing that allows other users on the same AppleTalk network to connect to your computer and read or copy files from your computer onto their own. In effect, your Mac becomes a file server to the other computers on your local network, and the other Macs on your local network become clients of your server.

There are many types of servers on the Internet, each one is designed to store, locate, and transfer a specific type of data to at least some of the approximately 20 million clients.

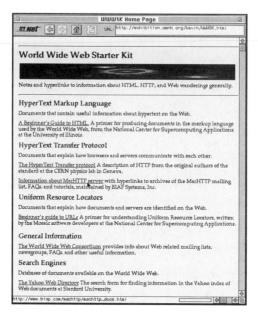

Figure 6.1   *You can set up your own Web server while reading this chapter.*

How the Web Communicates

What sets a Web server apart from all of the other servers on the Internet is the way that it communicates with Web clients using the HyperText Transfer Protocol, or HTTP.

Web servers listen for requests sent to them by client applications (your browser). These requests are structured around Uniform Resource Locators that identify the text, graphic, sound, or other file being requested. Web browsers can also request information that must be generated by a program separate from the Web server. We'll discuss these external programs later.

The Web server responds to this request by sending the item identified by the URL.

Occasionally, the server sends a message telling you that it cannot process your request because the file you asked for doesn't exist at that location, or because one of a few other errors occurred.

Because browser/server communication is kept short and sweet, the HTTP method allows many browsers to talk to the same server almost simultaneously.

HTTP communications involve four steps. The first two are initiated by the browser. The second two are initiated by the server. Let's examine the steps involved in retrieving the document at:

```
http://www.panix.com/~kcoffee/index.html
```

Step 1: Connection

The first step is the Connection initiated by the browser by sending a URL. The goal of the connection is to locate a Web server and open a channel to it through the Internet.

URLs always begin with an identifying communications scheme that indicates the type of service being requested. URLs addressed to Web servers always begin with the identifier **http://** followed by the network address of the computer, either expressed as a name or a number, for example: **http://www.panix.com.**

Because computers on the Internet run more than one server application at the same time, each of these processes requires its own "channel" for communicating over the network. These channels are called ports.

According to the Transmission Control Protocol (TCP) standard used by the Internet, port 80 is reserved for HTTP. This port number is automatically assumed (by your browser) to be the communication port for **http://** URLs.

A Web server can listen for connections coming through on other ports (other than 80), but in that case, the port number must be used as part of the address for that server and included in the URL, as in **http://www.panix.com:1080**.

Note

If a Web server is using a port number other than 80, it must use a port number that is greater than 1024, because every port below that number is already reserved for other uses on the Internet.

If you want to run two Web servers using the same computer, you must assign each to a different port and use these separate numbers in the URLs for those servers.

Step 2: Request

The second step is called the **Request**. This request appears as information that appears in the beginning of a message (the "header") that identifies the browser to the server and contains a partial URL, such as **/~kcoffee/index.html**.

Usually, browsers request files stored at the server. The method used in this kind of request is called the **GET** method. Web browsers automatically add this information to file URLs (see figure 6.2).

Headers sent by the browser include information about the HTTP version used by the browser. This version information may be used by the server to determine how to reply to the request, and whether to expect even more header information from the browser.

The request header gives the server other information about the request, including an acceptable modification date for the file being requested; the type of an authorization or encoding schemes to be used in the response; the types of data that the browser is programmed to process; and the human language of the documents that the browser is requesting.

HTTP headers enable information to get from point A to point B through the Web.

Figure 6.2   *Browsers and servers exchange header information during an exchange as shown in this MacHTTP log file.*

Step 3: Response

The third step is the **Response** that the server sends back to the browser in answer to the request.

The server sends out Response Headers that tell the browser about the server, including the HTTP protocol version it uses, the kind of server it is, and other information about the object it is about to send.

This header information might prompt the browser to perform some additional functions, like display a window in which you must enter a password, or a message that tells you why your request was not processed.

The response header also contains information about the object that you requested, including how big it is, what language it is written in, whether it is encoded or not, and when it was last modified. If your browser caches documents, this "last-modified" information might be used to determine whether the document should be downloaded.

Step 4: Close

The last step occurs at the end of the file transmission. When the file has been transferred, the Web server **Closes** its connection to the browser and goes back to its previous state of listening for requests.

There are two important points to remember from this description:

First, almost all communication between browser and server consists of these four steps, although there are new techniques being developed for keeping a connection open between clients and servers. Clicking on any of the hyperlinks in **http://www.panix.com/~kcoffee/index.html** constitutes a new request from the browser, even if it's to the same server.

Second, even though most of the header information involved in Web transactions is hidden from the user, these instructions are essential to how HTTP applications talk to each other. These various headers can be used by server interface programs that you might write to process fill-out forms, link requests to documents on other servers, conduct secure communication, or communicate with other programs on your server.

With this outline in mind, let's set up your Macintosh to be a Web server.

Server Logistics

As of this writing, the most prominent Web server application that runs on a Macintosh computer is MacHTTP and its commercial cousin WebSTAR, written by Chuck Shotton and BIAP Systems, Inc. In May 1995, StarNine Systems acquired the MacHTTP server and released an enhanced version of MacHTTP called WebSTAR. Both servers are discussed here, but the focus of this chapter is the MacHTTP 2.2 application, which is available as "shareware" and can be downloaded from the Internet (check an Info-Mac site in the directory **_Communication/tcp/mac-http-22.hqx**.

As you might expect from a Mac program, preparing a MacHTTP server requires a small time investment. Nevertheless, most Web servers aren't Mac servers. While Macs make excellent, inexpensive servers for small to medium sites, there is a limit to the number of connections they can accommodate as well as a practical limit to the number of transactions they can perform at one time. For these reasons, many sites have stuck with the pricey UNIX servers on which the Web has been primarily built, much to the delight of workstation vendors Sun Microsystems and Silicon Graphics.

MacHTTP, though, can do almost everything its UNIX-based ancestors are capable of, and having a commercial company behind WebSTAR should allow it to keep pace with its rivals.

Setting up MacHTTP is described in the next section of this chapter, but before you jump ahead, you need to learn some of the more mundane logistics of running a Web server on your Mac.

TCP/IP

Unlike a Web browser, the MacHTTP server application won't run without an open TCP/IP connection. This means your computer has to have the MacTCP control panel installed and communicating through a network driver.

Note

It is possible to use MacTCP to open a connection and run MacHTTP over a LocalTalk network. Each LocalTalk node requires the MacTCP control panel and an IP address. If the LocalTalk network is not connected to the Internet, the machines using MacTCP can be assigned bogus numbered addresses that mimic real IP addresses.

If your computer is not hooked into a network of any kind, but you have a copy of MacTCP installed, you can still test drive MacHTTP.

Files and Directories

Web servers locate files according to a directory tree that begins at the server's directory, this directory is known as the root. Uniform Resource Locators mark this hierarchy by placing a single slash mark between each directory level and between a directory name and the file name, like:

`/~kcoffee/index.html`

The Macintosh Finder displays directories as folder icons. Subdirectories are shown as folders nested inside other folders. On a Macintosh computer, the folder that contains the MacHTTP server application is considered the root level directory for that server.

Any file that you intend to serve must be in MacHTTP's folder or in a folder it contains. (MacHTTP can also work through an alias of a file if the alias is placed within the server's directory hierarchy.)

There is no hard rule about the number of folders that you can nest inside other folders, but you're sure to make a URL hard to remember (and type) if it leads through a half-dozen folders.

A typical MacHTTP server root directory is illustrated in figure 6.3.

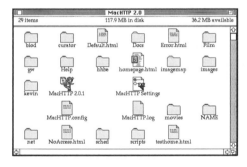

Figure 6.3   *A typical Web server hierarchy.*

This root directory contains several subdirectories, titled **images**, **Help**, **Film**, **hhbe**, and other equally descriptive names. It doesn't matter if no one but you understands the structure of your directories. If more than one person maintains the server, though, establishing some kind of organizing principle is advisable.

In the example shown in figure 6.3, directories are organized according to the content of documents. All of the files being served as part of an online exhibit about human biology and evolution are stored in the folder **hhbe**. All of the files that describe film and video exhibits are stored in the folder **Film**. This structure makes it easier to maintain the information on this server.

The directory names shown in this example are short. While you can use up to 31 characters for a Mac folder or file name, long names only make it difficult for users to remember and enter correctly in a URL.

You should also avoid putting "unsafe" characters, like ampersands or slash marks, in your file names. While the Macintosh file system can deal with any character in a file name except a colon, other systems are not so forgiving.

Macintosh browsers will try to encode any characters that are not safe for use on the Web. But using "unsafe" characters in file or directory names will present problems to users with other operating systems, especially if they try to enter one of your URLs manually in their own browser.

A good rule of thumb is that if the character cannot be used as normal text in an HTML document, you should avoid using it in a filename.

Hardware Requirements

Almost any model of Macintosh computer can be used to run MacHTTP. Not surprisingly, Macs with faster processors will operate more quickly than Macs with slower ones.

MacHTTP will run on either a 680x0 processor, found in Macintosh Quadras and earlier machines, or on a PowerPC processor used in the new Power Macs.

Brad Schrick has compiled a directory of links to Macs running MacHTTP and has catalogued these according to model type. His list ranges from Macintosh SEs all the way through Power Mac 8100s. If you're interested in sampling the results, you can find this listing at:

```
http://www.ape.com/machttp_talk/machttpservers.by.mac.html
```

In addition to faster central processors, newer Macs also use faster input and output circuits for accessing disk drives, which can reduce the response time for finding and reading file requests.

The MacHTTP server does not require a very large amount of RAM in order to run efficiently. The standard RAM partition setting (shown in the Get Info box) is 1150K. This will enable MacHTTP to handle 10 simultaneous connections efficiently.

MacHTTP can handle up to 48 simultaneous connections (the limit is set by MacTCP), but you should increase this RAM partition by 100K for each additional connection (above the initial 10). A busy server might use 20 simultaneous connections and about 2200K of RAM.

Add to this the amount of RAM required by any external server programs used to process forms or image maps. All told, your Macintosh Web server will use about 4 MB of RAM (in addition to the operating system and any other applications you intend to run).

By comparison, Netscape recommends allocating 5 to 8 MB of RAM for running its browser.

Network Connections

The unfair aspect in the otherwise egalitarian world of the Web is the cost of getting connected to the Internet. Most popular sites have direct, high-speed links to the Net that can cost thousands per month to maintain, far beyond the means of most individuals. A low-budget alternative to setting up your own server and Internet connection is to lease space on someone else's Web server.

Many local Internet Service Providers that offer dial-up modem and PPP/SLIP accounts for individuals and businesses are now offering space on central Web servers, too. You upload your Web documents to the central server and clients access your pages through URLs that point to that server.

While you don't get to control the Web server, this is usually the least expensive way to get your content on the Internet if you don't have access to a network that is already connected. Even if your network is already so connected, security precautions such as a firewall (an electronic gate intended to keep intruders out) can keep you "locked in." The downside to this plan is that most Internet Service Providers use UNIX-based computers and either the NCSA or CERN HTTPd server. If you go this route, be prepared to learn some basics about UNIX and its command-line interface.

A typical rate structure for this type of plan includes the monthly service fee for a dial-up or PPP/SLIP connection plus a storage charge (based on how many megabytes of disk space your Web documents need), plus a charge for the amount of data that your clients download. Depending upon the provider and their rate structure, this kind of Web publishing starts around $15/month. Some providers charge considerably more if you're doing overt advertising on the Web.

For example, Panix in New York City offers noncommercial subscribers space on their Web server for the cost of a basic account ($19/month). This includes 5 MB of disk storage and 62.5 MB of transfers to browsers outside the `panix.com` domain.

Information about this kind of service is available from the local provider. You can start by looking through the listing compiled by the NSF, mentioned previously.

If you can get your Mac onto the Internet, or if you wish to set up a Web site for internal use, though, the remainder of this chapter discusses MacHTTP, the most popular Macintosh Web server.

Connecting Your Mac Server

The most basic type of server connection is through a data modem and telephone line. Existing 14.4 and 28.8 Kbps modems are fast enough to serve text and GIF files, though users will notice that delivery time lags behind servers with faster connections to the Internet.

For practical purposes, though, Web servers that make their content available to the Internet must have a constant, or dedicated, connection to the Internet. Leased line connections are usually 56 kilobits per second, or twice as fast as 28 Kbps high-speed modems. Digital telephone connections using ISDN switched digital service can be used to achieve 128 Kbps, but usually carry a higher price tag and require a special (and not inexpensive) ISDN interface for your computer, usually in the form of an external box connected to the serial port or internal card for a desktop Mac.

Further up the ladder are services called T-1 and T-3, but these require even more specialized and expensive hardware (you can't jack in from the serial port on the back of your Classic or through an interface card in your 8100) and cost thousands of dollars a month to use. If your Mac is already part of an Ethernet with an Internet connection, though, you may already have this kind of high-speed access.

If you want to explore the possibilities for getting a dedicated (and faster) connection to the Internet, there are two main routes to take.

You can inquire with your local telephone company about leased line and ISDN rates and equipment. If it's an option, you should speak with more than one telephone company, you may be surprised to find differences in rate structures.

You also can contact one of the growing number of Internet Service Providers; businesses that specialize in setting up and maintaining Internet access for businesses and individuals.

You can download a listing of national, regional, and local Internet Service Providers, compiled by the National Science Foundation, at:

```
gopher://ds.internic.net/1/nsf
```

This NSF directory is also accessible through the AT&T InterNIC Directory and Database Service at:

```
http://ds.internic.net/ds/dspg01.html
```

Installing MacHTTP

MacHTTP 2.2 is available as shareware and can be downloaded from the BIAP Systems web server at **http://www.biap.com** or at an Info-Mac archive.

Information about WebSTAR and a limited demo version can be found at **http://www.starnine.com**.

MacHTTP is not free software. The educational license is $65, a noneducational license is $95 per installation. Complete licensing and technical information is available from the StarNine Web server.

Both MacHTTP 2.2 and WebSTAR support Apple Events, including a set of custom Web-specific events, that allow them to communicate with other Apple Event-aware applications (all System 7 "savvy" programs can understand the basic Apple Events).

MacHTTP and WebSTAR are also fully scriptable using AppleScript, and this scripting language also can be used to write small programs that work with MacHTTP to process input from fill-out forms, image map interfaces, or other custom routines.

The use and configuration of these applications are explained later in this chapter.

MacHTTP 2.2 is distributed as a compressed "fat" binary archive for use on either Macintosh II/LC/Quadra computers or Power Macs, and includes AppleScript system extension software and a folder of Scripting Additions that enable you to use AppleScript scripts and applications to extend the functionality of the basic server. The license for MacHTTP includes a license to use these AppleScript extensions.

If you are using System 7.1 or 7.5 on your Mac, you probably already have the AppleScript system software installed. You can determine this by looking for the AppleScript extension and the Scripting Additions folder inside the Extensions folder in your System Folder.

MacHTTP is published by StarNine Technologies, Inc., 2550 Ninth Street, Suite 112, Berkeley, CA 94710.

StarNine also publishes WebSTAR, an enhanced Macintosh Web server that is capable of multi-threading, linking processes to server actions, remote administration, and several other advanced capabilities.

You can download MacHTTP 2.2 from **http://www.biap.com** using your Web browser. The downloaded archive, **machttp.sit.hqx**, is a binary-encoded file that must be decoded using StuffIt Expander or a similar program. Once decoded, you will have a second archive titled **machttp.sit**. This is a normal StuffIt file that can be decompressed to produce a single folder titled **MacHTTP 2.2**. (Netscape and other browsers should handle all of this for you if you have StuffIt Expander listed as one of your helper applications.)

Installing the Software

The following steps assume that you have a copy of MacHTTP 2.2. The previous section describes how to obtain a copy of this program.

Once you have a copy of MacHTTP, the installation procedure is fairly simple and you should be up and running in no time.

1. Open the MacHTTP 2.2 folder. Inside the main MacHTTP 2.2 folder are two other folders, MacHTTP Software & Docs and Apple's Scripting System.

   MacHTTP Software & Docs contains the server application and will be the root level directory for your server.

2. If you don't already have AppleScript installed on your computer, open the folder titled Apple's Scripting System. Inside this folder are two more folders, For all Extensions folder and For Power Mac Extensions folder.

3. From the For all Extensions folder, copy the AppleScript extension, the Frontmost Extension, and the folder titled Scripting Additions into your Macintosh's Extensions Folder inside your System Folder.

4. If you are using a Power Mac, open the For Power Mac Extensions folder and copy AppleScriptLib and ObjectSupportLib to the Extensions folder inside your System Folder.

5. To complete your installation of the AppleScript system software you must restart your computer.

The MacHTTP Software & Docs folder contains the MacHTTP application, five plain text documents, the MacHTTP Settings file, and three folders containing Documentation, Tutorials, and Images (see figure 6.4).

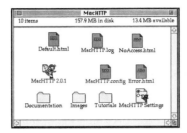

Figure 6.4   *The MacHTTP Software & Docs folder is the root-level directory for your Web server.*

Following is a breakdown of the items you will find in the MacHTTP Software and Docs folder:

- **MacHTTP 2.2** is the server application.

- **MacHTTP Settings** is a file used to record server preferences, including how the server status window is displayed, and any password accounts that you establish for your clients.

- **MacHTTP.config** is a text file that contains the configuration instructions for the server. It is read by the server every time it is launched.

- **MacHTTP.log** is a text file that records requests made to the server.

- **Default.html** is a default Index document. If used, browsers retrieve this document by sending a request to the root directory of the server.

- **Error.html** is the document that is returned to browsers as a result of a File Not Found error.

- **NoAccess.html** is the document that is returned to the browser if the URL requested is not permitted by the server.

- **Documentation** contains information on how to set up and operate the MacHTTP server. The documents are in HTML format and can be read locally by any browser, including MacWeb.

- **Tutorials** contains tutorials for learning how to use MacHTTP, setting up a secure server, and using and writing AppleScripts as Common Gateway Interface programs.

- **Images** contains a MacHTTP icon GIF that is displayed in some of the enclosed HTML files.

MacHTTP Software & Docs can be used as your root-level directory, and it is already set up for that purpose.

Files that you intend to serve with MacHTTP must be located within your root-level folder or a folder inside that root folder. MacHTTP does not look for files stored outside this folder hierarchy.

MacHTTP will recognize a file alias that points to a file outside the root hierarchy and will serve that file. However, the URL used in the request must be written for the alias, not for the original file. MacHTTP can only resolve an alias that points to a file, it cannot resolve an alias that points to a folder or volume.

Configuring MacHTTP

Before you begin using MacHTTP, you should make sure that the **MacHTTP.config** file contains the correct information for your server. Use BBEdit Lite to open the **MacHTTP.config** file (see figure 6.5).

The configuration file is a set of instructions read by MacHTTP every time it is launched. Each instruction line begins with a keyword. The text following the keyword acts as a configuration instruction.

Keywords that are not meant to be read as instructions can be "commented out" by typing a hash mark # at the beginning of the line. Lines that don't begin with keywords are ignored. Instructions are not case-sensitive.

Figure 6.5 *The* **MacHTTP.config** *file is a text document that provides operating instructions to the MacHTTP server application.*

You can create new or alternate **MacHTTP.config** files by using any plain text editor, as long as you write complete configuration instructions.

Most of the default settings written into the configuration file can be used "as is," but a few require some tweaking by you. If you need to change any settings, you should do so *before* you launch MacHTTP, because it reads these instructions when it starts up.

We've divided the explanation of configuration settings into three parts. If you want to get started quickly, the next section of this chapter will take you through the essential settings that you need to configure to get started.

Settings You Need to Get Started

VERSION 2.2 The version number shown on this line must match the version number of the application you are using with this file (most likely MacHTTP 2.2). The version number of the application can be found in the application's Get Info window (click once on the application and choose "Get Info" from the File menu; there is a line in this dialog box that will tell you about the application's version number). Using an older VERSION instruction with a newer version of the server application will result in erratic behavior. If you are using version 2.2 of MacHTTP, be sure to write VERSION 2.2 in the config file.

DEFAULT The Default instruction specifies the file format that will be assumed if no other file type identification is possible. The default instruction is text/ HTML, and you can leave this as is.

All files transferred on the Web are identified by a MIME file-type. Browsers send a request header that describes acceptable MIME file-types with every request to a server. Servers send a response header to the browser specifying the MIME file types that the server understands.

Web applications use filename suffixes as part of their method for matching MIME file-types to individual files. For example, a filename ending with .html is usually matched with the MIME file-type text/HTML. These suffix pairings are entered into server and browser instructions by you (or are entered as default settings for you by software authors).

The MIME types acceptable to your copy of MacHTTP server are written further down in the configuration file as a list of MIME file types. You can add or delete MIME file types in that set of instructions.

The Default instruction tells MacHTTP how to send a file for which it has no other MIME file-type information. Usually, Web software uses text/HTML as the default MIME file-type description.

INDEX default.html The Index document for your server is identified by this instruction. The Index document is the document that the server will send in response to a URL addressed to the root directory. Usually, administrators write a directory listing or "home page" for the server and use this document as the Index.

Note that this instruction has *nothing* directly to do with the **DEFAULT** instruction for MIME-type.

The default **INDEX** setting in the configuration file is the `Default.html` document included in the server folder. You can change this setting to any other document you want by replacing `Default.html` with the name of the new document.

In order to work through the server tutorial in this chapter, you should change this instruction to **INDEX welcome.html**. The `welcome.html` file is one of the Chapter 6 Tutorial documents on the companion disk.

Note

> Unlike Uniform Resource Locators, MacHTTP configuration instructions use the standard Macintosh pathname separator, a single colon, between folder and volume names.

The pathname for the **INDEX** file must be a simple pathname, without a preceding colon or slash character. The **INDEX** document must be located in the same folder level as MacHTTP.

ERROR The Error document is the message that your server will send in response to a URL request that cannot be located at your server. This is known as a type 404 or File Not Found error.

The syntax for this instruction is **ERROR:Error.html** Note that this and all file instructions, other than INDEX, use a MacOS pathname to the file, with colon separators between volumes, folders, and files. Since this file is located in the same folder as MacHTTP, the correct pathname is **:filename.html.**

You can write any special instructions into the text of this file. It is an ordinary HTML document. The default file is the `Error.html` file that was included in the server folder.

After you have reviewed your **MacHTTP.config** file for the VERSION and INDEX instructions described here, you are ready to start using the server. The rest of the settings in the configuration file can be modified later. If you want to get started right away, skip ahead to the section in this chapter titled "Serving Files—A Tutorial."

Don't forget to come back and review the rest of these settings instructions. They provide important options for your server.

Settings for Securing Your Server

MacHTTP 2.0 provides two methods for restricting access to your server: via the Internet access, or by using passwords. The tutorial section found later in this chapter discusses these issues further if you have trouble with the explanations.

Access by Address

The first method is to control access to the server according to the Internet address of the browser. The address of the requesting browser is obtained by MacHTTP during the connection process by reading TCP/IP segment header information.

This address-specific access is defined by the ALLOW and DENY instructions written in the configuration file. If any address security instructions are given, access will be automatically denied to all client addresses except those for whom specific ALLOW instructions have been given.

ALLOW is used to specify a client's domain name or IP number address or a range of client addresses that will be allowed to access the server, such as **ALLOW amnh.org**. The default instruction to MacHTTP is to allow access to all clients.

DENY is used to specify the client domain name or IP number addresses that are denied access to the server, such as **DENY caribou.amnh.org.**

Partial addresses can be used to specify a range of subnet addresses that are allowed or denied.

For example, the instruction **ALLOW amnh.org** enables **bullwinkle.amnh.org** or **moose.amnh.org** to access the server but will deny access to any machine addresses outside of the domain **amnh.org** (for example, **moose.nsso.com**).

The **DENY caribou.amnh.org** instruction denies access to the specific machine with that address. Additional ALLOW or DENY statements can be added to allow access to other addresses.

Numbered IP address ranges can be specified by using an asterisk character as a wild card for that digit position and any following positions.

For example, the instruction **ALLOW 129.106.3*** would allow access to any client with an IP address that began with **129.106.3** and include every address from **129.106.30.0** through **129.106.39.255**.

Realms and Passwords

The second type of access control used by MacHTTP protects specific files or directories at the server by assigning access privileges to specific user names and passwords.

Protected files and directories are assigned to a realm category at the server. This assignment is specified by REALM instructions in the configuration file.

REALM <match string> <menu name> indicates that **<match string>** is the name or part of the name of the file or folder to be protected, and **<menu name>** is the name of the realm that has been established for the file or folder.

When the text defined as the **<match string>** appears anywhere in a URL requested from the server, MacHTTP will send a 401 Authorization message to the browser. The browser should then display a dialog box that prompts the user for a name and password. The name and password are resubmitted to the server in a header for the URL request.

You can configure any number of REALM instructions. For example, the instruction **REALM docs documents** restricts access to any file or directory that contains the text docs in its URL. Requests for files in this realm will cause MacHTTP to request authorization from the browser. The browser will display a dialog for the user to enter a name and password and to submit this information back to the server.

This name and password is checked against a Password combination for the **documents** realm. Password combinations for realms are established using the Password command in the MacHTTP Edit menu. An example of configuring realms and passwords is given in the following tutorial.

Serving Files—A Tutorial

Once you have entered and saved the relevant instructions to the **MacHTTP.config** file, and have a domain name or IP numbered address to identify your Mac, you are ready to launch the server application and start publishing on the Web. All you need are some files to serve.

To help you with this, the folder Chapter 6 Tutorial on the WWWSK disk contains some basic text and GIF files that you can use to test-drive MacHTTP.

If you haven't read the section "Installing MacHTTP Server," you need to do so now. Otherwise, you're ready to pull away from the curb.

Step 1: The Root Directory

Some of the items for this portion of the tutorial have been prepared for you and can be found in the Chapter 6 Tutorial folder that came with the disk in this book. For the following steps to make sense, open the Chapter 6 Tutorial folder and familiarize yourself with its contents.

1. Move or copy the docs and scripts folders to your MacHTTP Software & Docs folder. In order for all of the hyperlinks in the tutorial documents to work correctly, these folders need to be at the same directory level as the MacHTTP 2.2 application (the root level).

2. Open the Tutorial images folder and copy the GIF files into the existing Images folder in your MacHTTP Software & Docs folder.

3. Copy the welcome.html document to the server's root level (copy it to MacHTTP Software & Docs folder).

At this point, your root-level folder should contain all of the folders and files shown in figure 6.6.

Figure 6.6   *The root-level directory of your server as set up for this Tutorial.*

Step 2: Configure MacHTTP.config

For this tutorial, the root level Index document for your Web server will be the **welcome.html** document.

Use BBEdit Lite to open the **MacHTTP.config** file and change the **INDEX** instruction line to read **INDEX welcome.html**. There should be a letter space, but not a colon, between the keyword INDEX and the document name.

The INDEX document is used by your server as the default document for the directory in which it resides. You can identify INDEX documents inside subdirectories by giving them the same name specified in your INDEX configuration instruction.

For example, if your server was running on a machine with the address **caribou.amnh.org**, the URL to your MacHTTP root directory would be **http://caribou.amnh.org**. Browsers sending that URL would retrieve the INDEX document in your root directory.

Index documents are typically used to provide hyperlinks to the contents of a server or directory.

Step 3: Open a TCP/IP Connection

Before you start up MacHTTP, you need to open a TCP/IP network connection. If you need help installing or configuring the MacTCP control panel, see the explanation in Chapter 2.

If you are already connected to a local Ethernet with a gateway to the Internet, you don't need to do anything special here. Your Mac is probably configured with MacTCP, and you can go ahead and launch MacHTTP. If you're not sure about MacTCP, ask your network administrator.

Note

> *You should also find out from your network administrator if your computer is located behind a "firewall." This firewall will prevent people from being able to access your server and it will appear that you have not configured MacHTTP correctly. Talk to your administrator about placing your computer "in front" of the firewall.*

If you are using a dial-up SLIP/PPP connection to the Internet, you should open the ConfigPPP or the SLIP control panel and dial into your service location. Once your connection is confirmed, you're ready to launch MacHTTP.

The IP number or domain address that you use for your TCP/IP connection also will be the address for your MacHTTP server, as in **http://166.84.247.149** or **http://caribou.amnh.org**.

Step 4: Launch MacHTTP

All set?

Double-click on the MacHTTP 2.2 application icon.

That's it.

As it's starting up, the server will configure itself to communicate through Port 80 at the IP address of your computer. The Status Window will open on your desktop, and shortly thereafter the following message (or something very close to it) will appear in the Status Window:

```
MacHTTP 2.2, Copyright ©1995 Chuck Shotton,
All rights reserved.

*** Check out WebSTAR, the ultimate upgrade to MacHTTP! ***
  http://www.starnine.com/

Loading MacHTTP.config...
680x0 (CW) Server is running on port 80.
```

Select **Verbose Messages** in the MacHTTP **Options** menu. This will provide you with some useful information about the server operations demonstrated in this exercise.

Step 5: Talk to Yourself

Now you need to connect to your server.

Launch Netscape and select the Open Location command from the File menu. The URL you need to use is **http://** followed by the domain name or IP number address assigned to your computer.

IP address information is entered and displayed in the MacTCP control panel in the IP Address field.

Send the URL. In a few seconds, the **welcome.html** page should be blazing across your browser window (see figure 6.7).

You're in service!

Step 6: Examine the Tutorial Documents

From the Welcome to My Server page, you can navigate to a few text files and GIF images created by the National Aeronautics and Space Administration. This information is borrowed from one of their Web servers for instructional purposes only.

Toward the bottom of the Welcome page is a hyperlink to NASA's Copyright Notice. Click on this link and read the notice, please (see figure 6.8).

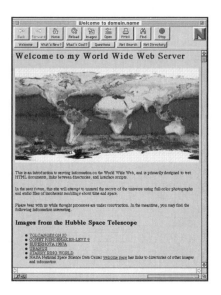

Figure 6.7   *The* `Welcome.html` *page that is included with the World Wide Web Starter Kit tutorial files.*

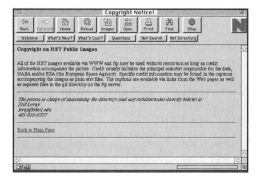

Figure 6.8   *Most of the GIF images included with this tutorial were produced by NASA's Hubble Space Telescope.*

Take a look at the other documents on your new server and watch the information that is recorded in the MacHTTP Status Window.

This information can be divided into the same four categories described earlier in this chapter.

The Connection is reported first, and includes the Internet address of your computer.

Under the line ###Received, you see the Request that your browser sent. Notice that this request starts with the line GET followed by the URL for the file you requested. This is followed by a series of Accept: lines indicating the MIME types that your browser understands. There will also be a line that indicates the User-Agent: which refers to your browser application.

The next several lines report on the MacHTTP Response to this request. You should see a line for each of the Response Headers that MacHTTP sends, followed by a report on the downloaded file size and the duration of the download.

Finally, the log reports that the connection was Closed, and records the date and time.

MacWeb also reports on connections in the location field at the bottom of the browser window (the status fields in Mosaic and Netscape also provide some connection information). This information is very brief, but it may be helpful to compare it with what's reported in the MacHTTP Status Window.

If your monitor screen is big enough, you can display both windows side by side and try to decipher how the two applications talk to each other.

While we've got things up and running, let's take a closer look at path names on your server.

Writing URLs Correctly

You are now looking at real HTML documents being served to your browser via HTTP. This is an ideal opportunity to examine Uniform Resource Locators and see how they relate to the file structure on a server.

1. Close your browser window. This should flush all of the documents currently saved in memory by your browser.

2. Use BBEdit to open the **supernova.html** file stored in the **docs** folder in your server's root directory.

At the top of the document are hyperlinks to two GIF files. The URLs pointing to these files are partial URLs that include a directory name and the file name, but not a host address. (You can use partial URLs to point to other documents on the same server.) These GIF files are stored inside the **images** folder inside your MacHTTP root directory.

For example, the larger GIF is addressed through the URL **HREF="/images/ SN1987A_Rings.gif"**, not **HREF="http://xxx.xx.xx.xxx/images/ SN1987A_Rings.gif"** (see figure 6.9).

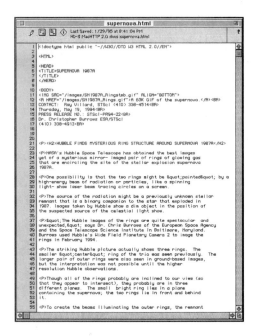

Figure 6.9   *The* **supernova.html** *document includes the anchor* **<A HREF="/images/SN1987A_Rings.gif">** *at the top of the document.*

Change this anchor to **<A HREF="SN1987A_Rings.gif">** and save your changes.

Re-open your client and send the URL for your server. In the Welcome document, click on the SUPERNOVA 1987A link and go to the document you just edited (see figure 6.10).

Click on the link A 63K GIF of the supernova.

The server reported an error message (see figure 6.11), because the hyperlink no longer points to the location of the file.

Your edit changed the link to point to a file that could either be in the root-level directory of the server, or in the same folder as the document that contains the hyperlink. There is no file named **SN1987A_Rings.gif** in either directory.

A proper URL describes the pathway to the document from the root directory of the server. Since **SN1987A_Rings.gif** is still located in the **images** directory, MacHTTP can't find it and the anchor does not work.

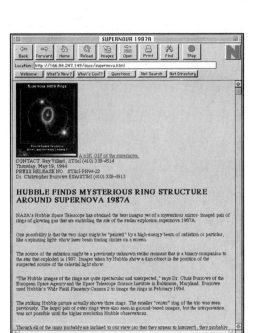

Figure 6.10   *The* `63K GIF of the supernova` *hyperlink is supposed to point to the file* **SN1987A_Rings.gif**.

Figure 6.11   *If the Uniform Resource Locator sent by the client cannot be located, the server will return an error message.*

Re-edit the **supernova.html** document and fix the anchor that points to **SN1987A_Rings.gif**, so that the pathname is restored to **/images/SN1987A_Rings.gif**.

MacHTTP can resolve URLs that point to files inside the root-level folder or to files in folders within the root-level folder. These folders are subdirectories of the main directory.

Because MacHTTP cannot resolve URLs pointing outside this root hierarchy, all other files and folders on your disk drive are relatively safe from unauthorized access.

Using Passwords

As open as the World Wide Web is, there may be times when you'd like to control access to files on your server. MacHTTP provides two methods for doing just that.

Writing ALLOW and DENY instructions into the configuration file enables you to restrict access to entire sections of the Internet. This might be appropriate for servers set up for use within an organization on a local area network, for example.

If MacHTTP is running, you should shut it down using the Quit command from the file menu. You can make changes to MacHTTP.config while the server is running, but you'll need to restart the server to load your new instructions.

In order to define a realm, you need to enter an instruction in the MacHTTP.config file. Open the MacHTTP.config document and scroll down to the two lines of example **REALM** instructions. You can modify one of these existing lines or write a new one, it doesn't really matter.

Type the following instruction into the MacHTTP.config document:

```
REALM docs documents
```

This instruction tells MacHTTP to restrict access to any file or folder with the text string **docs** in the URL. This will restrict access to every sample document in this tutorial, since they are all stored inside the folder **docs**.

This instruction also establishes a realm with the name **documents**. When you assign password access to the **documents** realm, you will be assigning access privileges for the **docs** folder, or any URL at the server that contains the text string **docs**.

Re-launch MacHTTP and load the new configuration instructions.

Now go to the Passwords command in the Edit menu and open the dialog window for editing User Passwords. The window displays a pop-up menu in the lower left corner that shows realm names that have been entered in the configuration file. The realm `documents` should be displayed in this menu.

Enter your name in the `Name` field and a password in the `Password` field and click the Add button (see figure 6.12). This name and password information is recorded in the `MacHTTP Settings` file.

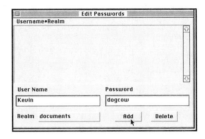

Figure 6.12   *Registering a User Name and Password with MacHTTP.*

Now use your browser to send the URL `http://<your-server-address-here>` to your server. When the index page for your server is downloaded, click on the link pointing to one of the example documents. All of these files are stored in the **docs** directory, which is now password protected in the `documents` realm.

When MacHTTP receives a request for one of these files, it will respond by sending a status code `401-Unauthorized` message to the browser.

When your browser receives this message, it will display a dialog box asking for a user name and password (see figure 6.13).

Enter your name and password and click OK. The name/password combination is submitted to the server where it is checked against the names and passwords recorded for the **docs** realm.

Assuming that you entered the correct name and password, the document you requested will be downloaded to your browser by MacHTTP.

The browser is responsible for getting your name and password, and it retains this information in its RAM partition. Any additional requests that you send to this server and realm will not require you to re-enter a name or password.

Requests sent for other protected directories on the same server, or requests to other protected servers, will receive a new 401 message and prompt the browser to display a new dialog box for a new name/password combination.

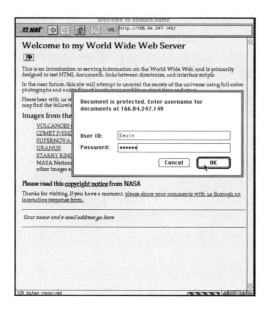

Figure 6.13 *MacHTTP sends a status code 401 to the browser. The browser displays a dialog box asking for your name and password.*

This concludes the first part of our lesson. As you've just seen, getting started with MacHTTP isn't a whole lot more complicated than launching it. The hard part is coming up with worthwhile documents, pictures, and other files to share.

To quit MacHTTP, use the File menu. Quit is your only option. If you have been using a modem connection to the Internet, you may want to close that, too.

CGIs Using AppleScript

Web servers do a very good job of listening for client requests and downloading files, but that's about all the file processing that a server is capable of performing.

Just as most browsers rely on external applications to handle any data files beyond basic **.html** and **.gif** documents, Web servers rely on external applications to perform any special processing of data they store or receive.

There is a standard way for external programs to communicate with Web servers called the Common Gateway Interface, or CGI. CGI programs can process information in a form, create a database query, or map parts of an image to different URLs. On a UNIX-based Web server, this kind of Common Gateway Interface would be written using Perl or the C programming language.

While you could write CGIs that work with MacHTTP using these languages, there is a better option. MacHTTP is written to understand the AppleScript language and to communicate with other Mac applications using messages called Apple Events.

AppleScript is a scripting language that enables you to control operations on your Mac without having to use a mouse or keyboard. It allows you to compile a series of written instructions into small scripts or programs. AppleScript is very easy to learn (compared to other languages) and you only need to know one scripting language for automating a variety of tasks. AppleScript scripts can also be compiled into self-contained programs.

Apple Events are messages sent from one application to another. They're used to request a service from another application or to perform a service that another application has requested. Apple Events also can be used to move data from one application or process to another.

MacHTTP supports a suite of Apple Events to communicate with a large number of other Macintosh applications, including those created with AppleScript.

In order to run AppleScript programs on your Mac, you need to install the AppleScript extension as part of your operating system. This extension contains the basic language and structure used for AppleScripts.

The AppleScript extension is distributed with MacHTTP 2.2, and is also included in most editions of System 7.1 and System 7.5. The AppleScript extension is stored in the Extensions folder nested in the System Folder.

Second, you need some of the Open Scripting Architecture Extensions (OSAX) that are used by AppleScript to expand its vocabulary. OSAXs are also called Scripting Additions, and consist of bits of code that are used by AppleScript scripts and other AppleScript-aware programs. OSAXs are stored in the Scripting Additions nested inside the Extensions folder (nested inside the System Folder).

The full MacHTTP 2.2 archive includes a basic set of Scripting Additions.

Third, and in order to *write* programs using AppleScript, you need a copy of the Script Editor program. This application allows you to edit, and compile AppleScripts as scripts or as self-contained programs.

The CGI described in this section is an AppleScript program. In order to compile the script for this program, you will need a copy of the Script Editor.

The Script Editor is not shareware or distributed over the Internet. It is included in System 7.5, and in some editions of System 7.1, including the one shipped with AV model Macs. It also is available in separate AppleScript packages published by Apple Computer as well as *The Tao of AppleScript*, by Derrick Schneider, published by Hayden Books.

These separate packages also include full descriptions of the AppleScript language and dialects and are very helpful for delving more deeply into scripting MacHTTP (or any other AppleScript-aware program).

The sample script shown in this chapter, **shortform.acgi**, is located in the `scripts` folder from the Chapter 6 Tutorial file collection.

AppleScript Spoken Here

The example form described below sends information to a Common Gateway Interface program. This CGI processes the information submitted by the form by writing it into a text file at your server. The CGI then sends a confirmation message back to the browser that submitted the form.

This small program relies on several OSAX extensions. An OSAX is an Open Scripting Architecture Extension.

`File I/O`, `Tokenize`, `DePlus OSAX`, and `Decode URL` are a few of the OSAXs that have been written to extend the function of AppleScript and MacHTTP. Collections of OSAXs are available on servers throughout the Web. All of the ones used in this chapter are available at:

```
http://www.biap.com/machttp/tools/
```

or at

```
ftp://gaea.kgs.ukans.edu/applescript/
```

File I/O enables a script to open, write to, and close a file. Script Tools comes with a complete documentation for File I/O and other OSAX, including the Choose Files & Folders, Gestalt, List Screens, Processes, Regular Expressions, Shutdown, and Speech OSAXs.

Decode URL is used to remove encoded characters that are inserted into Uniform Resource Locator strings.

Certain characters are not allowed inside a Uniform Resource Locator string and are replaced with special hexadecimal (base 16) notation preceded by the % character. Spaces, slashes, apostrophes, and several other characters are "escaped" in this manner.

The Decode OSAX converts the hexadecimal notation back to the original delimiter. It is written by Chuck Shotton, author of MacHTTP <cshotton@biap.com>.

Tokenize is used to remove or replace slashes, apostrophes and other delimiters, and can be used to process POST data containing multiple data items. A tokenize operation can translate a string of words into a series of words separated by commas, for example. Tokenize is included in the ACME Script Widgets collection written by Wayne Walrath <walrath@cs.indiana.edu>.

DePlus is used to replace the + delimiters placed in GET or POST arguments by some Web client applications, including NCSA Mosaic and Netscape. Including the command **dePlus textstring** or **dePlus some_variable** in your AppleScript will cause the script to remove all of the + characters from the argument string and replace them with spaces. DePlus is written by Jon Wiederspan <jonwd@tjp.washington.edu>.

FORM Interface Applications

As with browsers, part of the reason for not writing one monster server application is to keep Web software simple to set up and use.

MacHTTP works with external CGI programs that have been written specifically to run on a Macintosh. These can be programs written in "high-level" languages like C or converted ("ported") CGI scripts originally written for one of the UNIX-based Web server applications.

Common Gateway Interface programs are used to translate existing data files (stored at the server) into a form that can be sent to and read by browsers. CGI programs are also used to process data that has been sent by a browser and passed along to the CGI by the server. The CGI program is activated by the client request that usually consists of a URL pointing to the CGI program.

A Simple CGI

This example uses files and folders from the WWWSK disk.

1. If you haven't already set up your MacHTTP server with the tutorial files from the WWWSK disk, you need to do so now. Follow the steps outlined in the "Installing the Software" section at the beginning of this chapter.

    The MacHTTP 2.2 archive contains the folder MacHTTP Software & Docs. Shorten the name of this folder to MacHTTP. AppleScript doesn't treat ampersands as text characters, so leaving an ampersand in this folder name will cause your script to malfunction.

2. Check to be sure you copied the scripts folder in your MacHTTP root-level directory. Inside this folder are two AppleScript documents named shortform.acgi and shortform.text. They are identical scripts, but shortform.acgi has already been compiled and tested as an AppleScript applet.

3. Check to be sure you also copied the docs folder into your MacHTTP root directory. Inside this folder are several files, including shortform.html and results.txt.

4. This CGI program requires the File I/O, Tokenize, DePlus, and Decode URL OSAXs described earlier. You'll need to download these (use your browser) before you proceed with this exercise.

   These OSAXs must be stored in the Scripting Additions folder, inside the Extensions folder in your System Folder. You cannot compile or run `shortform.acgi` without these OSAXs.

Before you can run `shortform.acgi` successfully from your server, you need to make a modification to the script using the Script Editor program. This modification is not extensive, so don't worry. We'll take it step by step.

Here's what you do:

1. Launch the Script Editor program and use the Open Script command from the File menu to open shortform.acgi.

2. Script Editor displays the script inside an editing window. The displayed script should look like figure 6.14.

Figure 6.14   *An uncompiled copy of shortform.acgi in the Script Editor window.*

3. Find the line in the script that reads:

```
set rec to open file alias "HD-3:MacHTTP¬
2.2:MacHTTP:docs:results.txt" for update
```

This statement is supposed to point to the file **results.txt** inside your MacHTTP server directory. The script you copied from the WWWSK disk was written on my computer, so it points to a file on Kevin's computer in Brooklyn. Not good enough. You need to change this path name.

4. The pathname to `results.txt` is written inside quotation marks and uses colons to separate volumes, folders, and files.

The existing script locates the file beginning with the disk drive `HD-3`, followed by the folder `MacHTTP 2.0`, followed by the folder `MacHTTP`, followed by the folder `docs`, and finally ending with the file `results.txt`.

Your version needs to chart the path into your server folder using the actual names of your hard drive and folders that hold MacHTTP, leading to wherever you have your copy of the `docs` folder and the `results.txt` file.

For example, if your hard drive is named Macintosh HD, your copy of the MacHTTP 2.2 archive is on that top level of your hard drive, and you renamed your root level MacHTTP folder, the pathname in your script should be written as:

```
"Macintosh HD:MacHTTP 2.2:MacHTTP:docs:results.txt"
```

Note

This line in the script uses a standard Macintosh path name, not a Uniform Resource Locator. Use colons, not slashes, as separators. The path begins with volume (disk drive), not the root level of your MacHTTP directory.

5. After you've changed the path name, click the "check mark" button in the upper right corner of the Script Editor window. This is the Check Syntax button. The Script Editor will recompile the script and check its structure. Assuming that you didn't make any other changes, your script should compile without a problem.

If your script won't compile, check that you have copied the required OSAXs to the Scripting Additions folder in your Extensions Folder, and that the pathname in your script is correct and doesn't include any extra space characters (before or after the colon separators, for example).

6. Choose Save from the File command to save your changes.

Chapter 6
Web Publishing

Figure 6.15   `shortform.acgi` *after being compiled by the Script Editor.*

If you were creating this script for the first time, you would use the Save As command to save the file as an Application, checking the options for Stay Open and Never Show Startup Screen. Do not save it as Run-Only or as a Compiled Script.

If you chose Save As, make sure you save it under the name shortform.acgi and that it is still in the scripts folder of your server.

You're done. Now let's change gears for a minute and look at some more hypertext.

The <FORM>

The Chapter 6 Tutorial includes two plain text files in the docs folder. One is the form you will use with this exercise, **shortform.html**. The second is the file where your form data will be saved by the shortform.acgi program, **results.txt**.

Open shortform.html (use BBEdit Lite) and make sure that the **ACTION=** statement in the **<FORM>** element uses the correct URL to your **shortform.acgi** script. This should be the partial URL **/scripts/shortform.acgi**.

```
<HTML>
<HEAD>
<TITLE>A Lesson in Form</TITLE>
```

```
</HEAD>
<BODY>
<H1>Welcome to My Web Server</H1>
<P>Thanks for stopping by. Please take a minute to let me know
what you think.
<FORM ACTION="/scripts/shortform.acgi" METHOD=POST>
<P>Name:<INPUT NAME="name" SIZE="24">
<P>Address:<INPUT NAME="address" SIZE="30">
<P>City:<INPUT NAME="city">
<P>State: <INPUT NAME="state">
<P>Zip: <INPUT NAME="zip">
<P>Email address: <INPUT NAME="email">
<INPUT NAME="ID" VALUE="sample form" TYPE="HIDDEN">
<P>I use MacWeb: <INPUT NAME="macweb" TYPE="CHECKBOX">
<P>I use Netscape: <INPUT NAME="netscape" TYPE="CHECKBOX">

<P>Please rate this server:
<SELECT NAME="rating">
<OPTION>Very good
<OPTION>Average
<OPTION>Not that great
<OPTION>Poor
</SELECT>
<P>Your comments:
<P><TEXTAREA NAME="comments" COLS="72" ROWS="12"></TEXTAREA>
<HR>
<P><INPUT TYPE="submit"></FORM>
</BODY>
</HTML>
```

Now you have a form HTML document and a Common Gateway Interface script to process it. All that's left is to try it out.

The Test

Open a TCP/IP connection and launch MacHTTP.

Launch your browser and send the URL that points to **shortform.html** on your server. This should be `http://<your-server-address>/docs/`
`shortform.html`.

(You may need to enter your name and password if you left MacHTTP configured for the realm explained earlier in this chapter.)

Fill in the fields in the form and click on the Submit button. In a few seconds you should see a confirmation message in your browser window that tells you that your message was received (see figure 6.16).

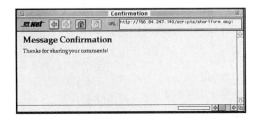

Figure 6.16   *The confirmation message sent from shortform.acgi.*

Take a look at the MacHTTP Status Window (Verbose Messages on) and examine the messages that went back and forth to your server.

The submitted form message begins with the POST URL. Skim down past the list of fields in the request header (Accept, Referrer, Content-type, and so on).

Just past the line for Content-length is the data you sent in the form. Each field entry of text data is tagged by the NAME value assigned to each of the various INPUT fields in shortform.html (see figure 6.17).

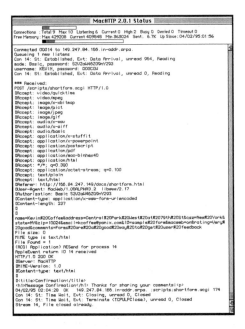

Figure 6.17   *The MacHTTP Status window records the exchange between the server and the CGI program.*

In the Status Window, you'll notice that your browser encoded any "unsafe" characters (like %, $, or #) submitted through the form by sending a percent sign followed by numbers or letters. These alphanumeric codes are actually hexa-decimal notation for ASCII text characters. If your browser is asked to send "unsafe" characters, it will always encode them this way.

A few lines below the submitted data, you'll also see two lines recording that MacHTTP sent and received Apple Event messages. The first of these Apple Event messages was sent by MacHTTP and triggered the Common Gateway Interface program to run. The second Event was sent by the CGI back to MacHTTP in the course of returning a confirmation message to the browser.

Toward the end of the transmission entry, you'll notice the confirmation mes-sage itself. Your browser received a "virtual" HTML document generated by the CGI program.

Now open the **results.txt** file in your docs folder. The shortform.acgi program writes the data it receives into this text file. If this is the first time you've run **shortform.acgi**, there should be one line of text in the file (see figure 6.18).

Figure 6.18   *The data from the form as recorded in the* `results.txt` *file.*

You'll note that the data written in **result.txt** doesn't look very much like the stuff that MacHTTP received. That's because shortform.acgi translated all of the encoded characters into something that you could read. The field entries from the form are recorded to **results.txt** as comma delimited text.

More Script Examples

AppleScript, in the right hands, is a powerful tool for extending your MacHTTP server. Two of those hands belong to Jon Weiderspan, who has written a set of scripting tutorials that are included in the Documentation folder distributed with the MacHTTP software.

Weiderspan's AppleScript tutorials are also available as "live" hypertext, with interactive examples and other useful information, at:

```
http://www.uwtc.washington.edu/Computing/WWW/CreatingASite.html
```

Image Map CGIs

Part of the appeal of the Web is its use of inline graphics and the user-friendly graphical interfaces of browsers like MacWeb, Netscape, and NCSA Mosaic.

Image maps are often part of a Web server's graphical interface with the browser, and work by using Common Gateway Interface programs to convert pixel coordinates on your screen into URLs (see figure 6.19).

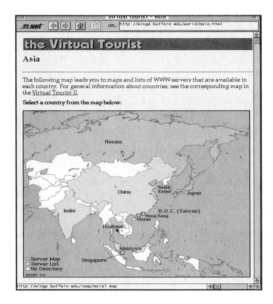

Figure 6.19   *Image maps link areas of an image to URLs to other objects on the Web.*

Image maps are marked up using the <IMG> element and the ISMAP attribute to identify an inline image as a clickable map. They can be used to turn small images on a page into hyperlink buttons, or they can be used to provide a more extensive user interface.

Properly designed image maps help make the Web even more accessible; improperly designed maps often have the opposite effect.

Two programs help you design and use an image map. The first program, WebMap, automates the process of recording image map coordinates. The second program, MapServe.cgi, is a self-contained Common Gateway Interface program that will process the image map coordinate information received from your browser via MacHTTP.

Before you proceed, you should download copies of these programs. Both are available as shareware ($20 each) from the authors.

WebMap is written by Rowland Smith, and can be found at:

```
http://www.city.net/cnx/software/webmap.html
```

MapServe.cgi is written by Kelly Campbell, and can be found at:

```
http://www.spub.ksu.edu/other/machttp_tools/mapserve/
```

After you have downloaded the two programs, copy MapServe.cgi to the scripts folder in your MacHTTP server directory. You can keep WebMap anywhere on your disk drive, it is used by you, not MacHTTP.

The image used in this exercise, **navbar.gif,** is already located in the images folder in your MacHTTP directory. You can use it to make a button bar for your **welcome.html** document.

But first, an explanation of how image maps work.

How an Image Map Works

Graphical computer interfaces operate on the principle that every pixel on screen can be described as a coordinate of its location. These coordinates are measured from the top left corner of the displayed object or screen. This is how the Macintosh operating system describes mouse locations and creates graphics, and this format is used by most other graphical programs and operating systems.

When a user clicks the mouse at a point on the screen, the location of the mouse click can be recorded as a set of x and y coordinates such as (245,198). A graphical interface maps these coordinates to specific actions, like closing a document window or emptying the Trash.

Through a Common Gateway Interface program, it is possible to use the same type of routine over the Web. Instead of just sending mouse coordinates to the local operating system, however, the browser also sends the coordinates through the Internet to a CGI program linked to a Web server.

Image maps are sometimes used in addition to standard anchored text mark-up. The hyperlinked text provides an alternate interface for nongraphical browsers or for browsers that are not autoloading images (see figure 6.27).

Figure 6.20   *The image map link to Hot Java in the upper right is duplicated by a standard text link further down the page.*

The HTML markup used to identify an image map in a document uses two nested elements.

```
<A HREF="/scripts/MapServe.cgi$navbar.map"><IMG SRC="/images/navbar.gif" ISMAP></A>
```

The inner image element, **<IMG SRC="/images/navbar.gif" ISMAP>** is used by the browser to download the graphic, just like any other inline image. The ISMAP attribute tells the browser that the image area is a clickable interface and that it should record pixel coordinates in response to mouse clicks within this image.

This element is then nested inside an anchor element, **<A HREF="/scripts/ MapServe.cgi$navbar.map"></A>** to create a hyperlink from the image to a Common Gateway Interface program and to the set of instructions that record the URL meanings for specific pixel coordinates in the image.

The hyperlink in this example points to a Common Gateway Interface program called **MapServe.cgi**.

The URL in the anchor follows this with a **$** sign to mark the next part of the URL as information intended for the CGI program. This information is the name of a document called **navbar.map**.

Programs that process image maps need a record of what the pixel coordinates mean. This information is recorded as a list of URLs and a series of numbers in a **.map** file.

The same CGI program can be used to process data from many different image maps, but each image requires its own map coordinates recorded in a **.map** file.

When the user clicks the mouse inside the image area, the browser measures the pixel coordinates of the mouse click and adds these to the end of the hyperlink, following a **?** character, as in:

```
GET /scripts/MapServe.cgi$navbar.map?89,7
```

Figure 6.21   *The button bar at the bottom of the page is an image map to three of the example documents from this book.*

The server receives the request for **/scripts/MapServe.cgi**, and launches that program. In this same message to the CGI, the server sends the name of the **.map** file and the appended pixel coordinates.

The CGI application processes this message by looking up the coordinates in the map file and finding the URL that is mapped to those pixel coordinates. It sends that URL back to the server.

If the URL is a location at the server, the server looks in its directories, finds the document and returns that document to the browser. If the URL is for a document somewhere else on the Internet, this URL is redirected by the server for the browser.

Seems like the long way around the block, eh?

Fortunately, thanks to the adroit efforts of several programmers, creating and serving image maps is considerably easier than describing them.

Before you move on to the descriptions of WebMap and MapServe, you should write the HTML markup just explained into your **welcome.html** document.

Just before your ADDRESS element, add the markup:

```
<A HREF="/scripts/MapServe.cgi$navbar.map"><IMG SRC="/images/navbar.gif" ISMAP></A>
```

This will display the file **navbar.gif** as an inline image at the bottom of your **welcome.html** page. Using the two programs I'm about to explain, you'll be able to set up **navbar.gif** as a clickable image.

WebMap 1.0.1

The first operation in creating an image map is to determine the pixel coordinates and Uniform Resource Locator addresses that will be mapped to it.

The URLs used in an image map are no different from the URLs used for any other hyperlink. If the link leads to a document on the same server, a partial pathname can be used. If the link leads to another server, a full pathname is required. Path names proceed from the root server directory, not from the directory that contains the CGI program.

WebMap cannot create graphics. Instead, it opens existing GIF or PICT format files and enables you to mark off areas of these files as "hot spots" for a clickable interface.

WebMap provides Mac-like drawing tools for describing circles, ovals, rectangles, and polygon areas.

Launch WebMap and use the File menu to open the navbar.gif file in your server's images folder. WebMap will open the navbar.gif file in a window and also display a small palette of editing tools.

Click once on the rectangle tool to select it. Next, click and hold the mouse down on a corner of one of the rectangle "buttons" in the navbar.gif image. Drag the pointer to select that rectangle area for use as a hot spot. Release the mouse button after you've outlined the clickable area with the selection tool.

The round or rectangular selection shapes can be resized or moved around the image either by dragging, or through keyboard commands. Polygons can't be resized or reshaped, but any of the items can be deleted.

Once a selection area is drawn over the image, an untitled URL item appears in the list window on the right. Double-clicking on the untitled URL item in this window opens a dialogue box for entering the URL to be associated with that clickable area (see figure 6.22).

Using the WebMap tools, define each of the rectangles shown in navbar.gif as a hot spot and map each to a partial URL for a document in your doc directory: /docs/jupiter.html, /docs/supernova.html, and /docs/cartwheel.html.

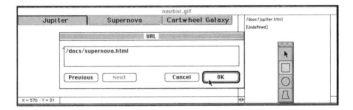

Figure 6.22 *WebMap provides an interface for defining "hot spots" in a graphic.*

A default URL can be specified for background areas of an image not covered by a hot spot. The default URL is set by using the Set Default command in the Edit menu. This displays a dialog box for entering the default URL. You don't need a default URL for this button bar exercise.

You also don't need to save the image file that WebMap opened and you used to define the map, but if you do save it, the geometric markers that you created are stored as resources in the image file and can be edited later to change the areas defined as hot spots.

All that you really need from this process is the .map file for navbar.gif (see figure 6.23). After you have defined the hot spots and URLs for the graphic, use the Export As Text command in the File menu to save the coordinate information and name the resulting file navbar.map. This file should be put in the Scripts folder on your server.

Figure 6.23   *A .map file created by WebMap for the graphic used in this exercise.*

There are two common formats for writing pixel coordinates as they are used on the Web. One format is used by the NCSA htimage program, the other is used by the CERN htimage program. You can specify which format WebMap will apply to your .map file by selecting one of the radio buttons in the Save dialog box when you save the file. The MapServe.cgi program uses the NCSA format.

.map files must be stored in the same directory as the Common Gateway Interface program that will process them. If you save the GIF that was marked up by WebMap, you can put it anywhere you keep inline graphics on your Web server. For this exercise, you will use the existing navbar.gif file as your clickable image.

Note

The numbers used to specify hot spots in a NCSA format image map are written as sets of numbers or number pairs.

Rectangles: top-left x,y bottom-right x,y

Circle: center x,y edge x,y

Oval: top-left x,y bottom-right x,y of bounding box

Polygon: vertice1 vertice2 vertice3 vertice4 etc.

MapServe 1.5

In order for an image map to work, the pixel coordinate data must be processed by a Common Gateway Interface application.

MapServe is a Macintosh version of the NCSA image map program. It supports rectangle, polygon, and circle parameters as specified for the NCSA program, as well as ovals as implemented by WebMap.

MapServe.cgi can be downloaded (using your browser) from:

```
http://www.spub.ksu.edu/other/machttp_tools/mapserve/
```

There is nothing to be configured or recompiled to use MapServe. It can be run from any location on a server. For the purpose of this exercise, you should copy MapServe.cgi to the scripts folder along with the navbar.map file because that is the location specified in the markup.

If you entered the markup described at the beginning of this section, your welcome.html document now includes this line of HTML:

```
<A HREF="/scripts/MapServe.cgi$navbar.map"><IMG SRC="/images/navbar.gif" ISMAP></A>
```

Use your browser to request the welcome.html document from your MacHTTP server. A button bar will appear at the bottom of the page . Each of the buttons acts as a hyperlink to a sample document included in the Chapter 6 Tutorial.

Clicking on any of the buttons sends the URL **/scripts/ MapServe.cgi$navbar.map** to MacHTTP.

MacHTTP passes this information on to MapServe.cgi. After it processes this information, MapServe.cgi gives MacHTTP the URL mapped to the pixel coordinates sent with the URL.

If the URL points to a document at this MacHTTP server, the document is returned to your browser. If the URL points to a document somewhere else in the Web, MacHTTP redirects this request on behalf of your browser. The complete transaction is recorded in the MacHTTP Status Window (see figure 6.24).

You can rename MapServe if you'd like, but the file extension **.cgi** must be retained in order for MacHTTP to launch the program and send it the coordinate data in the URL.

You also can use BBEdit Lite, or another plain text editor, to edit **navbar.map** and change the URL or pixel coordinate entries directly.

MapServe does not automatically quit after it has been launched by the server. When the application is open, it displays a log window showing the URLs received and sent by the program, as well as error messages that it may send as a result of malformed URLs.

All in all, MapServe is a great piece of CGI programming that greatly simplifies using image maps with your server.

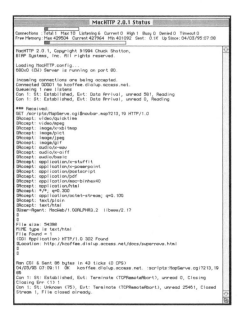

Figure 6.24   *The MacHTTP Status Window reports the progress of an image map request.*

Parting Bits

There are new tools being written for use with MacHTTP all the time. The best place to keep up with news about the server and Common Gateway Interface issues is through the **machttp-talk@academ.com** mailing list, administered by Chuck Shotton.

You can subscribe to the list by sending email to:

Majordomo@academ.com

In the body of the message, write:

subscribe machttp-talk *your_email_address*

The list is an open forum for discussing how to make the most of MacHTTP and WebSTAR. Frequently discussed topics include how to configure your server, how to extend the server through third-party tools, and how to use AppleScript with MacHTTP/WebSTAR.

As you've hopefully seen, setting up a Macintosh Web server is not quantum physics. The component software is available through the Internet. Configuring and operating the software requires only a moderate amount of time and expense.

If you have the content to provide, and a computer connected to the Internet, you can be up and running in less than 30 minutes. And then you, too, can send a new server announcement to NCSA's What's New page!

```
http://www.ncsa.uiuc.edu/SDG/Software/Mosaic/Docs/whats-new.html
```

Webward Bound

Now that you've seen the Web from the client view and the server view, it's time to look at it from a future view. As the bandwidth available for the Web grows, it will enable much richer presentation and interaction features than are available today. Today's hottest sites are the first baby steps in defining the Web of the future.

The Future of the Web

Analyzing the potential for future trends is challenging because much of the Web's content, hierarchy, and technology is continually updated and expanded. We can take our cue for promising indicators from the frontrunners in emerging technologies today. These innovations include the specifications for the proposed HTML 3.0, live and on-demand multimedia on the Web, and the promise of secure Web-based financial transactions. Even more importantly, an overview of trends in who comprises the Web's audience is in order, since user needs will drive which future uses of the Web will be most in demand.

Changing Demographics

Several academic and marketing groups have conducted surveys to collect information about Web demographics and usage. For example, the Graphics, Visualization, & Usability (GVU) Center of the Georgia Institute of Technology began conducting twice-yearly Web usage surveys via forms in 1994 as a public service. Its survey covers general demographics, Web and Internet usage, service providers, and purchasing behaviors, among other questions. The GVU researchers plan to oversee future surveys every April and October.

GVU's third Web survey, compiled in April 1995, showed significant changes from the demographics of the users who completed the two earlier surveys. While most respondents to GVU's earlier surveys had access to the Web through work or school, the April 1995 survey found a much greater representation of users who actively seek out Internet access via local or major providers and commercial online services.

The third GVU survey identifies a growing number of older users on the Web and more balanced gender ratios. According to the third survey, the median age of respondents was 35, almost four years greater than the corresponding figure from the second survey. Women comprised 15.5% of the respondents, a 10% increase from the first survey (in January 1994). GVU researchers predict this linear trend will continue, so that balanced female/male user ratios could possibly be achieved by the first quarter of 1997. A related GVU prediction is that as more major online services increase their Web and other Internet services, more balanced female/male user ratios are likely to occur.

The third GVU survey showed 80.6% of the respondents lived in the United States, 9.8% lived in Europe, and 5.8% were from Canada and Mexico. Respondents' primary computing platforms consisted of 52.0% Windows, 26.2% Macintosh, and 8.8% Unix; other computer platforms made up the remaining 13%. The most popular server was NCSA's at 38.6%, followed by MacHTTP (20.8%) and CERN's (18.5%). Among European respondents alone, the most popular server was CERN's at 34.9%.

Interestingly, the third GVU study also studied Web users who gained their access through the Prodigy online service. Prodigy users reported the greatest percentage of women on the Web (17.1%) and the highest estimated average income. Summaries of the GVU surveys can be found at:

```
http://www.cc.gatech.edu/gvu/user_surveys/User_Survey_Home.html.
```

Faster Connectivity

The Web requires high-bandwidth technology because of the memory-intensive applications it hosts, from audio to animation. Improving delivery speed is becoming an ever greater priority as Web traffic continues to grow exponentially.

Broadband technologies, such as Asynchronous Transfer Mode (ATM), offer high bandwidth and favorable economics; they are key to the next generation of networking solutions. ATM is one of the most stable emerging networking technologies; its networks use an entirely different encoding scheme from the Transmission Control Protocols used on the Internet and achieve much faster transmission rates as a result. ATM's great strength is its ability to consolidate multiple digital signals, including voice, data, and video.

The hardware required to build an ATM network is more complex (and expensive) than the routers and gateways now used on the Internet. But once ATM switches are in place, it is possible to encapsulate Internet Protocol packet data into ATM cells. The preferred physical network for ATM is fiber-optic cable. ATM backbones could replace many (if not all) of the existing electronic networks in a local area with one fiber-optic cable. Using this physical layer as the benchmark, ATM transmission rates begin at 155.5 megabits per second, and are capable of even greater throughput—well past one gigabit per second!

You can find much more information about Asynchronous Transfer Mode networks by checking the documents at:

```
http://www.whitetree.com/ATM_Reference.html
```

There are also other major networking projects underway that strive to increase transmission speeds past one gigabit-per-second. APPN (Advanced Peer-to-Peer Networking) research promotes networks that dynamically switch routing on-the-fly to optimize speed and efficiency. The APPN Implementors Workshop has additional resources at:

```
http://www.raleigh.ibm.com/app/aiwhome.htm
```

HIPPI is an ANSI switched-network standard with a dual-wide data rate of up to 1.6 gigabits per second; more information about HIPPI is available at:

```
http://www.esscom.com/hnf/html/whathnf.html.
```

HTML 3.0 and Beyond

HTML 3.0, which used to be called HTML+, has been evolving since November 1993, when it was first proposed by Dave Raggett as an assemblage of useful features omitted from the original HTML. These features included capabilities such as forms, math equations, and tables. As refinements to the draft specifications of HTML were added, the forms feature was included in the specs for HTML 2.0 (which is close to, but not yet, a published standard), and the other collected proposed features began being referred to as HTML 3.0.

The HTML 3.0 specifications are in a stage known as an Internet draft. The draft is under constant revision by the Internet Engineering Task Force (IETF) HTML Working Group. Although many Web users make reference to features of HTML 3.0, it will likely be at least a year or two before the HTML 3.0 specifications approach anything close to its final structure. The tags or features in the current set of specifications will probably be prioritized, with the less crucial (or perhaps most complex ones) set aside for review for what may be HTML 3.1 or beyond.

The HTML discussion is going on via the Internet, so if you'd like to observe the discussion, check out:

```
http://www.ics.uci.edu/pub/ietf/
```

This site includes links to current working documents, archives of mailing list discussions, and links to servers that can test your HTML documents, including the HTML Validation Service.

While Mosaic 2.0 and Netscape 1.1 support versions of table markup and some of the text and character elements and attributes suggested in the current proposals, most other browsers will ignore most of the other proposed HTML 3.0 tags described below.

The HTML 3.0 proposals can be grouped into one of three categories. The first category includes entirely new structures and global attributes for HTML. These changes are exemplified in style sheets, the **<STYLE>**, **<FIG>**, **<OVERLAY>** and **<DIV>** elements, the new use for **<LINK>** elements, and the new attributes that control text flow in a document. These represent the broadest changes to HTML.

The second category describes new formatting features that have been requested for some time, such as the **<TABLE>** and **<MATH>** elements.

The third group of changes streamlines existing HTML by removing unneeded elements and describes revised syntax for existing tags. This category includes proposals for list elements and the elimination of a few other tags.

The following descriptions should be read as snapshots of the developing parts of HTML. While we may refer to one or another element below as HTML 3.0, the information here is only meant to alert you to the direction that HTML is taking, and to provide some food for thought about how HTML might be used in your next-generation documents.

New Structures and Multipurpose Attributes

Since the Web's beginnings, the function of HTML has been to define the structure of documents. This structural approach follows the more general document markup standards called Standard General Markup Language, or SGML, from which HTML is derived. SGML is used to create standard languages (such as HTML) that indicate document format (mainly as it applies to text information) so that the information can be stored, read, or manipulated electronically without regard to the specific software or hardware being used.

As the role of the Web expands to incorporate graphics and other media, however, the desire to build graphical pages strains against the limitations of a text-oriented markup language. The new structural specifications for HTML 3.0 seem designed to bring HTML in line with strict SGML adherence while affording authors greater options for suggesting (but not imposing) the final appearance and design for their Web documents.

Style Sheets

Style sheets have been proposed as a more versatile method than setting browser preferences for defining the display of elements within a document. Style sheets are separate style language documents applied to one or many base documents through special markup in the base document.

Using style sheets, authors could define type sizes or typeface families, special character sets, background or foreground colors, or other display features. Style sheets would not replace display settings selected by individual browser users, but would provide additional information about how the document may be displayed.

As currently specified, style sheet documents could be attached or linked to Web documents and provide underlying formatting instructions for one or more HTML elements. The same style sheet could be used by many HTML documents, or many style sheets could be used by one HTML document.

Among the questions that remain to be answered are what language will the style sheet use, the final syntax for how the style sheet will be linked to a document, and how browsers should read the style sheet.

Discussions for what language should be used to write Web style sheets have focused on two entrants: a Web-based version of SGML's Document Style Semantics and Specification Language (DSSSL), called DSSSL-Lite; and CSS (Cascading Style Sheets) by Håkon Lie of the W3 organization.

You can read the draft specifications for CSS at:

```
http://www.w3.org/hypertext/WWW/Style/css/draft.html.
```

Regardless of the final mechanism chosen for HTML 3.0, style sheets will improve the graphical look of documents and provide some guarantee to the author that documents will be displayed according to the format intended.

Character Sets

In a multilingual Internet, several dozen alphabets are used, but currently there are few multilingual Web browsers. HTML was built around part of an International Standards Organization character set known as ISO 8859-1 (aka Latin-1). Consequently, virtually all existing browsers understand only a 127-character subset of Latin-1. Many of the rest of the characters in this set can be described using special "entity" markup.

The Latin-1 character set effectively limits HTML documents to languages that use a Roman alphabet. As one alternative, some authors incorporate display text as an inline graphic. This can result in documents that defeat the purpose of the markup language. Inline graphics are not text. Inline graphics cannot be defined using headings, or submitted in a **<FORM>**, or located by a search engine, or read by text-only browsers.

Extending a multilingual Web requires programming work on the part of browser authors. But fundamentally, standards makers for the Web need to agree on the use of one or more alternate character sets in the HTML specification.

The leading candidate for a new base character set is another ISO standard called 10646. ISO10646 is also the basis for a language standard called Unicode, a 16-bit character system being developed by a consortium of hardware and software manufacturers, including Apple, Digital Equipment Corporation, IBM, Lotus Development, Microsoft, NeXT, Symantec, Taligent, and other hardware and software companies. (The Newton MessagePad uses a version of Unicode as will Apple's next version of the MacOS, code-named Copland.)

ISO 10646 contains more than 34,000 distinct characters, called glyphs, in 24 scripts that can each be used to write one or more languages, including Chinese, Farsi, Arabic, Hebrew, and other non-Roman "alphabets."

Another strong selling-point (to current content providers) is that the existing Latin-1 character set maps directly to the first 255 character places in 10646. Because of this correspondence, documents and software written using a 10646 standard would be backwards-compatible with existing documents and would work with existing server software that understands headers and URLs that conform to Latin-1.

For more information about multilingualism and the Web, see:

```
http://www.echo.lu/other/norm.html
```

For an explanation of how to configure Netscape to access Japanese-language Web documents, see:

```
http://mtlab.ecn.fpu.ac.jp/ReadJap.html
```

or

```
http://condor.stcloud.msus.edu:20020/netscape.html
```

For an example of how your browser doesn't handle other alphabets, you can try the links at:

```
http://www.ics.uci.edu/pub/ietf/html/multilingual.html
```

More information about Unicode is available at the Unicode Home Page:

```
http://www.stonehand.com/unicode.html
```

Multipurpose Attributes

The following new proposals for attributes will be common to many HTML tags; this fits with the growing interest in applying style and other global definitions to documents.

LANG= would indicate the language and country code of a document through an International Standards Organization abbreviation, such as **en_uk** (English, United Kingdom) or **fr** (French). It is designed for use in many of the body tags.

CLASS= would specify subclasses for content elements, and provide the possibility of assigning styles to specific paragraphs or other parts of the body, as in `<P CLASS="STANZA">`.

ID would identify a document part as a target of a hyperlink, or to label elements with style definitions given in a separate style document. The `ID=` attribute would be used with any content element. Currently, `NAME=` is used to identify hyperlink targets.

NOWRAP is proposed to control line breaks in a heading or paragraph. It will be used along with `<BR>` to specify exact line breaks in a block of text. Currently, browsers automatically break lines at a space between words, depending upon the width of the browser window.

Text, headings, and paragraphs throughout a document will likely also be defined using new multipurpose attributes:

ALIGN=(LEFT ¦ CENTER ¦ RIGHT ¦ JUSTIFY) is proposed for use with paragraphs, headers, and other parts to align the element content on the page.

CLEAR=(LEFT ¦ RIGHT ¦ ALL) is proposed to control the display of text block elements, such as headings, in relation to floating elements, such as inline images. CLEAR=LEFT and CLEAR=RIGHT would mark a text block so that it would not break along one or the other side of the page. CLEAR=ALL would mark text so that it displayed below floating elements.

\<LINK\> and \<STYLE\>

In HTML 3.0, display style instructions will be added to documents by using the **\<LINK\>** element combined with a new **\<STYLE\>** element.

A **\<LINK\>** element points to a style document at the server that defines global style information for a document, as described above. Style documents described by **\<LINK\>** markup are downloaded by the browser. The LINK element could include a REL=StyleSheet attribute to identify the type of link and an HREF= attribute to point to a specific style document.

The **\<STYLE\>** element is used to assign formatting styles within a document using some type of style language; this tag would override the style sheet accessed via **\<LINK\>**. NOTATION is a proposed attribute for \<STYLE\> to declare the style language being used.

\<LINK\> could also include graphics like navigational toolbars that are shared by more than one document and intended to appear on every screen. The REL= attribute will be used to define the type of link, such as HOME, TOC, INDEX, GLOSSARY, COPYRIGHT, UP, NEXT, PREVIOUS, HELP, and BOOKMARK. These objects would be described by individual LINK elements, as in **\<LINK REL=NEXT HREF="doc33.html"\>**

Similarly, \<LINK\> could be used to insert banner graphics for documents using a REL=BANNER attribute. These style and graphic elements could be cached separately by browsers or proxy servers, conceivably speeding up document download times.

Tables

According to the W3 organization, tables were the most requested feature in suggestions for revisions to HTML. Variations of \<TABLE\> markup are already interpreted by Mosaic 2.0 and Netscape 1.1 and up. This existing markup corresponds generally to elements in the 3.0 proposal, but the attributes used in the existing markup do not.

\<TABLE\> aligns table cell contents and controls the position of document text before and after the table. Like the existing FORM element, the TABLE element contains a set of subsidiary elements and attributes.

A **BORDER** attribute specifies a border drawn around the element. The size of the border would be specified through <STYLE> information in the document head or through style sheets.

COLSPEC=(Lnumber,Cnumber,Rnumber) indicates column widths and alignment. Widths might be measured in en spaces, pixels, or as a fractional value of the table width. Table columns may also be adjusted for width and alignment on the page. Attributes could be applied to the entire table to control the flow of text within or around the table.

Within the major <TABLE> element, subsidiary elements control the display and content of **<TR>** table rows, **<TH>** table header cells, and **<TD>** table data cells, used together like this:

```
<TR><TH>Widgets</TH><TH>Whatsits</TH><TH>Things</TH></TR>
<TR><TD>45</TD><TD>62</TD><TD>89</TD></TR>
<TR><TD>19</TD><TD>23</TD><TD>65</TD></TR>
```

This markup displays three columns of numbers in two rows under the headings of Widgets, Whatsits, and Things.

In addition, the **CLASS=** attribute may be used with the <TR> element to assign the row as a **HEADER**, **BODY**, or **FOOTER** so that single-page display browsers can break a table into multiple pages.

Table elements will be adjusted for horizontal and vertical alignment, using the **ALIGN=(LEFT ¦ CENTER ¦ RIGHT ¦ JUSTIFY ¦ DECIMAL)** and **VALIGN=(TOP ¦ MIDDLE ¦ BOTTOM)** attributes. Display styles will be assignable to individual elements so that you can format individual cells, rows, or entire tables.

In addition, **ROWSPAN=** will control the number of rows spanned by the cell, and **COLSPAN=** will control the number of columns spanned by the cell.

<MATH>

HTML 3.0 proposes a series of <MATH> elements and attributes primarily geared to technical users. <MATH> is not for the faint-hearted or those with short attention spans. We'll forgive you if you skip over this description.

Like the existing <FORM> element, the <MATH> element contains a series of subsidiary elements that are only used within <MATH>, and standard character formatting tags take on unique meanings when used within a math element. For example, **<B>**, **<T>**, and **<BT>** will alter the default fonts used for constants and variables in an equation.

In addition, a series of math entities will be used to display functions, operators, relations, Greek letters, and other special math symbols.

The <MATH> element will be given the standard HTML 3.0 attributes for ID and CLASS, but not LANG. A BOX attribute will draw a box around the entire MATH formula.

<FIG>

Currently, inline images are marked up using <IMG SRC="some.gif"> and automatically downloaded along with the text of the document. HTML 3.0 proposes a completely new **<FIG>** element for displaying inline images and combining images with other graphic overlays, much like layers in a CAD or graphic program.

These new figures would also provide a method for marking up paragraphs, headings, and anchored text for display as part of or instead of a graphic.

Multilayered images would combine one or more <OVERLAY> elements within the <FIG> element, much the way <FORM> includes <INPUT> or <OPTION> in current HTML usage.

Figures could also use hypertext anchors and the SHAPE attribute to provide hot-spot information for graphics that are used as image maps or that would be direct hypertext links within the image.

In addition to these new hyperlink features, <FIG> supports a variety of attributes to control how graphics appear in Web pages, including attributes for horizontal alignment and image/overlay size (following and extending some current Netscape markup).

The <FIG> and <OVERLAY> combination opens up many possibilities for both display graphics and graphic interfaces in documents. For example, a basic graphic could serve as a navigation tool for multiple document collections by using separate text overlays with hot-spot information, and save download time in the bargain (since the basic <FIG> could be cached for use by multiple documents).

The basic markup for a photograph with overlaid text and button graphics might look like this:

```
<FIG SRC="newyork.gif">
  <OVERLAY SRC="map.gif">
  <P>New York from the air!
</FIG>
```

\<BACKGROUND\>

BACKGROUND= identifies an image through a URL to display behind the body as a background color or pattern. Netscape Navigator introduced support for the BACKGROUND= attribute in its 1.1 release.

\<BANNER\>

A new **\<BANNER\>** element is proposed for handling corporate logos, navigational aids, and other information that should not scroll with the rest of the document. This banner element would be included in the content of the document (as opposed to being referred to by the REL= attribute in a \<LINK\> tag).

\<CAPTION\> and \<CREDIT\>

Designed for use with figures and tables, \<CAPTION\> allows you to position text below a graphic using an ALIGN= attribute. A **\<CREDIT\>** element will be used to provide a credit line for a figure.

Mosaic and Netscape already include support for the \<CAPTION\> tag.

\<DIV\>

In the interests of making Web documents more modular, a new **\<DIV\>** element is proposed for delineating a document body into separate sections. Each section could be formatted differently.

For example, the tag \<DIV CLASS="ABSTRACT"\> would mark up a text block as a specific way with its own display characteristics. These defined display characteristics would help to distinguish it from the next section of the document.

Notes and Footnotes

An admonishment element, **\<NOTE\>** is used as a cautionary statement or warning, like the ones used in computer manuals that say CAUTION: DON'T STORE YOUR FLOPPY DISKS IN THE OVEN!

\<NOTE\> will be qualified with a ROLE= attribute and values for SIMPLE, NOTE, CAUTION, WARNING, or FOOTNOTE. Footnotes might display as pop-up notes.

The note marker (in the main text) would use the HREF= attribute to point to the note. The target note would be marked with an ID= attribute.

\<TAB>

Horizontal tabs will allow positioning text through a **\<TAB>** element and several attributes that describe the position of the tab settings in a document.

Logical and Physical Character Tags

A number of logical and physical character level elements have also been thrown into the HTML 3.0 pot for consideration. These elements, too, could be given attributes for ID, CLASS, and LANG.

New logical styles include:

\<DFN> identifies the defining occurrence of a term in a document.

\<LANG> alters the language context of some text.

\<AU> indicates the name of the document author.

\<PERSON> identifies the names of people that should be noted by indexing robots or other search programs.

\<ACRONYM> identifies an acronym.

\<INS> marks up inserted text (for example, in a revised version of a document).

\<DEL> marks up deleted text (for example, in a revised version of a document).

New physical styles include:

\<S> strikethrough puts a horizontal line through the text.

\<BIG> marks up the text for display in larger than normal type.

\<SMALL> marks up the text for display in smaller than normal type.

\<SUP> marks text as superscript, in a smaller type size.

\<SUB> marks text as subscript, in a smaller type size.

Both **\<SUB>** and **\<SUP>** will use **ALIGN=(LEFT ¦ RIGHT ¦ CENTER)** if they are written within a \<MATH> element.

\<SUP> and \<SUB> are currently used by NCSA Mosaic 2.0.

Character Entities

In a continuing effort to work around the limits placed on the default HTML character set, a whole series of special characters have been defined. HTML 3.0 adds the following special characters to the existing list:

&emap; denotes an em space (the width of the letter m).

  denotes an en space (one-half the width of an em space).

— denotes an em dash.

– denotes an en dash (one-half the width of an em dash).

  denotes a non-breaking space.

­ denotes a soft hyphen.

© denotes a © copyright symbol.

™ denotes a ™ trademark symbol.

® denotes a ® registered symbol.

Some of this markup, like © and ®, is already supported by current versions of some browser software.

Revisions to Existing Tags

This section lists the significant changes made in HTML 3.0 to tags you're already used to working with in HTML.

Lists

List elements will be streamlined to focus mainly on <OR> ordered, <UL> unordered, and <DL> definition lists. <DIR> directory and <MENU> lists are deprecated, meaning that you are advised to stop using them.

Every list element may use a list header **<LH>** element to mark up the title for the list. The <UL>, <OL>, and <DL> elements will also use the attributes for ID, LANG, CLASS, and CLEAR.

Ordered lists will use the attribute CONTINUE= to indicate that the current list elements continue a numbering sequence begun in a previous set of list elements. Style sheets could be used to specify alternate ordering schemes or styles: Roman or Arabic numerals, upper or lowercase letters, and so on.

Unordered lists **<UL>** are extended with a series of display attributes. **WRAP=(VERT ¦ HORIZ ¦ NONE)** sets up a multicolumn display of list items. **PLAIN** suppresses list item bullets. **DINGBAT=** specifies a dingbat from a set of available characters. **SRC=** identifies an inline graphic as the bullet for the list item.

Anchor Links

Hypertext anchors are a defining component of hypertext documents. HTML 3.0 proposes three changes to the **<A>** anchor element.

ID= will replace **NAME=** to identify target anchors in a document. Browsers will still interpret NAME so that existing documents continue to work, but the shift is toward the new attribute.

More significantly, a **SHAPE=** attribute specifies hot spots in <FIG> image maps. Anchors used in the new <FIG> figure element use CIRCLE, RECT, and POLYGON to define pixel coordinates. A DEFAULT value specifies the default URL for the figure background area.

In addition to embedding map information in documents, using anchors to define hot spots will allow authors to provide alternate hyperlinked text for nongraphical browsers (without having to write separate hyperlinked text).

The shape data might also be processed at the browser location instead of sending a request to a Common Gateway Interface program at the server, making image map interfaces much faster. See "Client-Side Scripting" later in this appendix for information.

TITLE= provides an informational name for hyperlinked objects. This TITLE might be displayed when you move the mouse over the link.

<ISINDEX>

The **<ISINDEX>** element has mainly been replaced by the use of forms. However, there are two proposed extensions to <ISINDEX> in HTML 3.0. An **HREF=** attribute would indicate the server handling the ISINDEX search, and a **PROMPT=** attribute would allow you to specify the message that is displayed as the search prompt.

PROMPT= is supported by some versions of the Netscape browser.

<BASE>

The **<BASE>** element might be extended to cite URLs for both the document and any inline images used in the document. Two BASE elements could be written, using <BASE HREF="http://etc.etc.etc/text.html"> to identify the document and <BASE ID=IMAGES "http://etc.etc.etc/image.gif"> to identify the graphics.

Rules

Line breaks **
** will be modifiable using ID=, LANG=, CLASS=, and CLEAR=, to control how line breaks work with the surrounding text.

Horizontal rules **<HR>** will use ALIGN=(LEFT ¦ CENTER ¦ RIGHT) to position the rule in the window. **WIDTH=(100)** specifies the width of the rule as a percentage of the width of the window. **SRC=(URI)** will be used to point to (and download) a custom graphic rule. The WIDTH attribute is used now by Netscape.

And speaking of width, the **<PRE>** element for preformatted text would be modified with the attribute **WIDTH=(NUMBER)** to indicate the width of the preformatted text.

Images

The existing <IMG> will add attributes for ID=, LANG=, and CLASS=. Three other new attributes are **WIDTH=(NUMBER)** to indicate the width of the image in pixels or en spaces; **HEIGHT=(NUMBER)** to indicate height in pixels or en spaces; and **UNITS=(EN ¦ PIXELS)** to indicate the units being specified for height or width.

The current version of Netscape uses WIDTH=PIXELS and HEIGHT=PIXELS markup to define an image window size within a document.

Forms

Forms were the major addition to HTML 2.0, and have provided a key user interface for entering and sending small amounts of information over the Web.

The proposed additions to HTML 3.0 enhance the way that forms work by providing markup for creating graphical menus, accepting stylus input, using input fields to upload existing files to a server, and automating the input process through the use of scripts run by the browser.

The <FORM>, <INPUT>, <TEXTAREA>, <SELECT>, and <OPTION> elements will also use the ID=, LANG=, and CLASS= attributes, just like other elements in HTML 3.0.

A **SCRIPT=** attribute refers to the URL of a script file that could be downloaded and run from the browser. This script controls the operation of the <FORM>, such as linking input to multiple INPUT fields, responding to mouse clicks over a graphic input interface, or to automatically enter dates, times, user names, browser type, or other information available from the browser or the operating system.

Three new **TYPE=** attribute values are proposed for the **INPUT** element.

TYPE=RANGE specifies a numerical range that is allowed for input in the field.

TYPE=FILE allows users to attach files as part of the form content and upload these to the server. An **ACCEPT=** attribute is added to the file input element to define the MIME file types that could be uploaded, for example:

```
<FORM ACTION="http://some.url.com/some.cgi" METHOD=POST>
File to upload: <input name=pictures type=file
accept="image/*">
<INPUT TYPE="SUBMIT" VALUE="UPLOAD">
</FORM>
```

On the server end of the transfer, a Common Gateway Interface script controlling the form input determines the final disposition of the uploaded file. This CGI could perform any number of operations along with the upload, such as checking for viruses and saving the file to the proper directory.

The file uploading proposal for HTML 3.0 is derived from an Internet Draft written by Larry Masinter and Ernesto Nobel, available at:

```
http://www.ics.uci.edu/pub/ietf/html/
```

TYPE=SCRIBBLE allows pen or stylus input to be recorded and submitted with the form. The image displayed as the "scribble" interface area would be downloaded through an SRC= attribute pointing to an image file.

A **DISABLED** attribute is proposed for the <INPUT>, <TEXTAREA>, <SELECT>, and <OPTION> entry elements for marking fields that can't be modified by the user. The browser would provide some kind of visual clue that a field is DISABLED (the field might be grayed-out).

An **ERROR** attribute is also proposed for the <TEXTAREA>, <SELECT>, and <OPTION> entry elements to point to an error message to be displayed if the data that has been entered in the text area is not appropriate for the field.

The HTML 3.0 **<SELECT>** element will support graphical menus that use hot spots to register menu options. The markup for a graphic interface would be similar to the markup for creating image maps, with a few new HTML 3.0 twists.

The image in the **<SELECT>** field would use an SRC= attribute to download the graphic and define the display area using ALIGN=, WIDTH=, HEIGHT=, and UNITS= attributes.

Individual hot spots are assigned to **<OPTION>** fields within the <SELECT> element by using the **SHAPE** attribute. This image map information could be processed by the browser instead of a CGI program at the server. This method also allows the <OPTION> menu choices to be displayed as text by browsers that can't display graphics, for example:

```
<OPTION VALUE="Red" SHAPE="rect 7,28,15,36"> Red
```

This describes a rectangular hot spot with the upper-left corner at pixel coordinate 7,28, and is 15 pixels wide by 36 pixels high. Clicking on this hot spot enters the value "Red" into the form.

Further Research

The latest version of the HTML 3.0 specifications can be found at:

```
http://www.ics.uci.edu/pub/ietf/html/
```

The HAL HTML Validation program will check your HTML against the current version of the proposal at:

```
http://www.hal.com/~markg/WebTechs/validation-form.html
```

Dave Raggett, Håkon W Lie, Henrik Frystyk, and Phill Hallam-Baker have written Arena, a test-bed Web browser for X-Windows that implements HTML 3.0-specific features.

The browser is available for Unix machines, but as of this writing a Macintosh version has not been released. Information and code can be found at:

```
http://www.w3.org/hypertext/WWW/Arena/
```

Client-Side Scripting

Another potentially exciting source of experimentation for both users and site designers is expanding the power and function of the client side of the Web.

Until now, Web browsers have functioned exclusively as client agents of servers, as they send short requests to servers in the form of Uniform Resource Locators or download and view files sent back over the Internet. Most of the advanced, interactive functions of the Web have been controlled exclusively by the server, or by Common Gateway Interface applications running at the server site. Forms and image maps are two common examples of functions traditionally executed on the server side.

This division of processing follows the standard client-server model. Databases by their very nature are central repositories of information. Search engines are complex programs that wouldn't run very quickly if parts of the process were farmed out around the Internet, dependent on the capabilities of miscellaneous client computers.

But other types of Web functions are not that processor-intensive. Image maps, for example, primarily require a small program to translate pixel coordinates into predefined URLs and forward the proper redirection instructions to the server. Why not process an image map from the client computer?

The MacOS, for example, is well-equipped to handle such tasks. It contains its own scripting environment and language that can be used to control programs and inter-application communications on a single machine or over an AppleTalk network. Most of the current crop of graphical browsers written for the Mac make some use of either this scripting language or the inter-application communications functions of the operating system.

In the same vein, most versions of the X-11/Unix system can send and receive instructions between processes running on networked workstations, and X-clients already make use of the Internet for some types of collaborative processing.

One of the next big areas of development on the Web will be using the existing framework of HTML and HTTP to make client-side processing a normal method for moving data around the world.

How Does It Work?

Let's look at the example mentioned just above: processing an image map.

The traditional client-server method for handling a mapped image is to embed an HTML anchor and image element in a document. The inline image is downloaded along with the document, and is linked by the anchor to a Common Gateway Interface application located back at the server. The client (browser) receives no information about what pixel coordinates correspond to what URLs for the image map. All it does is transmit the coordinates of mouse clicks according to the URL of the image anchor.

In the meantime, the user waits for a number of processes to take place. The URL has to be sent back to the server, then the server passes the map information along to a CGI. Next, the CGI correlates the pixel information with a listed URL and the correlated URL is passed back to the server. Finally, the server returns a document or URL—and then the user waits for another server to respond to the redirected URL.

As you know from Chapter 6, the actual amount of data stored in a map configuration file is miniscule, and is probably only a small fraction of the size of the image map GIF that the browser downloaded in the first place. Why not send the map coordinate data and URLs to the browser (embedded in the document) and let it call an applet on the client computer (or written into the browser) to look up and send the URL itself?

In fact there are many possible uses for client-side processing on the Web: slide-shows of graphic files; streaming audio or video to a client-side player while it's being transmitted over the Internet; applying special display formats to documents; perhaps even browser-launched database searches.

Client-side scripting is a logical extension of how browsers now use helper applications to process data. The difference is that client-side scripting will enable a much greater range of functions for the Web.

What's Out There Now?

There are several paths leading to client-side processing right now. Several Internet vendors have introduced their own environments for employing client-side scripts and establishing inter-application communications.

Apple's OSA and OpenDoc

Apple Computer's Open Scripting Architecture provides a system-level connection between applications running on the MacOS by way of Apple Events. Programs that use this OSA are scriptable, using the AppleScript language. Many TCP/IP client applications, including the Netscape and MacWeb browsers, already support Apple Events. The only ingredient missing is a standard syntax for client-side scripts in HTML documents.

One step beyond this is another Apple innovation called OpenDoc. Using the OpenDoc framework, applications are replaced by collections of shared programming routines. To borrow a term from the Web, OpenDoc software will be designed as universal "helper" components. Files and documents will no longer belong to a specific piece of software, and will be easily exchanged between different types of computers and operating systems.

Apple is also developing a series of Internet client components in a project code-named CyberDog. CyberDog is expected to be unveiled early 1996.

Java and HotJava

Meanwhile, Sun Microsystems, makers of Unix workstations, has released a version of HotJava, a browser that runs on top of its Solaris operating system and provides its own scripting environment. HotJava uses Sun's new programming language called Java.

HotJava browsers recognize special markup tags, written into HTML documents, that create an inline link to an applet at the server. The HotJava browser downloads this applet and uses it to perform an action. Like OpenDoc, the Java language is intended to be platform-independent, built on shared libraries of program code based on the C++ programming language.

Sun expects to release a Macintosh version of the HotJava browser sometime in late 1995 (perhaps in November), and Netscape Communications Corporation has announced that it will support the Java language in a future release of its browser Netscape 2.0.

Aretha

Another approach to client-side scripting is demonstrated by UserLand, the software developer that built its own Frontier scripting environment for the Mac before AppleScript was released. This updated environment, code-named Aretha, is designed especially for use on the Web and is available now in beta release and distributed freely over the Internet.

The Aretha/Frontier scheme relies on a copy of the Frontier script engine, running on the same machine as the browser, to interpret Aretha scripts written into HTML documents. In the Aretha scheme, the Aretha/Frontier engine and the browser talk to each other using Apple Events.

WebRunner

A third method for employing client-side scripts with Mac-based browsers has been developed by Eric Iverson and is represented by the WebRunner script engine.

WebRunner is an AppleScript-based helper program that uses AppleEvents to process AppleScript files downloaded in an HTML document, in much the same way that Aretha works using the Frontier scripting language.

More Information

The latest news about these scripting environments and their effect on the Web, can be found at the following Web sites:

AppleScript and AppleEvents

http://www.info.apple.com/dev/developerservices.html

OpenDoc

http://www.cilabs.org/

Java and HotJava

http://java.sun.com/

Aretha and Frontier

http://www.hotwired.com/Staff/userland/aretha/

WebRunner

http://www.pass.wayne.edu/~eric/applescript.html

Advanced Media

As Web site developers continue to push their servers' and browsers' capabilities to the limits, you'll continue to see more opportunities to download and play multimedia presentations alongside text displayed in the browser window.

In most of your encounters with Web-based multimedia, you'll find that audio and video data are not passed immediately to a helper application. First, the data is downloaded to disk and then the helper is launched to play the data file. But now ,the first generation of Web-based multimedia software with real-time playback are being introduced; these allow your browser to play sound or video files on your computer within seconds after the data arrives through your network connection.

Real-Time Audio and Video

Real-time video and audio are images and sounds that are received almost as soon as they are captured. Your local broadcast television news program is usually an example of "real-time" video.

Progressive Networks' RealAudio lets users download sound files that can be "streamed" to a copy of the RealAudio Player. RealAudio performs this work by creating a buffer in your computer's RAM and assembling the received audio data there before processing it through your built-in audio circuits. You hear the sound very shortly after your computer receives it. The first live broadcast was held in September 1995 when ESPN's web site broadcast a baseball game between the New York Yankees and the Seattle Mariners.

You can read more about the RealAudio product line at:

```
http://www.realaudio.com/
```

Shortly after RealAudio began garnering headlines for itself, Xing Technology's StreamWorks was released with even grander claims. StreamWorks supports live and on-demand audio and video over the Web, utilizing MPEG compression and Xing's own Low Bit Rate compression technology. Users can access StreamWorks-enabled sites via their regular browsers. A Windows version of the client software was released in August 1995, with the Macintosh version to follow later in the year. You can find about more about StreamWorks from Xing's Web site, at:

```
http://www.xingtech.com/
```

The Telemedia, Networks, and Systems (TNS) Group at MIT has modified a version of X-Mosaic to display continuously streamed video data. Instead of recording the file to disk first and then launching a helper application, the browser launches the helper application and displays the data immediately in a second window.

A description and demonstration are available through the `Cool Demos` link on the TNS Web server at:

```
http://tns-www.lcs.mit.edu/tns-www-home.html
```

However, you need a Unix workstation and a fast Internet connection to try it out.

Virtual Reality

Using off-the-shelf virtual reality software, it's possible to construct elaborate three-axis drawings with which you can walk through and around simulations of real or imaged objects. Now, products such as Apple's QuickTime VR and ParaGraph International's Home Space Builder are early entrants in the effort to bring VR applications to the Web.

At the first WWW Conference in the spring of 1994, Dave Raggett presented a paper outlining developing virtual reality interfaces for the Web. An informal group met to discuss the topic and out of these early discussions, an ad hoc group of engineers and software developers began devising the framework for VR on the Web, and building prototypical software to test it.

The resulting framework is called the Virtual Reality Modeling Language (VRML) and it describes simulated objects and user interactions with them. VRML borrows from many sources, including the Open Inventor file format developed by Silicon Graphics Inc. and Object-Oriented Programming environments, like C++ and NeXTStep. A draft of the VRML 1.0 specification was published at the second WWW Conference in the fall of 1994.

Web-based virtual reality is intended to provide a more intuitive interface to the Internet. The architects of VRML would like to make Web navigation resemble at least some of the actions normally used to get from point A to point B in the real world.

VRML addresses how to represent objects on the Web graphically as the user's perspective changes; it looks and works like a computer programming language (VRML is not a replacement for or alternative to HyperText Markup Language).

Almost all of the programming work for VRML has been done on top of the Unix operating system. Consequently, the first examples of VR software ran only on Unix workstations. More recently, versions of these programs have been rewritten to run on top of other operating systems including Windows 3.1 and Windows NT.

VR viewers are designed as either stand-alone client programs, or to be used as helper applications with existing 2-D browsers. Viewers recognize VR file objects identified with the MIME type **x-world/x-vrml**.

For an overview of VR on the Web and information about VRML, visit the Virtual Reality Modeling Language Forum located at:

```
http://vrml.wired.com/
```

Another important resource is the Virtual Reality Modeling Language Repository, which contains links to information, VRML libraries, and several 3-D viewer programs. The Repository is located at:

```
http://www.sdsc.edu/vrml/
```

Silicon Graphics has published a 3-D viewer called WebSpace that can be used by itself or run as a helper to a Web browser. Versions for many platforms, including a Macintosh PowerPC version, are in various stages of testing. The latest information about WebSpace is at:

```
http://www.sgi.com/Products/WebFORCE/WebSpace/
```

The San Diego Supercomputer Center has released a program called SDSC WebView that also functions as either a stand-alone VRML viewer or as a helper for a 2-D browser. Information about WebView is at:

```
http://www.sdsc.edu/EnablingTech/Visualization/vrml/webview.html
```

Apple Computer has released its QuickTime VR Player and made it freely available as a helper application for Web browsers. QuickTime VR requires the QuickTime 2.0 extension, which is available for Windows and Macintosh.

```
http://qtvr.quicktime.apple.com
```

Note

At presstime, QuickTime 2.1 was made freely available on the Internet via FTP from Apple's software support site. You can find QuickTime 2.1 at:

```
ftp://ftp.support.apple.com//pub/Apple_SW_Updates/US/Macintosh/System_Software/
Other_System_Software/QuickTime_2.1.hqx
```

Apple has also created an alternative to VRML called QuickDraw 3D that allows Web users to navigate three-dimensional spaces.

```
http://www.info.apple.com/qd3d
```

Security and the Web

Until recently, HyperText Transfer Protocol server software provided only very basic methods for securing a server from unauthorized access. Most current types of security measures are more than adequate for most installations, but they are only the first layer of security options that are possible on the Web.

There is widespread commercial interest in the Web and you can now browse for everything from boxer shorts to salsa on the Web. As interest in Web-based commerce and financial transactions continues to grow, more sophisticated encryption and authentication methods will be needed.

Firewalls

A firewall is a method for controlling access to a local network from a wide area network or Internet, or for controlling access out of a local network to the wide area network or Internet. The firewall principle is simple. If you establish a data gateway into or out of a network, you can control the traffic passing through the gateway.

There are two main types of firewall mechanisms. The first is a router-based firewall. Routers are dedicated computing devices that are used to connect separate networks together. Routers maintain address information about nodes on the connected networks. Some routers can even be configured to only pass data based on certain types of address information. These instructions can be a set of Internet Protocol address numbers, specific protocol header types, or other instructions programmed into the router.

The second type of firewall mechanism is called a host-based firewall and consists of an application hosted by the computer that acts as the surrogate or proxy network address for other computers on either side of the wall. This proxy computer is the recipient of all transmissions sent by computers inside the local network and relays this data to the outside world. Traffic from outside is addressed to the proxy, or is intercepted by the proxy and relayed to local nodes.

Neither type of firewall is guaranteed to be 100 percent effective against a clever person determined to penetrate the wall, but either type will provide a high level of security to the local network.

Of course, if you are interested in keeping everyone away from your World Wide Web server, the solution is simple enough; you can disconnect your local network from any other networks to create an internal Web. Otherwise, most Web servers (including MacHTTP) can be configured to only allow access to nodes within your local network's IP address sub-net range.

Usually, there is a need for users in a local network to be able to communicate with the outside world and for those outside the local net to get through to it. In order to provide network security in this situation, a firewall may make sense.

Proxies and HTTP

If local network security is a problem, a good solution is to configure a proxy Web server to handle HTTP traffic on the firewall host computer.

There are two main proxy applications in use on the Web. The first is a general purpose protocol server called SOCKS (not an acronym, just another bit of computer shorthand) that is usually run on Port 1080 as the intermediary for traffic coming to the firewall. SOCKS runs on top of a Unix operating system.

In order to use a SOCKS proxy, clients have to be "socksified" to communicate with the proxy server. The most recent versions of Mosaic and Netscape are already socksified, which is helpful because the alternative is compiling your own version of Mosaic.

You can get more information about SOCKS in the file directory at:

```
ftp://ftp.inoc.dl.nec.com/pub/security/socks.cstc/
```

The second type of proxy is the HTTPd proxy server, run on the Unix operating system and published by the CERN lab. HTTPd enjoys a few advantages that a SOCKS server does not.

If you administer a Macintosh network that runs a public Web server and requires firewall security, your only option is to set up one of these programs on a Unix-capable computer. Some, but not all, Macintoshes can run Apple's version of Unix, called A/UX, as their primary operating system and run Unix applications on top of A/UX. These include the Macintosh II, Centris, most of the Quadra models (not the 660AV or 840AV), and the Workgroup Server 9500. Power Macs cannot run A/UX, but a version of IBM's AIX operating system is promised for the future. Presumably, this would allow current or future Power Mac workstations to also run Unix software.

You shouldn't become overly concerned about the security of your MacHTTP/ WebStar server because under most conditions, Macintosh computers are much less vulnerable to malicious Internet users than are Unix systems, and MacHTTP/WebStar are also very secure applications.

The MacOS is primarily a single-user operating system, and unless you specifically turn on file sharing and allow full guest access, there is no way for anyone to "get into" your Mac. Understanding how file sharing works on networked Macs, and configuring them accordingly, is usually enough to safeguard your network.

Note that if you want to focus control on individual requests and responses to your server, a firewall may not provide the kind of security you're looking for. You may need a way to secure individual HTTP transmissions via encryption, which is discussed in the next section.

Encrypting the Web

Cryptography may sound spooky, but there is nothing particularly forboding about developing or using security methods on a computer or network. The exponential growth of the Web for diverse communications and commercial uses mandates that some type of security be rolled into the software. If the Web can provide you, or someone else, with valuable information, it should also be able to help protect that information.

A method needs to be employed that will perform encryption and authentication of requests and responses over the Web so that credit card numbers and other sensitive information will not be compromised. There are two proposed methods for securing transmissions through Web space: the Secure Sockets Layer protocol (SSL), and Secure HyperText Transfer Protocol (S-HTTP).

SSL

The Secure Sockets Layer protocol is a standard developed by the Netscape Communications Corporation, publishers of Netscape client and server applications. It operates as an interface between the application protocol (HTTP, NNTP, FTP, SMTP) and the network protocols (TCP/IP) to provide data encryption and authentication for messages, clients, or servers. Its underlying premise is to secure the network connection, so that there's no need to worry about the security of each individual transmission.

If you use the Netscape browser, you have probably already seen the evidence of SSL written into the browser. There is a Security section in the Preferences command, and an icon in the lower-left corner of the browser window that lets you know whether a document is secure or not.

Currently, the only software that implements SSL is published by Netscape, but other software developers may integrate SSL into their products in the future.

S-HTTP

Secure HTTP, or S-HTTP, is an extension to the existing HyperText Transfer Protocol standard proposed by the Enterprise Integration Technologies Corp. (EIT). S-HTTP also provides for various methods of message protection, including secure signatures, authentication, and encryption. Individual transmissions can be subjected to a challenge-response verification process as well.

Like SSL, S-HTTP objects would be defined by a new protocol scheme descriptor in the URL—in this case, `://`. Unlike SSL, S-HTTP would not automatically run through a separate port.

Secure HTTP also proposes several new elements and attributes for the HyperText Markup Language, to be used with form input and with anchors. These anchor attributes would be used to mark up an encrypted message within a regular HTML document so that a secure document could be referenced by a standard `<A></A>` anchor.

EIT has collaborated with NCSA to produce a new version of Mosaic and NCSA HTTPD that has a reference implementation of SHTTP.

For a copy of the Internet Draft for Secure HTTP, see the archive at:

```
http:///1id-abstracts.html
```

End Note

The World Wide Web has come a long way from its rather modest beginnings in 1989. It has truly established itself as the Internet delivery system for the foreseeable future.

Of course, if you had made that claim only two years ago, even hard-core Internet users would have considered it hyperbole. The future is never what it used to be, and the half-life of computer technology is increasingly brief.

The encouraging lesson here is to not underestimate the speed with which the new technologies discussed in this chapter are coming into fruition, and the potential for enabling researchers, Internet vendors, and experimenters to expand their known applications.

You're in a great position to jump right into the Web revolution. Good luck!

HTML Elements and Special Characters

This appendix should serve as a reference when writing HTML documents. While this section is not a tutorial, it will be a helpful reference when you write and view HTML source code.

HTML 2.0 Elements

The following list describes HTML 2.0 elements in alphabetical order, according to the following:

Element name

Element tag(s):	<Correct element notation>
Element may contain:	Attributes or elements that may be used within: or subordinate to this element.
May be used within:	Elements to which this element may be subordinated.
Required attributes:	Attributes required for the correct use of this element.

A	**[anchor]**
Element tag(s):	<A> </A>
Element may contain:	HREF="..." NAME="..." REL="..." REV="..." URN="..." TITLE="..." METHODS="..." characters...<IMG> <EM> <STRONG> <CODE> <SAMP> <KBD> <VAR> <CITE> <TT> <B> <I> </A>
May be used within:	<ADDRESS> <B> <CITE> <CODE> <DD> <DT> <EM> <H1> <H2> <H3> <H4> <H5> <H6> <I> <KBD> <LI> <P> <PRE> <SAMP> <STRONG> <TT> <VAR>
Required attribute:	HREF="..." or NAME="..."

ADDRESS	
Element tag(s):	<ADDRESS> </ADDRESS>
Element may contain:	characters... <A> <IMG> <EM> <STRONG> <CODE> <SAMP> <KBD> <VAR> <CITE> <TT> <B> <I> <P> </ADDRESS>
May be used within:	<BLOCKQUOTE> <BODY> <FORM>

B	**[bold type face]**
Element tag(s):	<B> </B>
Element may contain:	characters... <A> <IMG> <EM> <STRONG> <CODE> <SAMP> <KBD> <VAR> <CITE> <TT> <B> <I> </B>
May be used within:	<A> <ADDRESS> <B> <CITE> <CODE> <DD> <DT> <EM> <H1> <H2> <H3> <H4> <H5> <H6> <I> <KBD> <LI> <P> <PRE> <SAMP> <STRONG> <TT> <VAR>

BASE	
Element tag(s):	<BASE>
Element may contain:	HREF="..." >
May be used within:	<HEAD>
Required attribute:	HREF="..."

BLOCKQUOTE

Element tag(s):	<BLOCKQUOTE></BLOCKQUOTE>
Element may contain:	<H1> <H2> <H3> <H4> <H5> <H6> <P> <UL> <OL> <DIR> <MENU> <DL> <PRE> <BLOCKQUOTE> <FORM> <ISINDEX> <HR> <ADDRESS> </BLOCKQUOTE>
May be used within:	<BLOCKQUOTE> <BODY> <DD> <FORM> <LI>

BODY

Element tag(s):	<BODY> </BODY>
Element may contain:	<H1> <H2> <H3> <H4> <H5> <H6> <P> <UL> <OL> <DIR> <MENU> <DL> <PRE> <BLOCKQUOTE> <FORM> <ISINDEX> <HR> <ADDRESS>
May be used within:	<HTML>

BR **[line break]**

Element tag(s):	
Element may contain:	
May be used within:	<A> <ADDRESS> <B> <CITE> <CODE> <DD> <DT> <EM> <H1> <H2> <H3> <H4> <H5> <H6> <I> <KBD> <LI> <P> <PRE> <SAMP> <STRONG> <TT> <VAR>

CITE

Element tag(s):	<CITE> </CITE>
Element may contain:	characters... <A> <IMG>
 <EM> <STRONG> <CODE> <SAMP> <KBD> <VAR> <CITE> <TT> <B> <I> </CITE>
May be used within:	<A> <ADDRESS> <B> <CITE> <CODE> <DD> <DT> <EM> <H1> <H2> <H3> <H4> <H5> <H6> <I> <KBD> <LI> <P> <PRE> <SAMP> <STRONG> <TT> <VAR>

CODE

Element tag(s):	<CODE> </CODE>
Element may contain:	characters... <A> <IMG>
 <EM> <STRONG> <CODE> <SAMP> <KBD> <VAR> <CITE> <TT> <B> <I> </CODE>

May be used within:	\<A> \<ADDRESS> \<B> \<CITE> \<CODE> \<DD> \<DT> \<EM> \<H1> \<H2> \<H3> \<H4> \<H5> \<H6> \<I> \<KBD> \<LI> \<P> \<PRE> \<SAMP> \<STRONG> \<TT> \<VAR>

DD [definition list definition]

Element tag(s):	\<DD>
Element may contain:	characters... \<A> \<IMG> \ \<EM> \<STRONG> \<CODE> \<SAMP> \<KBD> \<VAR> \<CITE> \<TT> \<B> \<I> \<P> \<UL> \<OL> \<DIR> \<MENU> \<DL> \<PRE> \<BLOCKQUOTE> \<FORM> \<ISINDEX>
May be used within:	\<DL>

DIR [directory list]

Element tag(s):	\<DIR>\</DIR>
Element may contain:	COMPACT \<LI>
May be used within:	\<BLOCKQUOTE> \<BODY> \<DD> \<FORM> \<LI>

DL [definition list]

Element tag(s):	\<DL>\</DL>
Element may contain:	COMPACT>\<DT> \<DD>
May be used within:	\<BLOCKQUOTE> \<BODY> \<DD> \<FORM> \<LI>

DT [definition list term]

Element tag(s):	\<DT>
Element may contain:	characters... \<A> \<IMG> \ \<EM> \<STRONG> \<CODE> \<SAMP> \<KBD> \<VAR> \<CITE> \<TT> \<B> \<I>
May be used within:	\<DL>

EM [emphasis]

Element tag(s):	\<EM> \</EM>
Element may contain:	characters... \<A> \<IMG> \ \<EM> \<STRONG> \<CODE> \<SAMP> \<KBD> \<VAR> \<CITE> \<TT> \<B> \<I> \</EM>
May be used within:	\<A> \<ADDRESS> \<B> \<CITE> \<CODE> \<DD> \<DT> \<EM> \<H1> \<H2> \<H3> \<H4> \<H5> \<H6> \<I> \<KBD> \<LI> \<P> \<PRE> \<SAMP> \<STRONG> \<TT> \<VAR>

FORM

Element tag(s):	\<FORM> \</FORM>
Element may contain:	ACTION="..." METHOD="..." ENCTYPE="..." >\<H1> \<H2> \<H3> \<H4> \<H5> \<H6> \<P> \<UL> \<OL> \<DIR> \<MENU> \<DL> \<PRE> \<BLOCKQUOTE> \<ISINDEX> \<HR> \<ADDRESS> \<INPUT> \<SELECT> \<TEXTAREA>
May be used within:	\<BLOCKQUOTE> \<BODY> \<DD> \<LI>
Required attribute:	ACTION="..." METHOD="..."

H1   **[heading level 1]**

Element tag(s):	\<H1> \</H1>
Element may contain:	characters... \<A> \<IMG> \ \<EM> \<STRONG> \<CODE> \<SAMP> \<KBD> \<VAR> \<CITE> \<TT> \<B> \<I>
May be used within:	\<BLOCKQUOTE> \<BODY> \<FORM>

H2   **[heading level 2]**

Element tag(s):	\<H2> \</H2>
Element may contain:	characters... \<A> \<IMG> \ \<EM> \<STRONG> \<CODE> \<SAMP> \<KBD> \<VAR> \<CITE> \<TT> \<B> \<I>
May be used within:	\<BLOCKQUOTE> \<BODY> \<FORM>

H3   **[heading level 3]**

Element tag(s):	\<H3> \</H3>
Element may contain:	characters... \<A> \<IMG> \ \<EM> \<STRONG> \<CODE> \<SAMP> \<KBD> \<VAR> \<CITE> \<TT> \<B> \<I>
May be used within:	\<BLOCKQUOTE> \<BODY> \<FORM>

H4   **[heading level 4]**

Element tag(s):	\<H4> \</H4>
Element may contain:	characters... \<A> \<IMG> \ \<EM> \<STRONG> \<CODE> \<SAMP> \<KBD> \<VAR> \<CITE> \<TT> \<B> \<I>
May be used within:	\<BLOCKQUOTE> \<BODY> \<FORM>

H5	**[heading level 5]**
Element tag(s):	<H5> </H5>
Element may contain:	characters... <A> <IMG> <EM> <STRONG> <CODE> <SAMP> <KBD> <VAR> <CITE> <TT> <B> <I>
May be used within:	<BLOCKQUOTE> <BODY> <FORM>

H6	**[heading level 6]**
Element tag(s):	<H6> </H6>
Element may contain:	characters... <A> <IMG> <EM> <STRONG> <CODE> <SAMP> <KBD> <VAR> <CITE> <TT> <B> <I>
May be used within:	<BLOCKQUOTE> <BODY> <FORM>

HEAD	
Element tag(s):	<HEAD> </HEAD>
Element may contain:	<TITLE> <ISINDEX> <BASE> <META> <NEXTID> <LINK>
May be used within:	<HTML>

HR	**[horizontal rule]**
Element tag(s):	<HR>
Element may contain:	<HR>
May be used within:	<BLOCKQUOTE> <BODY> <FORM> <PRE>

HTML	
Element tag(s):	<HTML> </HTML>
Element may contain:	<HEAD> <BODY>
May be used within:	These elements are used to describe the entire document. <HTML> signifies the beginning of the document, while </HTML> signifies the end of the document.

I	**[italics]**
Element tag(s):	<I> </I>
Element may contain:	characters... <A> <IMG> <EM> <STRONG> <CODE> <SAMP> <KBD> <VAR> <CITE> <TT> <B> <I> </I>

May be used within:	\<A\> \<ADDRESS\> \<B\> \<CITE\> \<CODE\> \<DD\> \<DT\> \<EM\> \<H1\> \<H2\> \<H3\> \<H4\> \<H5\> \<H6\> \<I\> \<KBD\> \<LI\> \<P\> \<PRE\> \<SAMP\> \<STRONG\> \<TT\> \<VAR\>

IMG [image]

Element tag(s):	\<IMG\>
Element may contain:	SRC="..." ALT="..." ALIGN="..." ISMAP
May be used within:	\<A\> \<ADDRESS\> \<B\> \<CITE\> \<CODE\> \<DD\> \<DT\> \<EM\> \<H1\> \<H2\> \<H3\> \<H4\> \<H5\> \<H6\> \<I\> \<KBD\> \<LI\> \<P\> \<SAMP\> \<STRONG\> \<TT\> \<VAR\>
Required attribute:	SRC="..."

INPUT

Element tag(s):	\<INPUT\>
Element may contain:	TYPE="..." NAME="..." VALUE="..." SRC="..." CHECKED SIZE="..." MAXLENGTH="..." ALIGN="..."
May be used within:	\<FORM\>
Required attribute:	TYPE="..." NAME="..."

ISINDEX

Element tag(s):	\<ISINDEX\>
Element may contain:	\<ISINDEX\>
May be used within:	\<HEAD\>

KBD [keyboard input text]

Element tag(s):	\<KBD\> \</KBD\>
Element may contain:	characters... \<A\> \<IMG\> \<BR\> \<EM\> \<STRONG\> \<CODE\> \<SAMP\> \<KBD\> \<VAR\> \<CITE\> \<TT\> \<B\> \<I\> \</KBD\>
May be used within:	\<A\> \<ADDRESS\> \<B\> \<CITE\> \<CODE\> \<DD\> \<DT\> \<EM\> \<H1\> \<H2\> \<H3\> \<H4\> \<H5\> \<H6\> \<I\> \<KBD\> \<LI\> \<P\> \<PRE\> \<SAMP\> \<STRONG\> \<TT\> \<VAR\>

LI	**[regular list element]**
Element tag(s):	<LI>
Element may contain:	characters... <A> <IMG> <EM> <STRONG> <CODE> <SAMP> <KBD> <VAR> <CITE> <TT> <B> <I> <P> <UL> <OL> <DIR> <MENU> <DL> <PRE> <BLOCKQUOTE> <FORM> <ISINDEX>
May be used within:	<DIR> <MENU> <OL> <UL>

LINK	
Element tag(s):	<LINK>
Element may contain:	HREF="..." REL="..." REV="..." URN="..." TITLE="..." METHODS="..."
May be used within:	<HEAD>
Required attribute:	HREF="..."

MENU	**[menu list]**
Element tag(s):	<MENU></MENU>
Element may contain:	COMPACT <LI>
May be used within:	<BLOCKQUOTE> <BODY> <DD> <FORM> <LI>

META	
Element tag(s):	<META>
Element may contain:	HTTP-EQUIV="..." NAME="..." CONTENT="..."
May be used within:	<HEAD>
Required attribute:	HTTP-EQUIV="..."

NEXTID	
Element tag(s):	<NEXTID>
Element may contain:	N="..."
May be used within:	<HEAD>
Required attribute:	N="..."

OL	**[ordered list]**
Element tag(s):	<OL></OL>
Element may contain:	COMPACT <LI>
May be used within:	<BLOCKQUOTE> <BODY> <DD> <FORM> <LI>

OPTION

Element tag(s):	<OPTION>
Element may contain:	SELECTED VALUE="..." characters...
May be used within:	<SELECT>

P   [paragraph]

Element tag(s):	<P>
Element may contain:	characters... <A> <IMG> <EM> <STRONG> <CODE> <SAMP> <KBD> <VAR> <CITE> <TT> <B> <I>
May be used within:	<ADDRESS> <BLOCKQUOTE> <BODY> <DD> <FORM> <LI>

PRE   [pre-formatted text]

Element tag(s):	<PRE> </PRE>
Element may contain:	WIDTH="..." characters... <A> <HR> <TT> <B> <I> <EM> <STRONG> <CODE> <SAMP> <KBD> <VAR> <CITE>
May be used within:	<BLOCKQUOTE> <BODY> <DD> <FORM> <LI>

SAMP

Element tag(s):	<SAMP> </SAMP>
Element may contain:	characters... <A> <IMG> <EM> <STRONG> <CODE> <SAMP> <KBD> <VAR> <CITE> <TT> <B> <I> </SAMP>
May be used within:	<A> <ADDRESS> <B> <CITE> <CODE> <DD> <DT> <EM> <H1> <H2> <H3> <H4> <H5> <H6> <I> <KBD> <LI> <P> <PRE> <SAMP> <STRONG> <TT> <VAR>

SELECT

Element tag(s):	<SELECT></SELECT>
Element may contain:	NAME="..." SIZE="..." MULTIPLE <OPTION>
May be used within:	<FORM>
Required attribute:	NAME="..."

STRONG   **[strong emphasis]**

Element tag(s):   <STRONG> </STRONG>

Element may contain: characters... <A> <IMG>
 <EM> <STRONG>
                               <CODE> <SAMP> <KBD> <VAR> <CITE> <TT> <B>
                               <I> </STRONG>

May be used within: <A> <ADDRESS> <B> <CITE> <CODE> <DD> <DT>
                               <EM> <H1> <H2> <H3> <H4> <H5> <H6> <I>
                               <KBD> <LI> <P> <PRE> <SAMP> <STRONG> <TT>
                               <VAR>

TEXTAREA

Element tag(s):   <TEXTAREA> </TEXTAREA>

Element may contain: NAME="..." ROWS="..." COLS="..." > characters...

May be used within: <FORM>

Required attribute: NAME="..." ROWS="..." COLS="..."

TITLE

Element tag(s):   <TITLE> </TITLE>

Element may contain: characters...

May be used within: <HEAD>

TT   **[fixed width typewriter font]**

Element tag(s):   <TT> </TT>

Element may contain: characters... <A> <IMG>
 <EM> <STRONG>
                               <CODE> <SAMP> <KBD> <VAR> <CITE> <TT> <B>
                               <I> </TT>

May be used within: <A> <ADDRESS> <B> <CITE> <CODE> <DD> <DT>
                               <EM> <H1> <H2> <H3> <H4> <H5> <H6> <I>
                               <KBD> <LI> <P> <PRE> <SAMP> <STRONG> <TT>
                               <VAR>

UL   **[unordered list]**

Element tag(s):   <UL></UL>

Element may contain: COMPACT <LI>

May be used within: <BLOCKQUOTE> <BODY> <DD> <FORM> <LI>

VAR

Element tag(s):	<VAR> </VAR>
Element may contain:	characters... <A> <IMG> <EM> <STRONG> <CODE> <SAMP> <KBD> <VAR> <CITE> <TT> <B> <I> </VAR>
May be used within:	<A> <ADDRESS> <B> <CITE> <CODE> <DD> <DT> <EM> <H1> <H2> <H3> <H4> <H5> <H6> <I> <KBD> <LI> <P> <PRE> <SAMP> <STRONG> <TT> <VAR>

Supplemental HTML Elements

The following list indicates modified or supplemental HTML elements and attributes that are currently used by the Netscape 1.1 browser.

These extensions are not part of the current HTML Document Type Definition and are not necessarily supported by other browsers. Some of these elements and attributes may be included in a future version of HTML (HTML 3.0), but probably not without some modification.

Text

<BR CLEAR=(left | right | all)> This is used to modify the <BR> element so that the next line is placed in relation to the margins of the display window. Used in relation to the <IMG> attribute extensions described above.

<NOBR> No Break determines that text contained by <NOBR> </NOBR> will not allow line breaks as it is displayed.

<WBR> Word Break is used to indicate the location of possible break locations in a <NOBR> statement. <WBR> element does not force a line break. It notes the break location if one is needed for display by the client application.

<FONT SIZE=(1,7 | +,-)> is used to specify type size. The allowed range is 1 through 7, and may include positive or negative notation to indicate values relative to the default <BASEFONT> size.

<BASEFONT SIZE=(1,7)> is used to specify the type size referred to by <FONT SIZE= > statements. The default SIZE=3.

<CENTER> </CENTER> is used to specify alignment of text relative to current window margins.

ALIGN=CENTER can also be used to align text within a paragraph or heading element.

Lists

<UL TYPE=(disc | circle | square)> is used to determine the shape of bullets displayed in an Unordered List.

<OL TYPE=(A | a | I | i | 1)> is used to determine the outline notation used in an Ordered List. The default notation is numeric. The alternate orders are alphabetic (A) upper or (a) lower case and Roman numeral (I) upper and (i) lower case.

<OL START=(number | letter)> is used to determine the beginning note in an Ordered List, based on either the default notation, or the TYPE= notation. <OL TYPE=1 START=5> will display a list that begins with the numbered item 5.

<LI TYPE=disc | circle | square | A | a | I | i | 1> is used to determine the notation type of individual List Items and for all subsequent List Items in a list. The TYPE= value available is dependent upon the major list elements <OL> and <UL>.

<LI VALUE=(number | letter)> is used to determine the notation of an individual List Item and subsequent items in an Ordered List.

Images

<IMG ALIGN=(left | right)> is used to position an inline image at either side of a display window with following text wrapped along the alternate side of the window and below the <IMG>.

<IMG ALIGN=texttop> is used to align the image with the top of the tallest text in the line (this is usually but not always the same as ALIGN=top).

<IMG ALIGN=middle> is used to align the baseline of the current line with the middle of the image.

<IMG ALIGN=absmiddle> is used to align the middle of the current line with the middle of the image.

<IMG ALIGN=baseline> is used to align the bottom of the image with the baseline of the current line.

<IMG ALIGN=absbottom> is used to align the bottom of the image with the bottom of the current line.

<IMG WIDTH=(pixels) HEIGHT=(pixels)> is used to indicate the size in pixels of the inline image. If specified, the client application does not need to fully download the image in order to calculate the size required for display.

<IMG BORDER=(pixels)> is used to determine the thickness of the border shown around an image.

<IMG VSPACE=(pixels) HSPACE=(pixels)> is used to determine spacing between the image and other elements above, below, or to either side of the image.

Tables

<TABLE> </TABLE> is used to markup all elements and attributes used to describe a table. A table displays text or other data in rows and columns that are defined by subordinate elements used within these tags.

<TR> </TR> indicates a row of table data cells. There can be as many table rows as required to present the table.

<TD> </TD> is used to mark up each set of data as cells of data. Table data elements are written within the <TR></TR> element, and each data element is displayed as an column entry.

<TH> </TH> is used to markup table header cells, which display as column headings for the table.

<CAPTION> </CAPTION> is used to markup a caption for the table. Captions are written within the <TABLE> element, but below the last row of cells. Captions can be modified to either ALIGN=TOP or ALIGN=BOTTOM. The default alignment is TOP.

BORDER is used with <TABLE> to define a border for the entire table.

BORDER=(number) can be used to specify the pixel width of the border. The border outlines the table and runs between rows and columns.

ALIGN=(TOP | BOTTOM) defines the alignment of the caption in relation to the table row above it.

ALIGN=(LEFT | CENTER | RIGHT) defines the horizontal alignment of cell contents inside the table cell boundaries.

VALIGN=(TOP | MIDDLE | BOTTOM | BASELINE) defines the vertical alignment of cell content within the cell, or to specify that all cells in a row are aligned to the same baseline.

NOWRAP prevents cell content from wrapping within the cell.

COLSPAN=(number) specifies the width of the cell in columns. The default value is 1 column.

ROWSPAN=(number) specifies the height of the cell in rows. A cell cannot be higher than the existing rows of the table. The default value is 1.

CELLSPACING=(number) inserts spacing between cells in a table. The default spacing is 2.

CELLPADDING=(number) inserts space between the cell content and the boundary of the cell. The default padding is 1.

Other Elements

<ISINDEX PROMPT="text"> enables the document author to specify a message, other than the default message, that will appear before the text input field of the index. The default message is: "This is a searchable index. Enter search keywords."

<BLINK> </BLINK> is used to specify that the contained text will display against an alternately highlighted / normal background color.

<HR> displays a shaded engraved line drawn across the page.

<HR SIZE=(pixels)> used to set the thickness of the displayed horizontal rule.

<HR WIDTH=(pixels | percent)> used to set the width of the horizontal rule across the displayed page. The default width is the width of the displayed page. WIDTH= is a value in number of pixels or percent of display window.

<HR ALIGN=(left | right | center)> use to align the position of the horizontal rule relative to the side margins of the displayed page.

<HR NOSHADE> used to define the horizontal rule as a solid line.

Special Characters

This portion of appendix A describes characters that are reserved for mark-up purposes. While web browsers will let you code these items, it may not be able to interpret every character that you code for. If you set your Web browser for a font that doesn't include a particular character, the character displays as a small box.

Name	Syntax	Description
&reg	Registered Trademark	&reg
&copy	Copyright	&copy
Quote	&quot	double quote mark
Ampersand	&amp	ampersand
Less than	&lt	right angle bracket
Greater than	&gt	left angle bracket
Aacute	&Aacute	Capital A, acute accent
Agrave	&Agrave	Capital A, grave accent
Acirc	&Acirc	Capital A, circumflex accent
Atilde	&Atilde	Capital A, tilde
Aring	&Aring	Capital A, ring
Auml	&Auml	Capital A, dieresis or umlaut mark
AElig	&AElig	Capital AE dipthong (ligature)
Ccedil	&Ccedil	Capital C, cedilla
Eacute	&Eacute	Capital E, acute accent
Egrave	&Egrave	Capital E, grave accent
Ecirc	&Ecirc	Capital E, circumflex accent
Euml	&Euml	Capital E, dieresis or umlaut mark
Iacute	&Iacute	Capital I, acute accent
Igrave	&Igrave	Capital I, grave accent
Icirc	&Icirc	Capital I, circumflex accent
Iuml	&Iuml	Capital I, dieresis or umlaut mark
ETH	&ETH	Capital Eth, Icelandic
Ntilde	&Ntilde	Capital N, tilde
Oacute	&Oacute	Capital O, acute accent
Ograve	&Ograve	Capital O, grave accent
Ocirc	&Ocirc	Capital O, circumflex accent
Otilde	&Otilde	Capital O, tilde
Ouml	&Ouml	Capital O, dieresis or umlaut mark
Oslash	&Oslash	Capital O, slash
Uacute	&Uacute	Capital U, acute accent

Name	Syntax	Description
Ugrave	&Ugrave	Capital U, grave accent
Ucirc	&Ucirc	Capital U, circumflex accent
Uuml	&Uuml	Capital U, dieresis or umlaut mark
Yacute	&Yacute	Capital Y, acute accent
THORN	&THORN	Capital THORN, Icelandic
szlig	&szlig	Small sharp s, German (sz ligature)
aacute	&aacute	Small a, acute accent
agrave	&agrave	Small a, grave accent
acirc	&acirc	Small a, circumflex accent
atilde	&atilde	Small a, tilde
atilde	&atilde	Small a, tilde
auml	&auml	Small a, dieresis or umlaut mark
aelig	&aelig	Small ae, dipthong (ligature)
ccedil	&ccedil	Small c, cedilla
eacute	&eacute	Small e, acute accent
egrave	&egrave	Small e, grave accent
ecirc	&ecirc	Small e, circumflex accent
euml	&euml	Small e, dieresis or umlaut mark
iacute	&iacute	Small i, acute accent
igrave	&igrave	Small i, grave accent
icirc	&icirc	Small i, circumflex accent
iuml	&iuml	Small i, dieresis or umlaut mark
eth	&eth	Small eth, Icelandic
ntilde	&ntilde	Small n, tilde
oacute	&oacute	Small o, acute accent
ograve	&ograve	Small o, grave accent
ocirc	&ocirc	Small o, circumflex accent
otilde	&otilde	Small o, tilde
ouml	&ouml	Small o, dieresis or umlaut mark

Name	Syntax	Description
oslash	&oslash	Small o, slash
uacute	&uacute	Small u, acute accent
ugrave	&ugrave	Small u, grave accent
ucirc	&ucirc	Small u, circumflex accent
uuml	&uuml	Small u, dieresis or umlaut mark
yacute	&yacute	Small y, acute accent
thorn	&thorn	Small thorn, Icelandic
yuml	&yuml	Small y, dieresis or umlaut mark

Glossary of Internet Terms

This glossary of terms includes excerpts from Internet RFC 1392 and FYI 18, (January 1993), written by Tracy LaQuey Parker and Gary Scott Malkin and used with permission.

RFC 1392 provides information for the Internet community. It does not specify an Internet standard. Distribution of RFC 1392 is unlimited and is available in its complete form at: `http://ds.internic.net/ds/dspg1intdoc.html`

10BaseT   A variant of Ethernet which allows stations to be attached via twisted pair cable. *See also: Ethernet, twisted pair.*

802.x   The set of IEEE standards for the definition of LAN protocols. *See also: IEEE.*

Acceptable Use Policy (AUP)   Many transit networks have policies which restrict the use to which the network may be put. A well known example is NSFNET's AUP which does not allow commercial use. Enforcement of AUPs varies with the network. *See also: National Science Foundation.*

Access Control List (ACL)   Most network security systems operate by allowing selective use of services. An Access Control List is the usual means by which access to, and denial of, services is controlled. It is simply a list of the services available, each with a list of the hosts permitted to use the service.

acknowledgment (ACK)   A type of message sent to indicate that a block of data arrived at its destination without error. *See also: Negative Acknowledgment.*

address   There are three types of addresses in common use within the Internet. They are: email address; IP, internet or Internet address; and hardware or MAC address. *See also: email address, IP address, internet address, MAC address.*

address mask   A bit mask used to identify which bits in an IP address correspond to the network and subnet portions of the address. This mask is often referred to as the subnet mask because the network portion of the address can be determined by the encoding inherent in an IP address.

address resolution   Conversion of an internet address into the corresponding physical address.

Address Resolution Protocol (ARP)   Used to dynamically discover the low level physical network hardware address that corresponds to the high level IP address for a given host. ARP is limited to physical network systems that support broadcast packets that can be heard by all hosts on the network. *See also: proxy.*

Administrative Domain (AD)   A collection of hosts and routers, and the interconnecting network(s), managed by a single administrative authority.

Advanced Research Projects Agency Network (ARPANET)   A pioneering longhaul network funded by ARPA (now DARPA). It served as the basis for early networking research, as well as a central backbone during the development of the Internet. The ARPANET consisted of individual packet switching computers interconnected by leased lines. *See also: Defense Advanced Research Projects Agency.*

agent   In the client-server model, the part of the system that performs information preparation and exchange on behalf of a client or server application.

aiff   Audio file format used by Macintosh computers, and a typical file format found on the WWW.

American National Standards Institute (ANSI)   This organization is responsible for approving U.S. standards in many areas, including computers and communications. Standards approved by this organization are often called ANSI standards (e.g., ANSI C is the version of the C language approved by ANSI). ANSI is a member of ISO. *See also: International Organization for Standardization.*

anonymous FTP   Anonymous FTP allows a user to retrieve documents, files, programs, and other archived data from anywhere in the Internet without having to establish a userid and password. By using the special userid of "anonymous", the network user will bypass local security checks and will have access to publicly accessible files on the remote system. *See also: archive site, File Transfer Protocol.*

ANSI   See: American National Standards Institute

Appletalk   A networking protocol developed by Apple Computer for communication between Apple Computer products and other computers. This protocol is independent of the network layer on which it is run. Current implementations exist for LocalTalk, a 235Kb/s local area network; and EtherTalk, a 10M/s local area network.

application   A program that performs a function directly for a user. FTP, mail and Telnet clients are examples of network applications. Microsoft Word is an example of a word processing application.

application layer   The top layer of the network protocol stack. The application layer is concerned with the semantics of work (e.g., formatting electronic mail messages). How to represent that data and how to reach the foreign node are issues for lower layers of the network.

archie   A system to automatically gather, index, and serve information on the Internet. The initial implementation of archie provided an indexed directory of filenames from all anonymous FTP archives on the Internet. Later versions provide other collections of information. *See also: archive site, Gopher, Prospero, Wide Area Information Servers.*

archive site   A machine that provides access to a collection of files across the Internet. An "anonymous FTP archive site," for example, provides access to this material via the FTP protocol. *See also: anonymous FTP, archie, Gopher, Wide Area Information Servers.*

ARPA   See: Defense Advanced Research Projects Agency

ARPANET   See: Advanced Research Projects Agency Network

ASCII   See: American Standard Code for Information Interchange

au   Audio file format used on Sun and NeXT computers, and a typical file format found on the WWW.

Audio Interchange File Format (AIFF)   A sound format developed by Apple Computer.

authentication   The verification of the identity of a person or process.

bandwidth   Technically, the difference in Hertz (Hz) between the highest and lowest frequencies of a transmission channel. However, as typically used, it is the amount of data that can be sent through a given communications circuit.

baseband   A transmission medium through which digital signals are sent without complicated frequency shifting. In general, only one communication channel is available at any given time. Ethernet is an example of a baseband network. *See also: broadband, Ethernet.*

binary   A number format using only digits 0 and 1, as in 11001001.

BinHex   A file format where binary data is converted into ASCII text.

Bitnet   An academic computer network that provides interactive electronic mail and file transfer services, using a store-and-forward protocol, based on IBM Network Job Entry protocols.

bounce   The return of a piece of mail because of an error in its delivery.

broadband   A transmission medium capable of supporting a wide range of frequencies. It can carry multiple signals by dividing the total capacity of the medium into multiple, independent bandwidth channels, where each channel operates only on a specific range of frequencies. *See also: baseband.*

broadcast   A special type of multicast packet which all nodes on the network are always willing to receive. *See also: multicast.*

Bulletin Board System (BBS)   A computer, and associated software, which typically provides electronic messaging services, archives of files, and any other services or activities of interest to the bulletin board system's operator. Although BBSs have traditionally been the domain of hobbyists, an increasing number of BBSs are connected directly to the Internet, and many BBSs are currently operated by government, educational, and research institutions. *See also: Electronic Mail, Internet, Usenet.*

Campus Wide Information System (CWIS)   A CWIS makes information and services publicly available on campus via kiosks, and makes interactive computing available via kiosks, interactive computing systems, and campus networks. Services routinely include directory information, calendars, bulletin boards, and databases.

CERN   The European Particle Physics Laboratory, a sub-atomic particle accelerator lab in Geneva, Switzerland, and original developer/implementor of the HyperText Transfer Protocol and HyperText Markup Language.

CGI   A Common Gateway Interface application, used by a Web server to provide additional processes, such as indexing documents on a server, translating image-map coordinates to URL addresses, or processing a fill-out form.

checksum A computed value which is dependent upon the contents of a packet. This value is sent along with the packet when it is transmitted. The receiving system computes a new checksum based upon the received data and compares this value with the one sent with the packet. If the two values are the same, the receiver has a high degree of confidence that the data was received correctly.

circuit switching A communications paradigm in which a dedicated communication path is established between two hosts, and on which all packets travel. The telephone system is an example of a circuit switched network. *See also: connection-oriented, connectionless, packet switching.*

client A computer system or process that requests a service of another computer system or process. A workstation requesting the contents of a file from a file server is a client of the file server. *See also: client-server model, server.*

client-server model A common way to describe the paradigm of many network protocols. Examples include the name-server/name-resolver relationship in DNS and the file-server/file-client relationship in NFS. *See also: client, server, Domain Name System, Network File System.*

Common Gateway Interface See: CGI.

congestion Congestion occurs when the offered load exceeds the capacity of a data communication path.

cracker A cracker is an individual who attempts to access computer systems without authorization. These individuals are often malicious, as opposed to hackers, and have many means at their disposal for breaking into a system. *See also: hacker, Trojan Horse, virus, worm.*

Cyberspace A term coined by William Gibson in his fantasy novel *Neuromancer* to describe the "world" of computers, and the society that gathers around them.

DARPA See: Defense Advanced Research Projects Agency

Data Encryption Key (DEK) Used for the encryption of message text and for the computation of message integrity checks (signatures). *See also: encryption.*

Defense Advanced Research Projects Agency (DARPA) An agency of the U.S. Department of Defense responsible for the development of new technology for use by the military. DARPA (formerly known as ARPA) was responsible for funding much of the development of the Internet we know today, including the Berkeley version of Unix and TCP/IP.

dialup A temporary, as opposed to dedicated, connection between machines established over a standard phone line.

distributed database   A collection of several different data repositories that looks like a single database to the user. A prime example in the Internet is the Domain Name System.

DNS   See: Domain Name System

document   A file or unit of information sent from servers to clients; a document may contain plain or formatted text, inlined graphics, sound, other multimedia data, or hyperlinks to other documents.

domain   "Domain" is a heavily overused term in the Internet. It can be used in the Administrative Domain context, or the Domain Name context. *See also: Administrative Domain, Domain Name System.*

Domain Name System (DNS)   The DNS is a general purpose distributed, replicated, data query service. The principal use is the lookup of host IP addresses based on host names. The style of host names now used in the Internet is called "domain name," because they are the style of names used to look up anything in the DNS. Some important domains are: .COM (commercial), .EDU (educational), .NET (network operations), .GOV (U.S. government), and .MIL (U.S. military). Most countries also have a domain. For example, .US (United States), .UK (United Kingdom), .AU (Australia).

dot address (dotted decimal notation)   Dot address refers to the common notation for IP addresses of the form A.B.C.D; where each letter represents, in decimal, one byte of a four byte IP address. *See also: IP address.*

Electronic Frontier Foundation (EFF)   A foundation established to address social and legal issues arising from the impact on society of the increasingly pervasive use of computers as a means of communication and information distribution.

Electronic Mail (email)   A system whereby a computer user can exchange messages with other computer users (or groups of users) via a communications network. Electronic mail is one of the most popular uses of the Internet.

email address   The domain-based or UUCP address that is used to send electronic mail to a specified destination. For example, an editor's address is "gmalkin@xylogics.com".

encryption   Encryption is the manipulation of a packet's data in order to prevent any but the intended recipient from reading that data. There are many types of data encryption, and they are the basis of network security. *See also: Data Encryption Standard.*

Ethernet   A 10M/s standard for LANs, initially developed by Xerox, and later refined by Digital, Intel, and Xerox (DIX). All hosts are connected to a coaxial cable where they contend for network access using a Carrier Sense Multiple Access with Collision Detection (CSMA/CD) paradigm. *See also: 802.x, Local Area Network, token ring.*

European Academic and Research Network (EARN)   A network connecting European academic and research institutions with electronic mail and file transfer services using the Bitnet protocol.

external viewer   A software program used by a Web browser to view file formats that the browser itself does not support, also known as a helper application.

FAQ   Frequently Asked Question.

Federal Information Exchange (FIX)   One of the connection points between the American governmental internets and the Internet.

Federal Networking Council (FNC)   The coordinating group of representatives from those federal agencies involved in the development and use of federal networking, especially those networks using TCP/IP and the Internet. Current members include representatives from DOD, DOE, DARPA, NSF, NASA, and HHS. *See also: Defense Advanced Research Projects Agency, National Science Foundation.*

Fiber Distributed Data Interface (FDDI)   A high-speed (100M/s) LAN standard. The underlying medium is fiber optics, and the topology is a dual-attached, counter-rotating token ring. *See also: Local Area Network, token ring.*

file transfer   The copying of a file from one computer to another over a computer network. *See also: File Transfer Protocol.*

File Transfer Protocol (FTP)   A protocol which allows a user on one host to access and transfer files to and from another host over a network. Also, FTP is usually the name of the program the user invokes to execute the protocol. *See also: anonymous FTP.*

finger   A program that displays information about a particular user, or all users, logged on the local system or on a remote system. It typically shows full name, last login time, idle time, terminal line, and terminal location (where applicable). It may also display plan and project files left by the user.

flame   A strong opinion and/or criticism of something, usually as a frank inflammatory statement, in an electronic mail message. It is common to precede a flame with an indication of pending fire (i.e., FLAME ON!). Flame Wars occur when people start flaming other people for flaming when they shouldn't have.

FTP   See: File Transfer Protocol

Fully Qualified Domain Name (FQDN)   The FQDN is the full name of a system, rather than just its hostname. For example, "venera" is a hostname and "venera.isi.edu" is an FQDN. *See also: hostname, Domain Name System.*

gateway   The term "router" is now used in place of the original definition of "gateway." Currently, a gateway is a communications device/program which passes data between networks having similar functions but dissimilar implementations. This should not be confused with a protocol converter. By this definition, a router is a layer 3 (network layer) gateway, and a mail gateway is a layer 7 (application layer) gateway. *See also: mail gateway, router.*

GIF   The Graphic Image Format developed by CompuServe to store 8-bit color graphics in compressed form.

Gopher   A distributed information service that makes available hierarchical collections of information across the Internet. Gopher uses a simple protocol that allows a single Gopher client to access information from any accessible Gopher server, providing the user with a single "Gopher space" of information. Public domain versions of the client and server are available. *See also: archie, archive site, Wide Area Information Servers.*

hacker   A person who delights in having an intimate understanding of the internal workings of a system, computers, and computer networks in particular. The term is often misused in a pejorative context, where "cracker" would be the correct term. *See also: cracker.*

header   The portion of a packet, preceding the actual data, containing source and destination addresses, and error checking and other fields. A header is also the part of an electronic mail message that precedes the body of a message and contains, among other things, the message originator, date, and time.

hierarchical routing   The complex problem of routing on large networks can be simplified by reducing the size of the networks. This is accomplished by breaking a network into a hierarchy of networks, where each level is responsible for its own routing.

home page   The document initially displayed when starting up a Web browser, usually containing frequently used hyperlinks, personal notes, or other user-customized information. Also used to refer to the index page of a Web server, the main or directory document of a server. Also used to describe a personalized page on a Web server.

hop   A term used in routing. A path to a destination on a network is a series of hops, through routers, away from the origin.

host   A computer that allows users to communicate with other host computers on a network. Individual users communicate by using application programs, such as electronic mail, Telnet, and FTP.

hostname   The name given to a machine.

hotlist   A custom reference of World Wide Web documents, compiled by the user of a browser application and stored by that application as a preference file or HTML document.

HTML   HyperText Markup Language, the markup language used to define the various elements of a World Wide Web document

.html   The extension appended to a file that is written using the HyperText Markup Language.

HTTP   HyperText Transfer Protocol, the data transfer protocol used by Web servers and browsers to communicate with each other.

hub   A device connected to several other devices. In ARCnet, a hub is used to connect several computers together. In a message handling service, a hub is used for the transfer of messages across the network.

hyperlink   An HTML anchor element that links one document to another, or otherwise embeds a Uniform Resource Locator into a document. In a graphical browser, a hyperlink is displayed as a color highlighted and/or underlined word or graphic.

HyperText Markup Language   The collection of text markup elements used to format hyperlinked documents for use by HTTP applications.

HyperText Transfer Protocol   The transmission and software standard used by Web clients and server applications to transfer data. *See also: HTTP.*

inline image   A graphic image that is linked to a document using an HTML <IMG SRC=> element, and displayed inside the document window by the browser application.

Integrated Services Digital Network (ISDN)   An emerging technology which is beginning to be offered by the telephone carriers of the world. ISDN combines voice and digital network services in a single medium, making it possible to offer customers digital data services as well as voice connections through a single "wire."

International Organization for Standardization (ISO)   A voluntary, nontreaty organization founded in 1946 which is responsible for creating international standards in many areas, including computers and communications. Its members are the national standards organizations of the 89 member countries, including ANSI for the U.S.

internet   While an internet is a network, the term "internet" is usually used to refer to a collection of networks interconnected with routers. *See also: network.*

Internet (note the capital "I")   The Internet is the largest internet in the world. It is a three-level hierarchy composed of backbone networks (e.g., NSFNET, MILNET), mid-level networks, and stub networks. The Internet is a multiprotocol internet.

internet address   An IP address that uniquely identifies a node on an internet. An Internet address (capital "I"), uniquely identifies a node on the Internet.

Internet Architecture Board (IAB)   The technical body that oversees the development of the Internet suite of protocols.

Internet Protocol (IP)   The Internet Protocol is the network layer for the TCP/IP Protocol Suite. It is a connectionless, best-effort packet-switching protocol.

Internet Relay Chat (IRC)   A world-wide "party line" protocol that allows one to converse with others in real time. IRC is structured as a network of servers, each of which accepts connections from client programs, one per user.

IP address   The 32-bit address defined by the Internet Protocol. It is usually represented in dotted decimal notation. *See also: dot address, internet address, Internet Protocol, netw.*

ISDN   See: Integrated Services Digital Network

JPEG   The 24-bit image file format developed by the Joint Photographic Expert Group that stores digital photographic files in a compressed form.

Kerberos   Kerberos is the security system of MIT's Project Athena. It is based on symmetric key cryptography. *See also: encryption.*

Kermit   A popular file transfer protocol developed by Columbia University. Because Kermit runs in most operating environments, it provides an easy method of file transfer. Kermit is NOT the same as FTP. *See also: File Transfer Protocol.*

Knowbot   An experimental directory service. *See also: white pages, WHOIS, X.500.*

LAN   See: Local Area Network

layer   Communication networks for computers may be organized as a set of more or less independent protocols, each in a different layer (also called level). The lowest layer governs direct host-to-host communication between the hardware at different hosts; the highest consists of user applications. Each layer builds on the layer beneath it. For each layer, programs at different hosts use protocols appropriate to the layer to communicate with each other. TCP/IP has five layers of protocols. The advantages of different layers of protocols is that the methods of passing information from one layer to another are specified clearly as part of the protocol suite, and changes within a protocol layer are prevented from affecting the other layers. This greatly simplifies the task of designing and maintaining communication programs.

listserv   An automated mailing list distribution system originally designed for the Bitnet/EARN network. *See also: mailing list.*

Local Area Network (LAN)   A data network intended to serve an area of only a few square kilometers or less. Because the network is known to cover only a small area, optimizations can be made in the network signal protocols that permit data rates up to 100M/s. *See also: Ethernet, token ring, Wide Area Network.*

Lurking   No active participation on the part of a subscriber to a mailing list or USENET newsgroup. A person who is lurking is just listening to the discussion. Lurking is encouraged for beginners who need to get up to speed on the history of the group. *See also: mailing list, Usenet.*

MacTCP   System software from Apple Computer that enables the use of TCP/IP through Macintosh network interface circuits.

mail gateway   A machine that connects two or more electronic mail systems (including dissimilar mail systems) and transfers messages between them. Sometimes the mapping and translation can be quite complex, and it generally requires a store-and-forward scheme whereby the message is received from one system completely before it is transmitted to the next system, after suitable translations. *See also: electronic mail.*

mail path   A series of machine names used to direct electronic mail from one user to another. This system of email addressing has been used primarily in UUCP networks which are trying to eliminate its use altogether. *See also: email address.*

mail server   A software program that distributes files or information in response to requests sent via email. Internet examples include Almanac and netlib. Mail servers have also been used in Bitnet to provide FTP-like services.

mailing list   A discussion group in which people send messages to each other via email. Generally, a mailing list is used to discuss certain set of topics, and different mailing lists discuss different topics. A mailing list may be moderated. This means that messages sent to the list are actually sent to a moderator who determines whether or not to send the messages on to everyone else.

Metropolitan Area Network (MAN)   A data network intended to serve an area approximating that of a large city. Such networks are being implemented by innovative techniques, such as running fiber cables through subway tunnels. *See also: Local Area Network, Wide Area Network.*

MIME   See: Multipurpose Internet Mail Extensions

moderator   A person, or small group of people, who manage moderated mailing lists and newsgroups. Moderators are responsible for determining which email submissions are passed on to list. *See also: Electronic Mail, mailing list, Usenet.*

MPEG   Compressed video or multiple frame graphic format developed by the Moving Pictures Experts Group.

MUD   See: Multi-User Dungeon

Multipurpose Internet Mail Extensions (MIME)   An extension to Internet email which provides the ability to transfer nontextual data, such as graphics, audio, and fax.

Multi-User Dungeon (MUD)   Adventure, roleplaying games, or simulations played on the Internet. Devotees call them "text-based virtual reality adventures." The games can feature fantasy combat, booby traps, and magic. Players interact in real time and can change the "world" in the game as they play it.

name resolution   The process of mapping a name into its corresponding address. *See also: Domain Name System.*

National Research and Education Network (NREN)   The NREN is the realization of an interconnected gigabit computer network devoted to High Performance Computing and Communications.

National Science Foundation (NSF)   A U.S. government agency whose purpose is to promote the advancement of science. NSF funds science researchers, scientific projects, and infrastructure to improve the quality of scientific research. The NSFNET, funded by NSF, is an essential part of academic and research communications. It is a highspeed "network of networks" which is hierarchical in nature. At the highest level, it is a backbone network currently comprising 16 nodes connected to a 45M/s facility which spans the continental United States. Attached to that are mid-level networks and attached to the mid-levels are campus and local networks. NSFNET also has connections out of the U.S. to Canada, Mexico, Europe, and the Pacific Rim. The NSFNET is part of the Internet.

NCSA   National Center for Supercomputing Applications at the University of Illinois at Urbana-Champaign; developers of NCSA Mosaic.

netiquette   A pun on "etiquette" referring to proper behavior on a network.

network   A computer network is a data communications system which interconnects computer systems at various different sites. A network may be composed of any combination of LANs, MANs, or WANs. *See also: Local Area Network, Metropolitan Area Network, Wide Area Network, internet.*

network address   The network portion of an IP address. For a class A network, the network address is the first byte of the IP address. For a class B network, the network address is the first two bytes of the IP address. For a class C network, the network address is the first three bytes of the IP address. In each case, the remainder is the host address. In the Internet, assigned network addresses are globally unique. *See also: Internet, IP address.*

Network File System (NFS)   A protocol developed by Sun Microsystems, which allows a computer system to access files over a network as if they were on its local disks. This protocol has been incorporated in products by more than two hundred companies, and is now a de facto Internet standard.

Network News Transfer Protocol (NNTP)   A protocol for the distribution, inquiry, retrieval, and posting of news articles. *See also: Usenet.*

Network Operations Center (NOC)   A location from which the operation of a network or internet is monitored. Additionally, this center usually serves as a clearinghouse for connectivity problems and efforts to resolve those problems.

NNTP   See: Network News Transfer Protocol

node   An addressable device attached to a computer network.

octet   An octet is 8 bits. This term is used in networking, rather than byte, because some systems have bytes that are not 8 bits long.

Online Computer Library Catalog   OCLC is a nonprofit membership organization offering computer-based services to libraries, educational organizations, and their users. The OCLC library information network connects more than 10,000 libraries worldwide. Libraries use the OCLC System for cataloging, interlibrary loan, collection development, bibliographic verification, and reference searching.

packet   The unit of data sent across a network. "Packet" is a generic term used to describe unit of data at all levels of the protocol stack, but it is most correctly used to describe application data units.

Packet InterNet Groper (PING)   A program used to test reachability of destinations by sending them an echo request and waiting for a reply. The term is used as a verb: "Ping host X to see if it is up!".

Point Of Presence (POP)   A site where there exists a collection of telecommunications equipment, usually digital leased lines and multi-protocol routers.

Point-to-Point Protocol (PPP)   The Point-to-Point Protocol provides a method for transmitting packets over serial point-to-point links. *See also: Serial Line IP.*

port   A port is a transport layer demultiplexing value. Each application has a unique port number associated with it. *See also: Transmission Control Protocol, User Datagram Protocol.*

PostScript   A page description language developed by Adobe Systems.

Post Office Protocol (POP)   A protocol designed to allow single user hosts to read mail from a server. There are three versions: POP, POP2, and POP3. Latter versions are NOT compatible with earlier versions. *See also: Electronic Mail.*

postmaster   The person responsible for taking care of electronic mail problems, answering queries about users, and other related work at a site. *See also: Electronic Mail.*

PPP   See: Point-to-Point Protocol

Privacy Enhanced Mail (PEM)   Internet email which provides confidentiality, authentication, and message integrity using various encryption methods. *See also: Electronic Mail, encryption.*

protocol   A formal description of message formats and the rules two computers must follow to exchange those messages. Protocols can describe low-level details of machine-to-machine interfaces (e.g., the order in which bits and bytes are sent across a wire) or high-level exchanges between allocation programs (e.g., the way in which two programs transfer a file across the Internet).

Protocol Data Unit (PDU)   "PDU" is international standards committee speak for packet. *See also: packet.*

queue   A backup of packets awaiting processing.

QuickTime™   A compressed audio/video format developed by Apple Computer.

route   The path that network traffic takes from its source to its destination. Also, a possible path from a given host to another host or destination.

router   A device which forwards traffic between networks. The forwarding decision is based on network layer information and routing tables, often constructed by routing protocols. *See also: gateway.*

routing   The process of selecting the correct interface and next hop for a packet being forwarded. *See also: router.*

Serial Line IP (SLIP)   A protocol used to run IP over serial lines, such as telephone circuits or RS-232 cables, interconnecting two systems. *See also: Point-to-Point Protocol.*

server   A provider of resources (e.g., file servers and name servers). *See also: client, Domain Name System, Network File System.*

SGML   Standard Generalized Markup Language, a programming language for style sheets and documents.

SIG   Special Interest Group.

signature   The three or four line message at the bottom of a piece of email or a Usenet article which identifies the sender. Large signatures (over five lines) are generally frowned upon. *See also: Electronic Mail, Usenet.*

Simple Mail Transfer Protocol (SMTP)   A protocol used to transfer electronic mail between computers. It is a server to server protocol, so other protocols are used to access the messages. *See also: Electronic Mail, Post Office Protocol.*

Simple Network Management Protocol (SNMP)   The Internet standard protocol, developed to manage nodes on an IP network. It is currently possible to manage wiring hubs, toasters, jukeboxes, etc.

SLIP   See: Serial Line IP.

subnet   A portion of a network, which may be a physically independent network segment, which shares a network address with other portions of the network and is distinguished by a subnet number. A subnet is to a network what a network is to an internet. *See also: internet, network.*

subnet address   The subnet portion of an IP address. In a subnetted network, the host portion of an IP address is split into a subnet portion and a host portion using an address (subnet) mask. *See also: address mask, IP address, network address, host address.*

subnet mask   See: address mask

subnet number   See: subnet address

Switched Multimegabit Data Service (SMDS)   An emerging high-speed datagram-based public data network service developed by Bellcore and expected to be widely used by telephone companies as the basis for their data networks.

T1   An AT&T term for a digital carrier facility used to transmit a DS-1 formatted digital signal at 1.544 megabits per second.

T3   A term for a digital carrier facility used to transmit a DS-3 formatted digital signal at 44.746 megabits per second.

tags   A shorthand name for the formatting elements used in HyperText Markup Language, for example <TITLE>, <P>, <H1>, etc.

TCP   See: Transmission Control Protocol.

TCP/IP   Protocol Suite Transmission Control Protocol over Internet Protocol. This is a common shorthand which refers to the suite of transport and application protocols which runs over IP.

TELENET   A public packet switched network using the CCITT X.25 protocols. It should not be confused with Telnet.

Telnet   Telnet is the Internet standard protocol for remote terminal connection service.

terminal emulator   A program that allows a computer to emulate a terminal. The workstation thus appears as a terminal to the remote host.

terminal server   A device which connects many terminals to a LAN through one network connection. A terminal server can also connect many network users to its asynchronous ports for dial-out capabilities and printer access. *See also: Local Area Network.*

TIFF   Tagged Image File Format, developed to store digital image data.

TN3270   A variant of the Telnet program that allows one to attach to IBM mainframes and use the mainframe as if you had a 3270 or similar terminal.

token ring   A token ring is a type of LAN with nodes wired into a ring. Each node constantly passes a control message (token) on to the next; whichever node has the token can send a message. *See also: Local Area Network.*

topology   A network topology shows the computers and the links between them. A network layer must stay abreast of the current network topology to be able to route packets to their final destination.

transceiver   Transmitter-receiver. The physical device that connects a host interface to a local area network, such as Ethernet. Ethernet transceivers contain electronics that apply signals to the cable and sense collisions.

Transmission Control Protocol (TCP)   An Internet Standard transport layer protocol. It is connection-oriented and stream-oriented, as opposed to UDP.

Trojan Horse   A computer program which carries within itself a means to allow the creator of the program access to the system using it. *See also: virus, worm.*

twisted pair   A type of cable in which pairs of conductors are twisted together to produce certain electrical properties.

UDP   See: User Datagram Protocol

URL   Uniform Resource Locator, the Internet path information used to specify the location of a document, and comprised of a transfer method scheme, domain address, and directory information, as well as a filename.

Usenet   A collection of thousands of topically named newsgroups, the computers which run the protocols, and the people who read and submit Usenet news. Not all Internet hosts subscribe to Usenet and not all Usenet hosts are on the Internet.

User Datagram Protocol (UDP)   An Internet Standard transport layer protocol. It is a connectionless protocol which adds a level of reliability and multiplexing to IP. *See also: Transmission Control Protocol.*

virtual circuit   A network service which provides connection-oriented service regardless of the underlying network structure. *See also: connection-oriented.*

virus   A program which replicates itself on computer systems by incorporating itself into other programs which are shared among computer systems. *See also: Trojan Horse, worm.*

W3   See: World Wide Web

W3C   World Wide Web Consortium

WAIS   See: Wide Area Information Servers

WAN   See: Wide Area network

WG   Working Group

white pages   The Internet supports several databases that contain basic information about users, such as email addresses, telephone numbers, and postal addresses. These databases can be searched to get information about particular individuals. Because they serve a function akin to the telephone book, these databases are often referred to as "white pages." *See also: WHOIS, X.500.*

WHOIS   An Internet program which allows users to query a database of people and other Internet entities, such as domains, networks, and hosts, kept at the DDN NIC. The information for people shows a person's company name, address, phone number and email address. *See also: white pages, Knowbot, X.500.*

Wide Area Information Servers (WAIS)   A distributed information service which offers simple natural language input, indexed searching for fast retrieval, and a "relevance feedback" mechanism which allows the results of initial searches to influence future searches. Public domain implementations are available. *See also: archie, Gopher.*

Wide Area Network (WAN)   A network, usually constructed with serial lines, which covers a large geographic area. *See also: Local Area Network, Metropolitan Area Network.*

World Wide Web (WWW or W3)   A hypertext-based, distributed information system created by researchers at CERN in Switzerland. Users may create, edit, or browse hypertext documents. The clients and servers are freely available.

World Wide Web Consortium (W3C)   A committee established by Massachusetts Institute of Technology and the European Particle Physics Laboratory CERN in 1994, to guide development of software and standards for the World Wide Web.

worm   A computer program which replicates itself and is self-propagating. Worms, as opposed to viruses, are meant to spawn in network environments. Network worms were first defined by Shoch & Hupp of Xerox in ACM Communications (March 1982). The Internet worm of November 1988 is perhaps the most famous; it successfully propagated itself on over 6,000 systems across the Internet. *See also: Trojan Horse, virus.*

WWW   See: World Wide Web

WWW Worm   A benign computer program that automatically traverses servers on the World Wide Web and records document information for use in a retrieval database. The full name of this service is the World Wide Web Worm.

WYSIWYG   What You See is What You Get

X   X is the name for TCP/IP based network-oriented window systems. Network window systems allow a program to use a display on a different computer. The most widely-implemented window system is X11—a component of MIT's Project Athena.

XBM   X BitMap, a black-and-white image format used by UNIX-based computers running the X-Windows application interface.

X.25   A data communications interface specification developed to describe how data passes into and out of public data communications networks.

X.400   The CCITT and ISO standard for electronic mail. It is widely used in Europe and Canada.

X.500   The CCITT and ISO standard for electronic directory services. *See also: white pages, Knowbot, WHOIS.*

Yellow Pages (YP)   A service used by UNIX administrators to manage databases distributed across a network.

zone   A logical group of network devices (AppleTalk).

A Guide to Elements and Attributes

HTML is an evolving language and has changed significantly since its inception in 1989. The elements and attributes explained in this section are specified in the Document Type Description (DTD) for HTML 2.0.

Not every Web client application in use today is able to interpret all of the elements or attributes specified in Level 2. After all, there are millions of copies of a dozen or more programs out there. Luckily, none of the 2.0 elements or attributes causes a problem on a non-2.0 literate browser; browsers should ignore unprogrammed markup.

The IETF HTML Working Group discussions of HTML 3.0 have been going on since the autumn of 1994. As of this writing, a specification is expected sometime in late 1995. Included in proposals for HTML 3.0 are new elements for handling mathematics, tables, and more complex forms. Some of these new elements are explained in Chapter 7.

Regardless of changes to HTML in the near future, tens of millions of client applications will be able to correctly interpret what you write if you follow the definitions given below.

Elements

<A> Anchors mark up hyperlinks to other text or documents through Uniform Resource Locators. The URL is written as part of an HREF= attribute.

HREF= attributes can use full or partial Uniform Resource Locators, depending on the location of the target document in relation to the document that contains the hyperlink. The first example points to a document on the same server. The second points to a document on another server:

```
<A HREF="/directory/filename.html">linked text</A>
<A HREF="http://foo.dog.org/directory/filename.html">linked
text</A>
```

Text can be identified as a target for a hyperlink by writing a anchor that identifies itself with a NAME= value.

```
<A NAME="idname">target text</A>
```

The URL pointing to this type of anchor uses the named value to identify its target, and places a hash mark (#) separator between the URL for the document and the name of the target anchor.

```
<A HREF="/directory/filename.html#idname>linked text</A>
```

Hyperlinks to target anchors within the same document omit any URL and just use HREF="#anchorname".

Text written between <A> and </A> is displayed as highlighted text. Earlier versions of HTML anchor markup included attributes for REL=, REV=, TITLE=, and METHODS= in addition to an HREF= attribute but these attributes are rarely, if ever, used in an anchor and are not proposed for the HTML 3.0 specification. Anchors close with </A>.

<ADDRESS> marks up an address in a document—for example, the name and email address of the author, or an ordinary postal address. The address text is usually displayed in italics by the browser.

```
<ADDRESS>Kevin Coffee, kcoffee@panix.com</ADDRESS>
```

<B> Bold typeface is a typographical style element used to mark up text so that it is displayed in bold type.

```
<B>Bold is a physical text style</B>
```

\<BASE> is used within the \<HEAD> element to identify the full Uniform Resource Locator for a document. The \<BASE> element is written using an HREF= attribute to describe the document URL.

This \<BASE> URL provides a valid reference for any partial URLs that are contained in the document. If the document is moved from its original location, a \<BASE> URL maintains the functions of partial URLs in the document. There is no closing tag for \<BASE>.

\<BASE HREF="http://foo.bah.org/directory/document.html">

\<BLOCKQUOTE> is a logical style element used to mark up a body of type as quoted text. All text contained between blockquote tags is indented to the right.

\<BLOCKQUOTE>Blockquote is a logical style\</BLOCKQUOTE>

\<BODY> should be used to contain the content of an HTML document displayed by a browser. Body elements use the end tag \</BODY>.

**\
** creates a line break in displayed text but does not force a line space. \
 does not use an end tag.

\<CITE> is a logical style element used to mark up text as a literal citation. The text contained between citation tags is italicized or otherwise specially formatted for display by the browser.

\<CITE>Cited text requires an end tag \</CITE>

\<CODE> is a logical style element used to mark up a string as computer language. The text contained between code tags is displayed in a monospaced typeface.

\<CODE>Code requires an end tag \</CODE>

\<DD> Definition list Definition is used within a definition list element \<DL> to mark up text as a definition in a list of terms and definitions. Definitions are always written along with and following a Definition Term \<DT> element. Definitions are displayed below and indented to the right of terms in a definition list. Definition items do not use an end tag.

```
<DL>
<DT>Widget
<DD>The device used to exemplify a whatayacallit in an example.
<DT>Term
<DD>A word used to name an object or entity.
</DL>
```

<DIR> Directory lists mark up a series of items for display as a list, indented to the right of the surrounding text. List items in a directory list are marked with the <LI> tag.

```
<DIR>
<LI>A-H<LI>I-M
<LI>N-T<LI>U-Z
</DIR>
```

<DL> Definition Lists contains items that are displayed as a series of terms and definitions using the tags <DT> to mark terms and <DD> to mark definitions. (See <DD> above.) The <DL> element requires an end tag </DL>.

<DT> Definition Term marks text as a term being defined in a definition list. The <DT> element precedes the <DD> definition element in a definition list. (See <DD> above.) Definition Terms do not require an end tag.

<EM> is a logical style element used to mark up text to be displayed with emphasis. By default, emphasized text is displayed in italic type.

<EM>emphasis is a logical style</EM>

<FORM> is used to collect and send data to a Common Gateway Interface program on a server. The attributes used in a <FORM> element are ACTION=, METHOD=, and ENTYPE=.

Forms contain entry field elements <INPUT>, <SELECT>, and <TEXTAREA>.

When the ACTION= attribute in a form is the Uniform Resource Locator for a Common Gateway Interface program on a Web server, it must also be defined with a METHOD= attribute to indicate the method to be used by the CGI program, either GET or POST.

<FORM> elements cannot be written inside other <FORM> elements. Entry fields are enclosed between <FORM> and </FORM>.

<FORM METHOD=GET ACTION="http://foo.dog.org/directory/ script.cgi">

<H1> Headings mark up text as a text heading or subheading. There is a series of six heading elements used in order of priority, <H1> through <H6>. Headings require an end tag, </Hn>.

<H1>The Main Heading</H1>

<HEAD> is used for the placement of six types of elements that describe the entire document: <TITLE>, <ISINDEX>, <BASE>, <META>, <NEXTID>, and <LINK>.

Browsers do not display head elements. <HEAD> requires the end tag </HEAD>.

<HR> places a horizontal line in the document at the tag location. <HR> does not use an end tag.

<HTML> The HyperText Markup Language element describes the entire contents of a document as HTML text. All other text and elements in a document are written between <HTML> and </HTML>.

<I> Italic is a typographical style element used to mark up text for display in an italic type face.

<I>Italic is a physical style element</I>

<IMG> Image marks up an inline image and always includes an SRC= attribute pointing to the URL of the image file. Inline image URLs are processed at the time they are read by the browser.

<IMG> may also use the ALIGN= attribute to define alignment of adjacent text, so that any text before or after the element lines up with the TOP, MIDDLE, or BOTTOM of the image.

The ALT= attribute is written to provide alternate text that describes the image and is displayed instead of the image by text-only browsers.

The ISMAP attribute describes the image as a graphical interface that plots Uniform Resource Locators to pixel coordinates in the image area and sends these coordinates to a Common Gateway Interface program on the server. <IMG> does not use an end tag.

<IMG SRC="/images/image.gif" ALIGN="TOP" ISMAP>

<INPUT> is used to create an editable entry field in a fill-out form, and is used with the attribute NAME= to label the data entered in the field.

The size of an input field is specified by attributes for SIZE= and/or MAXLENGTH=, and to describe the field TYPE=. The default type is text entry, but other entry types can be specified, including CHECKBOX, HIDDEN, IMAGE, PASS-WORD, RADIO, RESET, or SUBMIT (see following definitions).

If the field entry type is SUBMIT, the field becomes a clickable button that sends the contents of the <FORM> to the location specified by the ACTION= attribute. <INPUT> elements do not use an end tag.

<INPUT NAME="address" SIZE="36" TYPE="TEXT' MAXLENGTH="36">

<ISINDEX> marks a document as a searchable index and enables searching of that index by keywords. The <ISINDEX> element should be generated by the server script that is executing the index search. <ISINDEX> is written within the <HEAD> element and does not require an end tag.

<KBD> Keyboard is a logical style element used to mark up text so that it is displayed in a monospaced typeface, to indicate text that should be entered using a computer keyboard.

<KBD>keyboard text is a logical style</KBD>

<LI> List item marks up individual list items in a <UL> unordered, <OL> ordered, <MENU> menu, or <DIR> directory list. Each list item is displayed as a single item within the list, indented to the right of surrounding text. There is no closing tag.

```
<OL>
<LI>banana
<LI>pineapple
<LI>grapefruit
</OL>
```

<LINK> is used to describe the relationship between one document and other documents, between the document and an index, between the document and an author, or some other relationship. <LINK> elements are optional and not widely used. This information may be displayed by a browser (capable of processing <LINK> elements), or used to enable some action between document A and the document referred to by a <LINK>.

Links are written using an HREF= attribute to point to the related document or object. The attribute REL= is used to indicate the type of relationship between document A and document B. The attribute REV= can be used to indicate a reverse relationship.

Current REL= values include "made" to indicate author, "owns" to indicate owner, "useindex" to identify a related index, "annotation" to indicate comment on another document, "reply" to indicate a reply to another document, "search" to point to a search form, "useglossary" to link to a glossary document, and "precedes," "supercedes," "history," and "subdocument" to indicate document revisions.

A proposed use of <LINK> in HTML 3.0 is to share common objects such as style sheets, toolbars, and other graphical display elements.

<LINK REV=made HREF="http://akebono.Stanford.edu/yahoo/ form.html">

\<MENU> marks up a series of items as a bulleted list. Menus are similar to unordered lists \<UL>. The single attribute COMPACT can be added to the tag to display a menu list with closer spacing between characters.

```
<MENU COMPACT>
<LI>20th Century
<LI>19th Century
<LI>16th Century
</MENU>
```

\<META> is a supplemental element written within the \<HEAD> part of a document to provide information useful for identifying, indexing, or cataloging the document by automated search programs (robots) and to SGML applications that cannot otherwise extract this information from the HTML elements within the document. \<META> is not used for normal server-browser requests and responses.

If the attribute HTTP-EQUIV= is written in a \<META> element, the value of this attribute is sent as an additional response header line by a Web server. \<META> should not be used to mark up information that can be provided through standard HTML markup. \<META> does not use an end tag.

\<META HTTP-EQUIV=Expires CONTENT="04 Dec 1993 21:29;02 GMT">

\<NEXTID> is a alpha-numeric identifier placed in the \<HEAD> part of a document by automated HTML editors. Do not enter a \<NEXTID> manually. \<NEXTID> does not use an end tag.

\<OL> Ordered list marks up a series of list items in numerical order beginning with the number 1. \<OL COMPACT> may be written to format an ordered list using tighter spacing between characters. \<OL> requires an end tag \</OL> (see \<LI> above).

\<OPTION> elements are used only within a \<SELECT> element to mark up each item in a list of items that are presented as a menu of possible entries in a \<FORM>.

\<OPTION> items are displayed as either a pop-up menu or a scrolling window. The attribute SELECTED is used to indicate a default selection. The attribute VALUE= is used to assign a value to the entry that is different from the text of the \<OPTION>. \<OPTION> does not require an end tag.

```
<SELECT>
<OPTION>banana
```

```
<OPTION>cherry
<OPTION>strawberry
</SELECT>
```

<P> marks a paragraph beginning on a new line. <P> may be used with or without the end tag </P>, but is typically used without an end tag.

<PRE> used to mark up preformatted text so that it is displayed as written in plain text and maintains all character and line spacing of the original text. Pre-formatted text is displayed in monospaced type by the browser. <PRE> text requires the end tag </PRE>.

```
<PRE>Pre-formatted text
    maintains the spacing of
    monospaced type</PRE>
```

<SAMP> is a logical style element used to mark up text as a string of literal characters using monospaced type.

<SAMP> uses the end tag </SAMP>.

<SELECT> entry fields are used within a fill-out form to create a list of entry choices as a pop-up menu or scrolling list. Each entry item is marked up using an <OPTION> element.

The MULTIPLE attribute is used within <SELECT> to create a scrolling list that allows multiple item selections. <SELECT> uses the end tag </SELECT>.

```
<SELECT MULTIPLE>
<OPTION>banana
<OPTION>cherry
<OPTION>strawberry
</SELECT>
<STRONG> is a logical style element used to mark up text for
extra emphasis.
<STRONG> requires the end tag </STRONG>
```

<TEXTAREA> creates a large text entry field in a fill-out form.

<TEXTAREA> is similar in function to <INPUT> and uses a NAME= argument to identify data entered in the field. The attributes ROWS= and COLS= are used to define the displayed size of the field. Browsers display scroll bars along the right and bottom of the field to allow viewing text. Up to 1024 characters can be submitted as the content of the field.

`<TEXTAREA NAME="comments" COLS="24" ROWS="6"></TEXTAREA>`

`<TITLE>` describes the title of a document within the document `<HEAD>`. Information entered as a `<TITLE>` element is retrieved by search engines, displayed in the client application title bar, and used for recording the document to a Hotlist or a Bookmark list.

`<TITLE>WWW Starter Kit Home Page</TITLE>`

`<TT>` Typewriter type is a typographical style element used to mark up text for display as monospaced type.

`<TT> Typewriter type is a physical style</TT>`

`<UL>` Unordered list marks up a list of items for display as a bulleted list, similar to a `<MENU>` list.

```
<UL>
<LI>get the groceries
<LI>do the laundry
<LI>polish the doorknobs
</UL>
```

`<VAR>` is a logical style element used to mark up text as a variable parameter, as used in computer language.

`<VAR> Variable is a logical text style</VAR>`.

Attributes

`ACTION=` identifies the URL destination for the `<FORM>`. When the `ACTION=` is an HTTP URL, like a Common Gateway Interface program, the `METHOD=` combined with `ACTION` must be a valid HTTP `METHOD`. Ordinarily the method is either `GET` or `POST`.

`<FORM METHOD=POST ACTION="script/survey.cgi">`

`ALIGN=` controls the flow of text around an inline image. Your choices are ALIGN=TOP | MIDDDLE | BOTTOM.

ALIGN= determines how text that comes before or follows an `<IMG>` tag lines up with the image on screen. Text that precedes the `<IMG>` ends at the image. Text that follows the `<IMG>` begins at the image. The image is treated as if it were another character in the line of type. Type doesn't reform in a column on either side of the image.

`ALIGN=` is also used within an `<INPUT>` element if the element is `TYPE=IMAGE`.

```
<IMG SRC="/directory/image.gif" ALIGN="BOTTOM">
<INPUT TYPE="IMAGE SRC="/image/button.gif" ALIGN="Bottom">
```

`ALT=` identifies a text phrase as an alternate description for an `<IMG>` inline image. The text phrase is displayed by text-only browsers (instead of images) and by newer graphical browsers when Autoload Images is turned off (in the browser preferences).

```
<IMG SRC="/directory/house.gif" ALT="a 24K  picture of our
house">
```

CHECKED identifies that a CHECKBOX or RADIO input selector should be checked as the default selection.

```
<INPUT NAME="frequent" TYPE=CHECKBOX CHECKED>
```

COLS= specifies the display width of a `<TEXTAREA>` entry field as the number of characters wide. `COLS=` does not control the amount of data that can be entered in the field.

```
<TEXTAREA NAME="comments" COLS=48 ROWS=24>
```

COMPACT is a one-word attribute that can be used in either a `<MENU>` or `<OL>` list element to call for compact type spacing in the list.

```
<MENU COMPACT>
```

CONTENT= identifies document information within a `<META>` element (see above) and is paired with the attribute `HTTP-EQUIV=`. META is a special purpose element intended for use by automated programs, and the information written in META is usually special purpose information for that program. META is not used for normal browser/server transactions. Response Headers are usually generated by a Web server.

```
<META HTTP-EQUIV=Expires CONTENT="15 Mar 1996 12:12:30 GMT">
```

ENCTYPE= identifies the format of data being submitted by an `ACTION=` attribute if that format cannot be implied with the URL and/or file extension indicated. ENCTYPE specifies the format of the submitted data according to an Multipurpose Internet Mail Extension (MIME) type. It is not used for normal browser/server transactions.

```
<FORM METHOD=POST ACTION="http://foo.bah.com/directory/
newprogramtype" ENCTYPE="application/x-www-form-urlencoded">
```

HREF= identifies a hyperlink reference using a Uniform Resource Locator for the linked file in an <A> element. It is also used to identify a URL written in a <BASE> or <LINK> element.

```
<A HREF="http://foo.bah.com/directory/document.html">
<BASE HREF="http://foo.bah.com/directory/document.html">
<LINK REV="made" HREF="http://foo.bah.com/directory/form.html">
```

HTTP-EQUIV= specifies a customized response header that is attached to the information written in a CONTENT= attribute. It is used only within a <META> element to convey special information for use by an automated search program (robot). It is not used for normal browser/server transactions. Response headers are usually generated by a Web server (see Chapter 6).

```
<META HTTP-EQUIV=Expires CONTENT="15 Mar 1996 12:12:30 GMT">
```

ISMAP marks an <IMG> element as user interface. An image map sends a Uniform Resource Locator request that has been mapped to specific pixel coordinates in the image. The user triggers a URL request by clicking on these mapped parts of the graphic.

ISMAP is only active if the <IMG> URL points to an image map program on a Web server.

```
<IMG SRC="/scripts/image.gif" ISMAP>
```

MAXLENGTH= is added to an <INPUT> field if you need to specify the maximum number of characters that should be submitted in a field.

```
<INPUT NAME="name" SIZE=24 MAXLENGTH=24>
```

METHOD= is required in a <FORM> element to identify the process that is being requested by the form. There are two main methods used with a form, GET and POST. The GET method is ordinarily used for submitting a query to a database. The POST function is normally used for adding information to a file of some type, and the contents of the form are sent as the body of a message.

```
<FORM METHOD=POST ACTION="script/survey.cgi">
```

METHODS= is rarely used. Its purpose was to indicate the HTTP methods used by <A> and <LINK> elements. The attribute can describe several methods separated by commas. Method information is normally supplied by the URL. The METHODS attribute is not proposed for inclusion in HTML 3.0.

MULTIPLE is added to a <SELECT> field so that multiple <OPTION> selections can be selected and appear in a scrolling window.

<SELECT MULTIPLE>

N=*n* is added to a <NEXTID> element as the alphanumeric identifier for the document. <NEXTID> elements make sense only to programs that automatically generate HTML and should not be added manually.

NAME= is used in an <A> to identify specific text in a document as the target of a hyperlink. The NAME can be used as a partial URL within the same document or can be added to a larger URL used in a different document. Links that point to NAME anchors precede the NAME with a # character.

```
<A HREF="#zither">
<A HREF="http://foo.bah.com/directory/document.html#zither">
<A NAME="zither">
```

NAME= is added to the entry field elements of a <FORM> to identify the field and its data when they are submitted as part of the form. NAME is used in <INPUT>, <SELECT>, and <TEXTAREA>.

<INPUT NAME="address">

REL= is used to specify the relationship between the current document and another document or object pointed to by a <LINK> URL. These relationships describe the history of the document, the document author, glossaries, or indexes referred to by the document. <LINK> is used only within a document <HEAD>.

<LINK REL=made HREF="http://foo.bah.com/direct/search.html">

REV= may be used to specify a relationship between one document and another document that is the reverse of REL=.

<LINK REV=made HREF="http://foo.bah.com/direct/form.html">

ROWS= specifies the display height of a <TEXTAREA> entry field by number of characters high. ROWS= does not control the amount of data that can be entered in the field.

<TEXTAREA NAME="comments" COLS="48" ROWS="24">

SIZE= specifies the display width of an <INPUT> entry field when it is not the default width (20 characters). The value in SIZE= indicates number of characters.

SIZE= specifies the display height of a <SELECT> entry field when it is not the default height (I character).

`<INPUT NAME="address" SIZE="36">`

SRC= points to the source URL of an inline image written as an <IMG> element.

`<IMG SRC="/images/image.gif">`

TITLE= is added to an <A> or <LINK> element to identify the <TITLE> of a document pointed to by the anchor or link URL, and used for display purposes by browsers. TITLE= is not supported by current Mac browsers.

TYPE= identifies the field type of an <INPUT> entry field. The default type is text. Other types of entry fields are: checkbox, hidden, image, password, radio, reset, submit, and text. Descriptions of these follow.

TYPE="CHECKBOX" creates a Boolean (on/off, either/or) entry field that is displayed as a checkbox. The additional one-word attribute CHECKED can be added so that the default value of the checkbox is checked.

`<INPUT NAME="option" TYPE="CHECKBOX" CHECKED>`

TYPE="HIDDEN" creates a hidden field used to hold data that should be submitted along with the rest of the form. Hidden fields are not editable by the form user.

`<INPUT NAME="survey number" TYPE="HIDDEN" VALUE="27">`

TYPE="IMAGE" creates an graphic button identical in function to TYPE="SUBMIT". Clicking on this button sends the form input to the URL specified by the ACTION= attribute.

The image for the button is treated as an inline image request and is identified as SRC= URL. The image can be aligned with adjacent text by adding an ALIGN= attribute.

`<INPUT TYPE="IMAGE" SRC="image/button.gif" ALIGN=MIDDLE>`

TYPE="PASSWORD" can be used to hide text entered into a field by displaying bullets instead of characters.

`<INPUT TYPE="PASSWORD" NAME="password" SIZE="12">`

TYPE="RADIO" is used to create a Boolean (on/off, either/or) entry field that is displayed as a radio button. Radio buttons are normally used in groups to present a series of alternate entries.

Each TYPE=RADIO field uses the same NAME= name, but a unique VALUE= value. Only one value in the series can be submitted in the form. CHECKED can be added to specify one of the buttons as the default selection.

```
What model of computer do you use?
Quadra 840AV <INPUT NAME="user Mac" TYPE="RADIO" VALUE="1">
Powerbook 180 <INPUT NAME="user Mac" TYPE="RADIO" VALUE="2">
Classic <INPUT NAME="user Mac" TYPE="RADIO" VALUE="3">
```

TYPE="RESET" creates a button that clears any data entered in form entry fields, or reset fields to their default values.

<INPUT TYPE="RESET" VALUE="Reset">

TYPE="SUBMIT" creates a button that triggers the ACTION and METHOD indicated by the <FORM>. Adding an attribute for VALUE="text" labels the button with the specified text.

<INPUT TYPE="SUBMIT" VALUE="Submit">

TYPE="TEXT" creates a field for entering text data. This is the default type for <INPUT> fields.

VALUE= assigns a value in text or numbers to an entry field. This data is shown as the default entry for a text field, or it is the value submitted by a Boolean entry field, or it is the value assigned to a hidden field. VALUE= is used to assign a value to an <OPTION> entry field that is different from the name of the <OPTION>.

```
<INPUT NAME="country" SIZE="5" VALUE="France">
<OPTION NAME="USA" VALUE="domestic">
```

WIDTH= assigns a line length used to display text inside a <PRE> element. The width of the line is indicated by number of characters. The default line length of text in <PRE> is 80 characters per line.

<PRE WIDTH="60">

Index

A

E

M

Q-R

V-W

Index